# Intertextuality in Faulkner

# Intertextuality in Faulkner

Michel Gresset and
Noel Polk,
Editors

UNIVERSITY PRESS OF MISSISSIPPI
Jackson

This book has been sponsored by the
University of Southern Mississippi

**Library of Congress Cataloging in Publication Data**
Main entry under title:

Intertextuality in Faulkner.

   Papers delivered at the Second International Faulkner
Colloquium, held in Paris, April 2–4, 1982.
   Includes index.
   1. Faulkner, William, 1897–1962—Criticism and inter-
pretation—Congresses.   2. Allusions in literature—
Congresses.   I. Gresset, Michel.   II. Polk, Noel.
III. International Colloquium on Faulkner (2nd : 1982 :
Paris, France)
PS3511.A86Z848   1985        813'.52        84-21943
ISBN 0-87805-249-6

# Contents

# Intertextuality in Faulkner

# Introduction

## Faulkner between the Texts

That one cannot find the word "intertextuality" in any but the most recent dictionary of literary terms does not prove that the thing (let us call it the practice) has not been part of literary activity ever since the first book was written: indeed, the Bible (itself admittedly an intertextual nexus) may be considered as a well-nigh inextinguishable source of intertextuality in the field of English and American literature: the biblical connection is even one of the most outstanding characteristics of American literature.

This is also to say that intertextuality is part and parcel of culture in general. It is not only useful, it is necessary to state from the start that no quotation is innocent of a meaning which, though it may escape the writer's conscious mind, in no way escapes the cultural web in which we are all caught—in which, indeed, most of us thrive, at least professionally.

That the Bible can be held as the fountainhead of all intertextuality (as of all translation) is implicit in the following, secularized use of the word by the writer who may well have been the first of the moderns to lay his finger on intertextuality as a key operation in literary activity—and it is all the more revealing as he can hardly be associated with white anglo-saxon protestantism. In *Variations on a Subject,* Mallarmé writes that

> all books, more or less, contain the fusion of a certain number of repetitions: even if there were but one book in the world, its law would be as a bible simulated by the heathens. The difference from one work to the next would afford as many readings as would be put forth in a boundless contest for the trustworthy text among epochs that are supposedly civilized or literate.

3

The "fusion of some operative repetition," indeed: literally, "intertextuality" means the weaving of (part of) one text into another.

In scope, intertextuality extends all the way from the "operative repetition" of one single word to the use of a whole book as an "inter-web" of meaning. One good example of the first can be found in Faulkner's subtle quotation (although, without quotation marks, can it still be called a quotation?) of the verb "to fade" taken from Keats's "Ode on a Grecian Urn" in "Pantaloon in Black." The best example of the second is most certainly Joyce's extended use of the *Odyssey* in *Ulysses*. Halfway between these extremes, I would place the intertextual diffusion of the whole of Keats's "Ode" throughout *Light in August*.

In point of fact, however, the three preceding examples are all one: they all consist in an anastomosis which connects two texts and then itself (the connection) becomes one of the constituents of the later text. This is the most obvious aspect of intertextuality that Roland Barthes has chosen to generalize about, to systematize as what he calls "a prerequisite for any text":

> Every text is an intertext; other texts are present in it, at variable levels, in more or less recognizable forms: the texts of the previous culture and those of the surrounding culture; every text is a new fabric woven out of bygone quotations. Scraps of code, formulas, rhythmic patterns, fragments of social idioms, etc. are absorbed into the text and redistributed in it, for there is always language prior to the text and language around it. A prerequisite for any text, intertextuality cannot be reduced to a problem of sources and influences; it is a general field of anonymous formulas whose origin is seldom identifiable, of unconscious or automatic quotations given without quotation marks.[1]

In this statement, Barthes deliberately extends the concept of intertextuality to make it sound almost limitless. Not only does it appear that I cannot write if no one has written before me (a proposition likely to shatter the dividing line between creative and critical writing), but reading itself may well appear, under

this light, as an intertextual activity: I cannot rea
wish I had written.

This is exactly what Quentin and Shreve sou...
*Absalom, Absalom!,* a book about such textual weaving, and v...
likely to remain unmatched as an intertextual novel *and* as a
discourse on intertextuality. To consider only, and briefly, its
title: even before opening the book, the reader is literally summoned as witness to the grief (or is it shock? Could it not also be
some happy recognition, or even a cry of ecstasy?) expressed by
the sheer repetition of a mere biblical name: thus the reader
cannot fail to wish to raise the question implicit in the interjection: whose voice is it which can thus be heard at the edge of the
text? One searches the book itself for an answer.

Even less unambiguously intertextual was the original title of
*The Wild Palms—If I Forget Thee, Jerusalem.* As with *As I Lay Dying,*
one is confronted from the outset with a subordinate clause
which is *not* followed by a main clause; the title is therefore a
proposition left dangling, and so begging for a completion
which only the reading of the book can accomplish.

However, there are also, if I may say so, perfectly ambiguous
intertextual titles in Faulkner's corpus: *Sanctuary,* for instance, is
a religious term; but it is also pagan, or pre-Christian; what part,
category, or segment of the text does it refer to (if it must refer
to anything)? It is as if the title were between quotation marks,
and the problem were to fit it into the text. Most of Faulkner's
titles can thus be said to raise a question of intertextuality.

After the King James version of the Bible, Shakespeare is
certainly the most plundered corpus in the history of English
literature. But who could now use the words "great expecta-
tions" without automatically (as Barthes has observed) directing
the reader's inner, cultural gaze to Dickens?

One more example, perhaps the best possible one for showing
"external" intertextuality at work in Faulkner: Eula's response to
Labove at the end of the well-known scene in *The Hamlet* (II, 1, i)
which could be described as "Courting as Wrestling": "You old
headless horseman Ichabod Crane." The direct allusion to "The

Legend of Sleepy Hollow" shows how literally true is Julia Kristeva's assertion that "Every text takes shape as a mosaic of citations, every text is the absorption and transformation of other texts. The notion of intertextuality comes to take the place of intersubjectivity, and poetic language is to be read as dual—at least."[2] Indeed, can we not say that the act of bringing together two texts (Faulkner's and Irving's) begets a third one, to be written, or woven, by the reader's imagination around the motif of the puritanical schoolteacher confronted with the upsurge of his own sexual desire? Like a rock falling into a pool (one of Faulkner's favorite images, particularly in *Absalom, Absalom!*), the intertextual impact can be said to ripple across the stagnant waters of our literary memories almost without an end: all literature becomes a huge intertext if one thus programs the conflict between nature and culture (or any other major theme) into the stock of all of one's former readings.

Faulkner was not only one of the most daring practitioners of intertextuality; on one occasion at least, he even went so far as to anticipate our present-day literary theoreticians. The reading of the ledgers in section iv of "The Bear" is no less than a highly elaborate reading contest between Cass and Ike, the two cousins confronted with three texts out of which they are determined to call forth the truth: a) the ledgers themselves, or the documents of history; b) the Bible, or the monument of the Law; c) Keats's "Ode on a Grecian Urn," or the poet speaking. Thus is achieved what Faulkner might call a "stereoptical" *tour de force*—which is exactly, I suggest, what should be the effect of a well-tempered intertextuality.

What most of the papers in the Second International Faulkner Colloquium, held in Ecole Normale Supérieure in Paris on April 2-4, 1982, were about was not only Faulkner's consummate art in weaving an intertext in and out of novels ranging from *Sanctuary* to *The Wild Palms;* nor was it only his skill in varying this parameter; it was also his extraordinary capacity to carry from one work to another (in other words, and quite strictly speaking, to *iterate*) words, phrases, motifs, "bygone citations, scraps of code, formulas, rhythmic patterns, fragments of social idioms" as well as "unconscious or automatic quotations" including auto-quotations. In short, this collection is concerned not only with Faulkner's intertextual relations with other authors, but also with his capacity *to write his own work as an intertext.*

In this perspective the notion of reference must of course recede somewhat, even though it is everywhere present, say, in the Snopes trilogy, or even (though to a lesser degree) in *A Fable.* As Paul Ricoeur puts it,

> The suspense which defers the reference merely leaves the text, as it were, 'in the air,' outside or without a world. In virtue of this obliteration of the relation of the world, each text is free to enter into relation with all the other texts which come to take the place of circumstantial reality referred to by living speech. This relation of text to text, within the efface-ment of the world about which we speak, engenders the quasi-world of texts or literature.[3]

Under the light of modern literary theory, Faulkner's repeated statements become blindingly clear: for instance, the "obit and epitaph" he suggested to Malcolm Cowley in his letter of 11 February 1949: "He made the books and he died," and the no less famous ending of his interview with Jean Stein: ". . . by sublimating the actual into apocryphal . . . I created a cosmos of my own."[4] In other terms, what Faulkner never ceased to dream about, even to *The Reivers*, was the "ideal text" described by Roland Barthes:

> this text is a galaxy of signifiers, not a structure of signifieds; it has no beginning; it is reversible; we gain access to it by several entrances, none of which can be authoritatively declared to be the main one; the codes it mobilizes extend as far as the eye can read, they are interminable . . .[5]

Thus indeed, as Mallarmé knew very well, intertextuality may well be seen not only as the basis, but as the very essence of literature.

The first set of three papers devoted to the study of *Sanctuary* is particularly illustrative of the many possible uses of intertextuality. In "The Space between *Sanctuary*," Noel Polk tries it as a tool to pry open the process of revision that took place at the end of 1930. After examining some of the "inter- and intra-textual relationships between the two versions," Polk soon reaches the conclusion (and convinces us) that "the space between *Sanctuary* is filled with an entire teeming, fecund, even honeysuckled Faulknerian world that perhaps only these intertextual relationships can give us access to." In a way to be expected only from one inured to the reading of the texts in manuscript and typescript, he goes as far as suggesting that the "novels and stories of 1927-1931 . . . form a veritable spider's web of intimate connections, a fascinating web . . . of intertexts."

Whether or not we agree with André Bleikasten's "clinical" interpretation of both Emma Bovary and Temple Drake as essentially and primarily *hysterical* women, we can hardly deny his assumption that Faulkner himself, by quoting the French novel almost at the outset of his own, has laid the first stone of the building of *Madame Bovary* into "one of the intertexts of *Sanctuary*." Bleikasten's use of the notion of "metaphorical isotopy" or of "semantic analogy" between the two novels leads to the emergence of "an intertext of intertexts. In this case at least, external and internal intertextuality are impossible to dissociate, since the encounter of Flaubert's and Faulkner's texts is beyond doubt also the encounter of two internal intertextualities."

As for my own study of the ending of *Sanctuary* as "the paradigm of all 'dying falls'," and for the shock of recognition (or the surprise of "inter-readability") I received when I perceived how both structurally and semantically comparable to the former is the "dying fall" of Samuel Beckett's *Murphy*, it is, of course, on the face of it, a case of external intertextuality, all the more typical as it "clearly cannot be reduced to a problem of sources and influences." However, it also enables one to propose the notion of "inter-structurality," of which one can hardly find a better illustration than in the same two "dying falls": not only do they provide "a closure to the space of the novel," but, by blurring the focus of the male narrator's observation of a young woman into a vanishing-point, and by adding a final touch of voice or music to the novel, it "allows time to become the qualifier of space," thus providing the transition out of the world of fiction back into the everyday, not without a highly symbolist sense of "longing with little hope."

Reverting to internal intertextuality, Patrick Samway addresses himself scrupulously to "The Search for Jason Richmond Compson: A Question of Echolalia and A Problem of Palimpsest." Beginning with an awareness of the methodological and even epistemological nature of the issue of the existence of Quentin's father in, between, and outside of the three texts by which we "know" him, Samway takes his clue from modern hermeneutical studies of the New Testament, only to find that "we cannot look through the various layers of Faulkner's works and discover a person who once had an ontological existence." The "layers" in question are, of course, "That Evening Sun," in which Samway establishes convincingly that Quentin's voice is "mimetic," *The Sound and the Fury,* in which it becomes "constitutive," and *Absalom, Absalom!* in which, we might add, it is precisely intertextual. Halfway through his paper, Samway finds himself confronted with the difficult problem of the relationship between *The Sound and the Fury* and *Absalom, Absalom!;* in dealing with it, he steers a middle course between two extreme positions illustrated here by John Irwin and by Michael Millgate. "By abandoning the structure of both novels and creating an oscillating third text, which is conceived of as a composite of the two novels Faulkner did write, Irwin has created a curious, but dubious methodology"—because, he points out, as does Polk, "What Irwin forgets is that there are real intertexts between these two novels: *As I Lay Dying, Sanctuary, Light in August, Pylon,* plus more than fifty short stories published between 1929 and 1936." Of Millgate's opposing views that "each Faulkner text must be considered a unique, independent, and self-sufficient work of art, not only capable of being read and contemplated in isolation but actually demanding such treatment," Samway remarks that these views, "while ideally desirable, are almost impossible to maintain in terms of a practical, comprehensive approach to Faulkner's works." In conclusion, he warns against being content with "using a string of quotes" when dealing with any of the often philosophical issues that make up most of what we know of Mr. Compson's "character."

Out of a second triad of papers also devoted to internal intertextuality and concentrating on the novel in which we may well see the radical necessity of studying the text *as* intertext, two use Mikhail Bakhtin's appropriately relevant distinction between monological and dialogical discourse, or between "discourse that is simply assertive of claimed truth" and "discourse that by its nature takes other speech, other voices, into account." In "Oratory and the Dialogical in *Absalom, Absalom!*," Stephen Ross, after showing very convincingly that Faulkner, no less than the political members of his family, went to the school of Southern oratory, takes a stand against those who "emphasize the differences among the narrators" of the novel, and argues that "the narrative discourse with its monological overvoice creates tremendous authority" which, he says, does not mean "that *Absalom* in fact becomes monological, or that it loses its polyphonic complexity," but rather that one is dealing with "a polyphonic text, one traversed by many voices, that is made more difficult to explicate because of a discursive rhetorical gesture—the gesture of masking voices within a single oratorically derived overvoice." Thus he can oppose "the orator's monological, or monomaniacal, word" to what he calls "dialogical violence," which, in a few well-known instances such as the mirror-like dialogue between Quentin and Henry at the end, "strips the mask of univocality behind which the orator hides."

Even more strictly and technically Bakhtinian is Olga Scherer's article, which focuses on what she calls, clearly enough, "A Polyphonic Insert: Charles's Letter to Judith." Like Mr. Compson's letter to his son, this letter is "polylogical, even though unlike Mr. Compson's written document, which virtually *frames* the body of the novel. . . [it] *is framed* by the body of the novel"—particularly at the central place where it occurs, at the end of chapter iv. Her conclusion, couched in no less precise terms, is that it is Judith ("that silent listener, that invisible interlocutor—that other self perhaps—whom Dostoyevsky has taught us to appreciate as one possessing the greatest contaminating *and* contesting capacity") "who, by recuperating the overlapping zones of her fiancé's different facets, makes it possible for him to speak chiefly through those zones."

The gist of Nancy Blake's ambitious contribution is also contained in her title: "Creation and Procreation: The Voice and the Name, or Biblical Intertextuality in *Absalom, Absalom!*," the purpose of which is "to examine the distinction established throughout Faulkner's text between two sets of binary oppositions: between creation and sexual reproduction on the one hand, and between the voice that I will relate to the Lacanian signifier and the name on the other." Not unlike Stephen Ross, Nancy Blake considers that all of the novel's narrators "are simply mouthpieces for a voice that is unique, singular, and indivisible," because indeed all the voices "become anonymous in the telling." She then observes that Faulkner's text seems both to proclaim that "The name is a destiny" and "to destroy any expectation of a body behind, beside, or underneath the all-powerful name." In brief, according to the author, negation is the great force at work throughout the novel, particularly the negation of time and sexuality, which "results in a static, frozen, mesmerized world, immortal because lifeless" (here she might have referred to the Keatsian intertext). In her conclusion she resorts to Lacanian doctrine: "Faulkner's *Absalom, Absalom!* can be read as an examination of the effects of the name as manifestation of the universal fear of desire. The book presents the central figure of a primal father outside of desire. Sutpen is eternal because he has lost everything. . . . Avoiding the encounter with the other, denying the necessity of division, Sutpen puts off his own encounter with castration and engenders a series of doubles fixed like Henry and Quentin in a dizzying repudiation of life and light," so that, in the final analysis, "if procreation is denied, if creation is impossible, Faulkner's text has only the power to negate." From the Keatsian to the Mallarmean intertext (the dream of *Igitur*), the arc is complete indeed.

One may not agree with François Pitavy's justification of the rejection of the title *If I Forget Thee, Jerusalem* on the ground that it was "too visible a marker of intertextuality" (why not then reject *The Sound and the Fury*?), but one can hardly disagree with his assertion that *The Wild Palms* appears as one of "Faulkner's densest and richest intertexts"; this novel is a perfect example of both internal and external intertextuality, though of course not quite in the same way as *Madame Bovary* and *Sanctuary*. Pitavy's argument is that "the Bible does not function here as a text within a text, as the Word among words, but rather as a pattern—a chart—*informing* the circular, regressive structure of the novel," and his conclusion, not unexpected after the title "Forgetting Jerusalem: An Ironical Chart for *The Wild Palms*," is that "Harry Wilbourne's and the convict's constricted and empty Jerusalems are thus ironical inversions of the one that kept the Jews sitting by the rivers of Babylon, weeping." Pitavy ingeniously suggests that Faulkner may have felt the need of the contrapuntal narrative of "Old Man" only *after* he wrote the sentences in which Harry Wilbourne views the prospect for his life "as if [it] were to lie passively on his back as though he floated effortless and without volition upon an unreturning stream." Working from the evidence of the late (July 1938) letter to Haas announcing the "good title," Pitavy then argues that the title does not necessarily antedate the novel: "The discovery of the title may have been the sudden realization that the Bible was providing the adequate chart for the novel—that the intertext already at work in the text had indeed a name." He concludes with Borges's provocative idea of the descendant's influence upon the predecessor: "To a reader of *The Wild Palms*, Psalm 137 will never be the same again."

In "*The Wild Palms*: Degraded Culture, Devalued Texts," Pamela Rhodes and Richard Godden have endeavored to wed the intertextual/intratextual approach to an argument about the reification of perception drawn from the Marxian concept of *commodity* as taken up by the Frankfurt School. In the first part of their essay, intertextuality is explored in relation to the Hollywood novels of the early thirties, particularly with Horace McCoy's *They Shoot Horses, Don't They?*, published in 1935, and of which Faulkner had a paperback copy in his library. The authors find that, like McCoy, Faulkner allows his escapees to seek an exit from commodity, and to quest for a form of authentic experience—to no avail, of course. The second third of the paper might be summed up in the authors' excellent albeit provocative suggestion of a synopsis for *The Wild Palms:* "Brief spells of happiness, paid for by woman's death. Unhappy ending, used to affirm indestructibility of life"—and the theoretical weight of the whole paper is found to bear on their brief comment: "The culture industry would approve." In the third part, it is the intratextual relationship which is explored, i.e.—once more—what Faulkner himself called, and what the authors find it is not enough to call, the "counterpoint" provided by "Old Man." In it, they see "Faulkner's realization that the coefficient of commodity fetishism and of man's dissociation from his own labour is a flattening of perception itself." It is not enough to call it a "counterpoint" because, they argue, "the intratextual network of the novel is part of Faulkner's argument about commodity." Thus the conclusion is both that "to follow Harry in turning Harry into a tragic hero is to accede to the degraded consolation that a maimed life is better than nothing," and that "'Old Man' . . . leaves the oral tale of the proletariat [as represented by the Tall Convict] as confined and impotent as Harry's reverie."

The last two speakers in the colloquium have addressed themselves to more general, or more encompassing, topics, so that it seems appropriate that they be placed at the end of this collection. In "Intertextuality and Originality: Hawthorne, Faulkner, Updike," John T. Matthews announces "purposeful digressions" on the Gospel, *The Scarlet Letter, As I Lay Dying,* and *A Month of Sundays,* with the aim of assessing the conditions for originality in the light of "the speaker's double bind: ruled by intertextuality and aspiring to originality" (Julia Kristeva). Taking his cue from the episode of Jesus's sympathy with the adulterous woman (John 8), the author suggests that it stems deeply from "the paradox of his humanity," and that his strange, "only recorded act of writing ['on the ground, as though he heard them not'] . . . resembles distantly but sharply the transgressive subversiveness of adultery. The brilliance of Jesus' gesture is to transform the appearance of shameful lawbreaking into an occasion for upholding the law, to translate apparent destruction into fulfillment." Only then does Matthews examine briefly his triad of works which, he contends, all "inquire into the conventions, the customs, of writing, and in so doing, they cast and recast the recognition that the originality of a work is constituted in the movement that displaces its origin, that textuality is always intertextuality, and that, in the master image of all three novels, adultery represents the constitution of authenticity through a proscribed act." Hester, Addie, and Reverend Marshfield are all in search of "an immanent word that is not *déjà lu*," of something authentic which presupposes "the adulteration of self in adultery."

There is great merit in the fine and wise simplicity of Professor's Ohashi's talk. After papers written on particular aspects of Faulkner's work in more or less technical language, it is both refreshing and invigorating to hear from one whom we may call the dean of Faulkner studies in Japan, the author of a three-volume study of Faulkner, express his conviction that "there can be found out an intertextual network of scenes, characters, or images inherent in the working of Faulkner's imagination," and at the same time that this "intertextual relation or network . . . cannot be static . . . but must be kinetic or dynamic." In other terms, what his paper is after is a reconciliation of sheer repetition and mere change into "what we may call a 'temporal intertextual relationship'." In his own terms, indeed, even if Professor Ohashi is "certain that Faulkner succeeded in conquering or transcending the time obsession after writing *Absalom, Absalom!*," it remains as a sort of challenge to reconcile "that whole intertextual network inherent in Faulkner's works" and the dynamic working of the 'time element in his imagination. In my opinion, the answer lies not so much, or not only, in Faulkner's "repetitions or self-parodies" (the Eula-Jody-Hoake relationship in *The Hamlet* can indeed be shown to be a comic version of the Caddy-Quentin-Dalton Ames relationship in *The Sound and the Fury*), perhaps not even in Ohashi's assertion that in his later works "he was always trying to stand on the time present" and searching for "new" time and values; it lies rather, as it were incidentally, in what Ohashi calls the "wholeness" of the novels: "—if not literally whole, yet whole in the sense that he continually summed up what had already been treated." Here most certainly lies what is perhaps the inmost single idiosyncrasy of Faulkner's literary creation, so that the most intertextual of his texts, from this point of view, must be the map of Yoknapatawpha at the end of *Absalom,* the "Compson Appendix," "Mississippi," and *The Reivers.*

Of course, much remains to be done with this relatively new and extremely stimulating concept of intertextuality, not only because its theoretical extension is almost infinite, but because, with Faulkner, in particular, its field of application is well-nigh inexhaustible. Indeed, intertextuality seems to have been woven into Faulkner's writing from the start: it is only to think of the way his poetry absorbs all kinds of other texts, and his early prose presents such a fascinating double as "The Hill" and "Nympholepsy."

Here, then, is a first collective contribution, itself, as must be, intertextual to a certain, loose, extent—were it only for the reason that whatever working definition each of us gave of the notion for its use in his paper, all the contributors shared the conviction that Faulkner's work is intertextual *par excellence.* And no wonder: after all, is he not the writer who used the word *apocrypha* in order to describe his own work?

Michel Gresset

---

NOTES

1. Roland Barthes, "Texte [Théorie du]" in *Encylcopaedia Universalis,* vol. XV (Paris, 1973).

2. Julia Kristeva, *Semeiotikè: Recherches pour une Sémanalyse* (Paris: Le Seuil, 1973).

3. See note 17 of *"The Wild Palms:* Degraded Culture, Devalued Texts."

4. Respectively, *Selected Letters of William Faulkner,* ed. Joseph Blotner (New York: Random House, 1977), p. 285, and *Lion in the Garden: Interviews with William Faulkner, 1926–1962,* eds. James B. Meriwether and Michael Millgate (New York: Random House, 1968), p. 255.

5. See note 20 of *"The Wild Palms:* Degraded Culture, Devalued Texts."

# The Space between *Sanctuary*

*Noel Polk*

There is no need to rehearse here the details of the writing and revision of *Sanctuary;* they are well-known. What we do not know, of course, is *why* Faulkner revised it: why, having in 1929 pronounced the original version sufficiently finished for his immediate post-*Sound and Fury* standards, which were very high indeed; why, reading it in October of 1930, he found it bad enough to insist upon revising it completely, even paying part of the costs of resetting it for the privilege, so as to make of it something that "would not shame *The Sound and the Fury* and *As I Lay Dying* too much."[1] The question does not yield easy answers and may not, finally, yield any answers that are not too highly speculative to be useful. It is nevertheless a tantalizing and important question for the Faulkner field, because it is becoming more and more obvious that the two versions of *Sanctuary* are, like sex and death, the front and back doors to an incredible Faulknerian world that we have not yet sufficiently understood. Clearly *Sanctuary* cost him a great deal—much more, the evidence of the manuscript suggests, in the original writing than in the revising; just as clearly, the materials of *Sanctuary* were far more significant to him than his smart-aleck indictment of it— "the most horrific tale I could imagine"[2]—allows.

Perhaps his reasons for revising were purely artistic; perhaps, on the other hand, mixed with the artistic reasons were a sufficient number of more personal reasons, simple or complex, denied to us now because there is still a great deal we do not know about Faulkner's life during this period.[3] We may be able, however, to understand Faulkner's need to revise *Sanctuary* by looking at the novel(s) through the curtained and opaque window Faulkner inadvertently provided for us in the work that he accomplished during the nearly eighteen months that elapsed between the two versions and by looking at the total complex of his achievement between the time of his first conception of *Sanctuary,* probably somewhere between 1925 and 1927, and the 1930 work of revising. Consider that between 1927 and 1931 Faulkner wrote *Flags in the Dust;* wrote *The Sound and the Fury;* wrote *Sanctuary;* wrote *As I Lay Dying;* revised *Sanctuary;* revised the Quentin section of *The Sound and the Fury;* and wrote and/or revised about thirty short stories, some of them among the best he would ever write. In quantity alone, this record is astounding; in quality, it is perhaps unparalleled. What he accomplished in the eighteen months between the two versions of *Sanctuary* is easily equal to what many major writers produce in a decade; it should not be too hard, then, to believe that what Faulkner taught himself about his craft during that year and a half is enough to account for his dissatisfaction with the early version.

We cannot, however, account for the two *Sanctuary*s simply by reference to chronology of composition, because in spite of a lot of factual information from this period, we still are not sure exactly when he wrote what; even if we accept strictly the order of composition indicated by dates on the manuscripts and on the short story sending schedule he kept during this period, we still cannot—or rather *I* cannot—demonstrate a straight line of artistic or thematic development from one end of the period to the other. Besides, the dates on the sending schedule could not possibly represent the order of composition; they seem rather to be the dates Faulkner recorded sending them out to magazines: even with his speed, he did not write "Mistral," "Pennsylvania Station," and "The Leg" on November 3, 1928![4] There is not, right now, enough evidence to prove when these and other stories were written, although it seems clear enough that many of them, at least early versions of many of them, were written in Europe or in the months immediately following his return to Mississippi.

We can, however, with some certainty trace the origins of *Sanctuary* to his time in Paris. In one letter home he described what seems to have become *Sanctuary*'s final scene: he reported having "written such a beautiful thing that I am about to bust—

2000 words about the Luxembourg gardens and death," and he spoke of having done 20,000 words on his novel.[5] It is not clear whether the 20,000 words and the 2,000 words are part of the same work, but it is at least possible that they are somehow related. The description of Temple Drake in the Luxembourg Gardens as it appears in *Sanctuary*, however, is a mere 344 words long.[6] Assuming that Faulkner was telling the truth, we may well ask what became of the other portions. Are they lost? Was he referring to *Elmer*? Did they become part of *Sanctuary*? Did those 20,000 or 2,000 words become part of *Flags in the Dust*, a novel with many important connections to *Sanctuary*?[7] Even though one might persuasively argue that *Sanctuary* is at least in part an attempt to salvage some of the Benbow material Faulkner had to delete from *Flags*, it is probably more useful, finally, to think of *Flags* and *Sanctuary* as having an even more intimate, even symbiotic, relationship in their origins somewhere very early in Faulkner's career.

At least part of *Sanctuary*, then, seems to have been written before *The Sound and the Fury*, perhaps before *Flags*, perhaps even before *Soldiers' Pay* and *Mosquitoes*. Add to this possibility the fact that during the winter and spring of 1929 Faulkner revised heavily the Quentin section of *The Sound and the Fury*,[8] and it is possible to demonstrate a close compositional relationship among *Flags*, *Sanctuary*, and *The Sound and the Fury* that may well symbolize the degree to which all three spring from the same matrix. Further, although *Sanctuary* had been rejected by his publisher (perhaps *because* it had been rejected), much of that novel's matter—themes and images in multiple variations—found its way into short stories and into *As I Lay Dying* in ways that suggest the peculiar quality of Faulkner's imagination during the early part of the period.

What I would like to do in this essay is to look at the space between *Sanctuary*, the *Sanctuary* texts and intertexts, to speculate a bit about the differences between the two works, and to propose that the intermediate works are in fact a kind of filter through which Faulkner pushed the nightmare phantasms of *Sanctuary*, with the result, even if not the intended one, of exorcising them completely or at least of rendering them so obvious that Faulkner could—perhaps had to—suppress them. I will leave it to someone else to suggest that what Faulkner meant when he said *Sanctuary* was *bad* was that it was actually worse than bad: it was intolerably *close*.

## I.

The early *Sanctuary* is Horace's book entirely: his profoundest anxieties and insecurities, his deepest fears, his darkest fantasies lurk everywhere inside his tawdry, uneventful, bourgeois existence; everything that is crystallized in his relationships with all the women in his life is projected outward from his mind into the grotesque shapes of those characters from the Memphis underworld who inhabit his nightmare, for nightmare it surely is. Nearly all of *Sanctuary* takes place in darkness, in halls dimly lighted or completely dark, in houses hiding dark secrets, in tunnels formed by trees or hedges; faces appear and disappear, appear again and blur in and out of focus, and combine in crucial passages, such as the one in which Temple and Ruby and Narcissa and Horace's mother and Popeye all become one in Horace's mind. *Sanctuary*'s nightmarish qualities are an important part of its meaning. A good deal of the novel can best be understood by approaching it through the general terms laid out by Freud in his monumental study *The Interpretation of Dreams*[9] and other works. I hasten to say that it is no purpose of mine in this essay to argue whether or how much Freud Faulkner read. There is on the one hand, of course, no known proof that he read any; there is, on the other hand, a great deal of indirect evidence that he knew much about Freud's theories. And there are a number of enigmas in *Sanctuary* that make more sense if they can be understood in terms of Freud's analyses of dreams, regardless of the degree of Faulkner's formal acquaintance with Freud's work.

That *Sanctuary* is a nightmare is rendered explicitly a number of times, nowhere more so than in the following passage, which occurs during Horace's return to Jefferson after he has been to Memphis to hear Temple's story at Miss Reba's whorehouse. He had caught the predawn train to Memphis earlier in the day; as he walks back home away from the station he has the sensation that

> there had not been any elapsed time between: the same ges-
> ture of the lighted clock-face, the same vulture-like shadows in
> the doorways; it might be the same morning and he had
> merely crossed the square, about-faced and was returning; all
> between a dream filled with all the nightmare shapes it had
> taken him forty-three years to invent. (SO, p. 219; SR, p. 266)

All of these "nightmare shapes" become "concentrated" in the "hot, hard lump" of undigested coffee in his stomach, which in turn becomes the immediate physical cause of the nausea that overtakes him only minutes later when he returns to his home and sees the blurring face of Little Belle in the photograph. In the spectacular conclusion to that scene, Horace vomits; and as he does so he *becomes* Temple Drake and Little Belle: *he* "plunged forward and struck the lavatory and leaned upon *his* braced arms while the shucks set up a terrific uproar beneath *her* thighs." Likewise, the coffee he vomits, which is something "*she* watched . . . black and furious go roaring out of *her* pale body" (SO, p. 220; SR, p. 268; italics supplied), identifies him specifically with Popeye, who to Horace smells black, "like that black stuff that ran out of Bovary's mouth" (SO, p. 25; SR, p. 6); it also connects him, not incidentally, to other characters in the novel who vomit, Uncle Bud and Temple's Ole Miss co-ed friend. Thus in the nightmare recapitulation of all that Temple has told him, in the dreamwork's condensation of its materials, Horace becomes Temple, Little Belle, and Popeye: he is at one and the same time male, female, androgynous; the seducer and the seduced; the violater and the violated; the lover and the protector; father, brother, sister; son, lover, destroyer.

What is the source of all this? There is no clue in the 1931 text, in which this scene survives unchanged from the early version. There is another scene, however, cancelled in the revision, which fuels some speculation. This is the paragraph that occurs shortly after the beginning of Chapter 12, when Horace once again passes the jail and looks up at the window in which sit the hands of the condemned Negro murderer. The jail window and the Negro murderer are very important points of reference for Horace, much more important in the first than in the revised version; the first version in fact *begins* with the oft-noted description of that window, in which Horace sees the Negro murderer's hands lying peacefully. Seeing them, Horace recalls in astonishing, graphic, detail the peculiarly violent nature of the Negro's murder of his wife. We needn't be surprised that the murder should interest Horace or that he should so strongly identify with the murderer. Doubtless part of him admires the Negro's neat, simple, passionate solution to his marital troubles, and perhaps in his fantasies he wishes he were aggressive enough, masculine enough, passionate enough, to solve his own problems so completely. Likewise, the Negro's present situation, safely incarcerated as he is in the sanctuary of the jail, is one that attracts Horace: unlike Horace, he is free of trouble and worry, free of all striving. He has nothing more troublesome to do than merely wait to die. Further, there may be in Horace's mind some relationship between the Negro murderer and Popeye—that "black man"—who is at the book's end also in jail, waiting peacefully, fretlessly, to die; it is a connection the reader cannot help making. Further still, as we shall see, Horace's complete identification with the Negro may also be a function of his feeling that he himself deserves, even wants, an appropriate punishment, from an appropriate figure, for his guilt over his murderous and incestuous fantasies, most, as nearly everybody has noted, directed toward his sister, who not for nothing is named Narcissa. In nothing is Horace more akin to Quentin Compson than in this cluster of facts and fantasies.

The passage in question was excised completely in the revision:

> Each time he passed the jail he would find himself looking up at the window, to see the hand or the wisp of tobacco smoke blowing along the sunshine. The wall was now in sunlight, the hand lying there in sunlight too, looking dingier,

smaller, more tragic than ever, yet he turned his head quickly away. It was as though from that tiny clot of knuckles he was about to reconstruct an edifice upon which he would not dare to look, like an archaeologist who, from a meagre sifting of vertebrae, reconstructs a shape out of the nightmares of his own childhood, and he looked quickly away as the car went smoothly on and the jail, the shabby purlieus of the square gave way to shady lawns and houses—all the stability which he had known always—a stage upon which tragedy kept to a certain predictableness, decorum. (SO, pp. 141–42)

This is a very important passage in the early text, equally for the way it reveals the nightmare images that haunt Horace's conscious mind as for the way in which it reveals his strategies for evading all those things he doesn't want to confront directly: what he sees through that window obviously conjures up for him some childhood nightmares so powerful that he looks away immediately, self-protectively, directing his eyes and his body toward the maternal home, back toward "all the stability which he had known always."

This impulse toward evasion is in fact the pattern that begins Horace's involvement with the Memphis underworld, the underbelly of his own tepid, middle-class existence. Standing at the curtained window of his office in Kinston, looking at the "green-snared promise of unease" just outside in the ripening garden, he thinks first of the rankness of his marriage to Belle, and then, inevitably, of Little Belle: at which point he leaves the window, goes to Little Belle's room, takes her picture out of its frame, and sets out walking to Jefferson, back, ostensibly, to the security of his childhood home; he tells himself that he is counting on Narcissa's "imperviousness." Yet there is considerable evidence in the early *Sanctuary* that Horace's childhood was not by any means so serene as he remembers and that his conscious memory of that childhood as stable and secure is yet another evasion of certain truths, never directly articulated in the novel, that he does not want to face. It is precisely on the way home that all his nightmares in fact come to life: in the reflecting waters of

that mysterious pond, just away from the road, kneeling, a twentieth-century Narcissus, Horace comes face to face with all the
conflicting elements that compose his inner life. Popeye, whose
face merges with his in the water, and at whom he stares,
petrified with fright, or fascination, for two hours, is much more
Horace's double than has generally been allowed: he is at once
Horace's twin, his alter ego, at the same time his id and his
superego; he is at once the reductio ad absurdum of Horace's
darker sexual impulses as well as the punishing, vengeful father.

Again, one could ask, what is the source of all this? There is
yet another significant scene in the first version, deleted in revision, which may help us understand Horace in these passages.
The scene occurs in Chapter 5 of the early text. Horace leaves
the Sartoris household where his sister and Miss Jenny live, returns to Jefferson determined to open up their childhood home,
the house where he and Narcissa grew up, and on which he has
secretly paid the taxes for the past ten years. He approaches the
old house through a "fence massed with honeysuckle," an association with Quentin Compson we cannot miss; he walks over a
lawn whose "uncut grass" has gone "rankly and lustily to seed."
As he wanders about the yard he feels it as a "tight and inscrut-
able desolation"—desolation, significantly, in the midst of all
that suffocating fecundity—in which he moves "in a prolonged
orgasm of sentimental loneliness" (SO, p. 61). The house hardly
inspires in him the serenity and stability he thinks he has always
known there; quite the contrary. He seems to "hurdle time and
surprise his sister and himself in a thousand forgotten pictures
out of the serene fury of their childhood." He examines the
windows of the house, which have remained exactly "as he had
nailed them up ten years ago":

> The nails were clumsily driven. . . . Rusted, mute, the warped
> and battered heads emerged from the wood or lay hammered
> flat into it by clumsy blows. From each one depended a small
> rusty stain, like a dried tear or a drop of blood; he touched
> them, drawing his finger across the abrasions. "I crucified
> more than me, then," he said aloud. (SO, pp. 61–62)

He pulls the nails with a hammer, opens the shutter, to let in light and, going from room to room, discovers his conscious past, a highly evocative tableau, his invalid mother at the center of it:

> It seemed to him that he came upon himself and his sister, upon their father and mother, who had been an invalid so long that the one picture of her he retained was two frail arms rising from a soft falling of lace, moving delicately to an interminable manipulation of colored silk, in fading familiar gestures in the instant between darkness and sunlight. (SO, pp. 62–63)

We are unquestionably being directed to take those tightly nailed windows as eyes, symbolically nailed tightly shut upon something, some traumatic scene, some pain, particular or general, associated with Horace's childhood in this house, which he has suppressed from his memory; clearly he has seen something that has traumatized him, filled him not just with fear but also with disgust and self-loathing. Exactly what he has seen we are never told, but given Horace's obsessions as they manifest themselves throughout the book, it seems clearly to be something sexual and just as clearly to have happened at home: I propose, simply, that Horace has been traumatized by what Freud called the "primal scene," or some variation of it. There are an arresting number of similarities between *Sanctuary* and Freud's "Wolf Man" case history,[10] which is his analysis of a young man who as a child had dreamed of waking in the middle of the night to see the window of his room open suddenly and inexplicably and reveal to his eyes a tree in which five white wolves were sitting, staring at him. Under analysis, the Wolf Man reveals that as a child he had awakened from sleep in his crib to see his father and mother engaged in what appeared to be anal intercourse— that is, his mother on her hands and knees and his father behind her. The child's immediate response was to defecate, in his bed. His long-range response was to suppress the incident entirely, both what he saw and what he did; but the incident emerged, fighting its way past the mind's censorious guards, transformed into something acceptable to, even while it troubled, the conscious mind. From the patient's childhood dream of the staring wolves, Freud builds an analytical edifice that involves the young man's family in ways that ring all sorts of bells for the reader of Faulkner—a mother in ill health, a depressed and frequently absent father, an older, dominating sister who as a child initiates him into children's sexual curiosity; further, the analysis establishes the Wolf Man's guilt over what he has seen, his shame over his defecation, his incestuous desire to have his father make anal love to him, and his simultaneous desire to be punished by his father for his sin. When he becomes Temple Drake, Horace fulfills his own rape fantasy; and it may be, finally, that Horace's and Uncle Bud's and Temple's co-ed friend's vomiting, as well as Temple's obsession with urination and defecation at the Old Frenchman Place, can be understood only by reference to the Wolf Man.

Horace's nightmare does not, of course, take the form of such a static visual tableau. He does not see through his window a set of white wolves; through his office window in Kinston he sees and smells the rife, fecund, suffocating, honeysuckled world of his own garden; as he continues watching through that window, the window to his own inner life, that same garden turns into the foul, rank, overgrown jungle that surrounds the Old Frenchman Place where, in the corn*crib*, Temple, his female self, is violated by Popeye as, in Temple's mind, blind Pap looks on. Horace's dream, then, substituting and transforming and inverting the actual experience, manufactures out of whatever he saw, whatever he felt, whatever he is suppressing, a world of dark fantastic characters and shapes that correspond to something in his hidden life. It is a fantastic world indeed, full of dark places and bizarre, grotesque shapes, which make the imagination of Quentin Compson seem, by comparison, a clean, well-lighted place.

There are two more scenes, one deleted from, one retained in, the revised text, which together support if they do not absolutely confirm such speculations about Horace's childhood trauma, whatever it was, and perhaps provide a base upon which we can build some generalizations about mothers and windows and doors and children and sex in Faulkner's work of this period. The first scene occurs in both versions. It is the wonderfully funny, if grotesque, scene at Miss Reba's, after Red's funeral, when Miss Reba and the two visiting madames indulge themselves in a bit of socializing; they sit around swilling beer and gin and talking about Red, Temple, and Popeye. Overhearing this conversation is the pathetic, lonely little boy, Uncle Bud, already practically an alcoholic, whose central form of amusement appears to be snitching drinks on the sly from the ladies. The madames are of course talking shop, discussing sex: normal sex, abnormal, voyeurism, and monkey glands. During their conversation Uncle Bud moves about "aimlessly" to the window where, like Horace Benbow in other passages, he peers out "beneath the lifted shade" (SO, p. 246; SR, p. 303). A few pages later, after more talk of drinking and sex, the ladies become aware that Uncle Bud has gotten drunk: exasperated, Miss Myrtle "grasp[s] the boy by the arm and snatch[es] him out from behind Miss Reba's chair and [shakes] him. . . . 'Aint you ashamed? Aint you *ashamed?*'" she screams at him: "Now, you go over there by that window and stay there, you hear?" (SO, p. 250; SR, p. 309). In this rather carefully executed scene, shame and windows are thus associated, the association emphasized by the fact that the word "ashamed" occurs half a dozen times in this scene, the only scene in the novel where the word is used.

The scene ends with Uncle Bud's vomiting, an act which, as we have already suggested, may serve to connect him directly to Horace; given other associations between the two, we may also be being invited to see the whole episode, which otherwise seems to be significantly outside the central narrative of the novel, as a kind of parable of Horace's childhood, if not actually a dream's distorted re-presentation of it.

If we can accept the scene as in some way rendering an episode in Horace's childhood or at least as crystallizing some quality, some essence, of that childhood; if we can entertain this notion, it becomes very tempting to see Miss Reba, by the same token, as a dreamwork version of Horace's mother. There are several reasons for suggesting this. In the early version, but not in the revision, for example, Faulkner may have intended to associate Miss Reba and Horace's mother more directly through the specific terms of a curious tree in the yard of the old Benbow house, scene of many of Horace's fondest recollections. The tree is

> old and thick and squat, impenetrable to sun or rain. It was circled by a crude wooden bench, onto the planks of which the bole, like breasts of that pneumatic constancy so remote from lungs as to be untroubled by breath, had croached and over-bosomed until supporting trestles were no longer necessary. (SO, p. 64)

Is this the self-sufficient mother, all-powerful, all-maternal, not needing the support of husband or of anybody else? It is clearly a maternal tree and may suggest that Horace was mothered to death as a child; this is, not incidentally, what Narcissa seems well on her way to doing to her son; and it is what Horace thinks Ruby is doing to her child when he accuses her of holding it too much, though the reader of the revised text only cannot understand *why* Horace thinks this. Later, in Chapter 13, the fat, wheezing, constantly breathless Miss Reba is described as having huge billowing breasts, a bosom of "rich pneumasis" (SO, p. 168; SR, p. 170): she moves through the room with the two dogs "moiling underfoot" like playful children and talks in a "harsh, expiring, maternal voice" (SO, p. 169; SR, p. 171). Further, if as we have suggested in Horace's nightmare Popeye is Horace's father[11]—the judge, the respectable family man become, by the substitution and inversion of the dreamwork, the impotent voyeur, the outlaw, the bootlegger, but still the punishing, vengeful father who in the dream kills the son for the Oedipal consummation; if Popeye is by inversion and repression and substitution Horace's father, it is not at all too much to consider that Miss Reba is, by the same process of inversion and substitution, Horace's mother: the frail, lifeless, shallow-breathing invalid mother become the robust, breathless, dominating madame of a brothel. This is a substitution that both hides and symbolically reveals exactly those attributes of his mother he wants to block from his memory—precisely that world, that is, upon which he nailed those windows shut, for the sake of those more pleasant memories he wants to retain of his childhood.

The equation—Popeye-Father, Miss Reba-Mother—is not, however, quite so simple or as simplistic as it would seem, for there is another scene in the original version, deleted in revision, in which Horace's mother, his sister, his wife, Ruby—all the objects of his sexual fantasies—and Popeye, who with the women represents Horace's failed masculinity, become fused, condensed in his imagination into one horrifying, repulsive image. Sleeping alone in the family house one night, he wakes up suddenly; the scene evokes Freud's Wolf Man:

> On the second night he dreamed that he was a boy again and waked himself crying in a paroxysm of homesickness like that of a child away from home at night, alone in a strange room. It seemed to him that not only the past two days, but the last thirty-five years had been a dream, and he waked himself calling his mother's name in a paroxysm of terror and grief. . . .
>
> After a while he could not tell whether he were awake or not. He could still sense a faint motion of curtains in the dark window and the garden smells, but he was talking to his mother too, who had been dead thirty years. She had been an invalid, but now she was well; she seemed to emanate that abounding serenity as of earth which his sister had done since her marriage and the birth of her child, and she sat on the side of the bed, talking to him. With her hands, her touch, because he realised that she had not opened her mouth. Then he saw that she wore a shapeless garment of faded calico and that Belle's rich, full mouth burned sullenly out of the halflight, and he knew that she was about to open her mouth and he tried to scream at her, to clap his hand to her mouth. But it was too late. He saw her mouth open; a thick, black liquid welled in a bursting bubble that splayed out upon her fading chin and the sun was shining on his face and he was thinking He smells black. He smells like that black stuff that ran out of Bovary's mouth when they raised her head. (SO, p. 60)

Thus Horace's repression of *something* connected with aggression and sex and death and disgust and his mother is made explicit; it is not unreasonable, then, to think that Horace's mother may have been much more closely akin to Caroline Compson than to the frail, wraith-like woman he insists upon remembering. Given many other relationships between Horace and Quentin Compson, and between the novels in which they appear, we might look backward to the relationship between Caroline and Jason Compson for some sense of the nature of Horace's parents' relationship and of their effect on their children. Indeed, if John T. Irwin wanted some real doubling and incest, some real repetition and revenge, he might well have explored the Horace/Quentin relationship in *The Sound and the Fury* and the original *Sanctuary*, which seem to me far more intimately related than *The Sound and the Fury* and *Absalom, Absalom!*[12]

*Sanctuary* drips with windows and doors, houses in which dark secrets are darkly hidden, where relationships between parents and between parents and children are founded upon suspicion and domination and sexual repression. In the early *Sanctuary*, as in *The Sound and the Fury*, as, indeed, in *Mosquitoes* and *Soldiers' Pay*, in *As I Lay Dying* and in a great deal of the short fiction of the mid- to late-twenties, sex and death and women are indissolubly associated; and Horace is, no less than Quentin Compson, no less than the entire Bundren family, no less than many other of Faulkner's protagonists of this period, simply overwhelmed by an invalid mother—this image rises screaming, insistent and peremptory, out of Faulkner's work of the twenties, and it will be worth a brief digression here to reflect on this fact.

Over and over again throughout Faulkner's work there are significant mothers: in the early years mothers who dominate and oppress—Mrs. Compson, the redoubtable Mrs. Bland, Addie Bundren, perhaps Horace's mother, certainly Narcissa; in the middle years are mothers, beginning as early as Caddy Compson, the very heart's darling herself, who abandon their children—Caddy, Dewey Dell Bundren (who wants to abandon it before it is even born), Laverne Schumann, Charlotte Rittenmeyer; in the later years this image gives way to mothers like the more ambivalent Temple Drake Stevens of *Requiem for a Nun* who, whatever else can be said about her, at least doesn't plan to abandon her *infant* child when she runs off with Pete and does plan to leave her older child with its father, who she knows will care for him; and in *The Town* there are Eula Varner Snopes, who literally sacrifices herself for her child, and Maggie Mallison Stevens, probably the healthiest, sanest, most good-humored, most *normal* female in all of Faulkner's work.

By contrast, fathers play a relatively minor role in the fiction. They are mostly weak, impotent, henpecked, peripheral, frequently absent and/or replaced by surrogate grandfathers, uncles, or older cousins. I do not forget strong fathers like Temple Drake's, or John Sartoris of *The Unvanquished,* or the foster father Simon McEachern or the fanatical Old Doc Hines in *Light in August;* nor do I forget Thomas Sutpen himself. Fathers are thus either weak unto despair, or strong unto destruction, or both, and it may be significant that there is, finally, no father in all of Faulkner, early or late, to match the heroic strength of Eula Varner Snopes or the healthy normality of Maggie Mallison. It may or may not be significant that Faulkner did not have much respect for his own father, who died in 1932; by the same token, it may or may not be significant that Faulkner's mother lived almost as long as Faulkner did and that he was clearly devoted to her, although Jay Martin has recently argued that under the surface of that relationship all was not so calm as that devotion might indicate.[13]

## II.

After Smith rejected *Sanctuary,* Faulkner was left holding not just an unpublished novel, but a whole world which he apparently could not exorcise, a myriad of images that he remained preoccupied with, or at least continued to use almost compulsively, perhaps for reasons he himself did not completely understand, in the months that followed. I can best suggest the relationship of the original *Sanctuary* to the works radiating outward from it by pointing, in closing, to a connection with *As I Lay Dying.* The occasion for the connection is the following amazing passage, which occurs in both versions of *Sanctuary.* In it Temple describes to Horace Benbow part of her experience at the Old Frenchman Place:

> I hadn't breathed in a long time. So I thought I was dead. . . . I could see myself in the coffin. I looked sweet—you know: all in white. I had on a veil like a bride. . . .

Then she describes her reaction to Popeye:

> . . . I'd lie there with the shucks laughing at me and me jerking away in front of his hand and I'd think what I'd say to him. I'd talk to him like the teacher does in school, and then I was a teacher in school and it was a little black thing like a nigger boy, kind of, and I was the teacher. Because I'd say How old am I? and I'd say I'm forty-five years old. I had iron-gray hair and spectacles and I was all big up here like women get. . . . And I was telling it what I'd do, and it kind of drawing up and drawing up like it could already see the switch. (SO, pp. 216–17; SR, pp. 263–64)

Thus Temple, repressed, or at least unpublished, in her first appearance, becomes Addie Bundren—though to what extent this character became Addie Bundren *because* she was repressed in her Temple Drake avatar we probably will never know. But the other terms Temple uses to describe the self she creates in her fantasy extends the first *Sanctuary*'s connection to other works of the period: she has both the large maternal bosom of Miss Reba and of the tree in the Benbow yard, and the sinister iron-gray hair of the numerous repressive and repressed women in the fiction of this period. Perhaps in this latter detail we are most suggestively reminded of the remains of Emily Grierson's murderous yet withal pathetic and frustrated love for Homer Barron: the speck of iron-gray hair left on the pillow beside his skeleton.

The image of the gray-haired old woman, repressing or repressed, or both, appears throughout the fiction of this period in various combinations with windows in which their peering faces are framed or with pillows out of which their sallow faces stare, dominant. From that central image are splayed out in all directions significant connections to recurrent symbols, which may themselves come directly from Freud: windows, doors, stairs, curtains, veils, and eyes, all appearing in the service of the dominant themes of sexual frustration and impotence, and the sickness begotten of the fear of sexual experience. Note, for example, Miss Zilphia Gant's mother, and then Miss Zilphia herself, looking out of their small house through barred windows at the playground/prison outside; Miss Emily Grierson with her face framed by the window in which she constantly sits looking out at Jefferson's passing life; the white-haired mothers and grandmothers in "Ellie" and "The Brooch" who dominate their children from their bedrooms; Minnie Cooper in "Dry September" has been victimized by an invalid mother; even Miss Jenny, in "There Was a Queen," gray-haired and wheelchaired, invalided by age, watches the peculiarly "manless" Sartoris world through a window: the significance of the image for the entire period may be indicated by the fact that it supplied Faulkner an early title for this important story: "Through the Window."

The novels and stories of 1927–31 thus form a veritable spider's web of intimate connections, a fascinating web, if you will, of intertexts: touch the web at one point and you send thrilling little vibrations into nearly all the other parts.

When Faulkner found himself confronted, unexpectedly, if we may believe him, with the *Sanctuary* galleys in the fall of 1930, we may surmise that at least part of what he was dissatisfied with was that it did not reflect his current concerns—one might say his current obsessions, whatever their sources. He found himself stuck with a throwback, felt obliged not only to bring it in line with his current interests, but perhaps, consciously or unconsciously, to repress much of that portion of his earlier self, both his artistic and his personal self, that he saw reflected in that early version.

By the time he received those galleys, he had worked his way through, out of, those images and themes that occur in the space around the early *Sanctuary* with such compulsive regularity. By the fall of 1930 they seem to have been brought under some control, to have lost some of their urgency, if not to have disappeared completely. That is, the differences between the early *Sanctuary* and *Light in August* may be traceable to the differences between such intense, internalized stories of repression and frustration as "Ellie" and "A Rose for Emily" at the early end of the period and, at the late end, such stories as "Lizards in Jamshyd's Courtyard," "Red Leaves," and "Mountain Victory," for example, which, whatever one thinks of their relative quality, can at least be recognized as less sexually intense, more open, more spacious, more external in their focus than the earlier stories.

What Faulkner did to *Sanctuary* was precisely to cut or alter those passages that call attention too explicitly to Horace's childhood, his incestuous fantasies, his parents, his nightmare, and his relationship to Popeye. We are in the revision taken directly, as quickly and efficiently as possible, out of Horace's cloyingly introspective mind; what is rendered as stream of consciousness in the first version is often recast as direct quotations from Horace's conscious mind. In the first version of the scene at the pond, for example, we first see Popeye from Horace's point of view; in the revised version we rather see Horace through Popeye's eyes. From being "Horace" or "Benbow" in the first version of the scene, he becomes "the man" in the second. Finally, it is very much worth noting that while deleting all this material about Horace's background, his childhood, and his parents, the one extended passage Faulkner added to the revision was about Popeye's childhood, his background: it is a short biography in which we learn about his itinerant absent father, his "invalid" mother, and his crazy, pyromaniac grandmother. This addition is strictly in keeping with Faulkner's other efforts to put Horace at some distance from the reader and, perhaps, from himself; in this passage he simply transfers the essence of Horace's childhood directly into Popeye's: there, at least, it *seems* more appropriate.

### III.

I do not know whether from observations like these one can conclude anything about Faulkner's reasons for revising *Sanc-*

*tuary:* whether his reasons were personal or artistic, the extent to which they represent a conscious or unconscious repression of some very significant material. The psycho-biographer might argue that Faulkner meant a great deal more than he knew when he wrote that he didn't want *Sanctuary* to "shame" *The Sound and the Fury* and *As I Lay Dying;* he might and doubtless now will pursue the possibility that many of Horace's nightmares, and some of his background, were very close to Faulkner's own and that, seeing his own traumas so baldly, so clear and unveiled through the open window of those galleys, Faulkner had, consciously or unconsciously, to suppress them. The New Critic may well argue that the revised *Sanctuary* is a "better" work of art than the early one; there is much to support such a position. I will not fuel either argument here. What I will assert, however, is that the first *Sanctuary* is, at least for the time being, in so many ways a more interesting book than the second, and that taken together, in their inter- and intratextual relationships with each other and with the other novels and stories in the space between, the two versions form a single literary text that is far more significant than either of the versions taken singly. We cannot now, I believe, pretend to understand either *Sanctuary* without also coming to terms with the other. And it seems to me obvious that there are ways in which all the texts of these years form a single intertext which holds important meanings for the study of Faulkner's work. The space between *Sanctuary* is filled with an entire teeming, fecund, even honeysuckled Faulknerian world that perhaps only these intertextual relationships can give us access to.

---

NOTES

1. *Essays Speeches & Public Letters,* ed. James B. Meriwether (New York: Random House, 1965), p. 178.
2. *Essays Speeches & Public Letters,* p. 177.
3. See the relevant portions of Joseph Blotner, *William Faulkner: A Biography* (New York: Random House, 1974), and the 1984 revised and reduced one-volume edition, which contains some significant new information about Faulkner's life during this period; Judith Bryant Wittenberg, *Faulkner: The Transfiguration of Biography* (Lincoln: University of Nebraska Press, 1979); and David Minter, *William Faulkner: His Life and World* (Baltimore: Johns Hopkins University Press, 1980).

4. James B. Meriwether, *The Literary Career of William Faulkner* (Princeton: Princeton University Library, 1961), pp. 167–80. See also Max Putzel, "Faulkner's Short Story Sending Schedule," PBSA, 71 (January–March 1977), pp. 98–105. For other significant discussions of Faulkner's short story career, see Meriwether, "The Short Fiction of William Faulkner: A Bibliography," *Proof I*, ed. Joseph Katz (Columbia, S.C.: University of South Carolina Press, 1973), pp. 293–329; Meriwether, "Faulkner's Correspondence with *Scribner's Magazine*," *Proof 3*, ed. Joseph Katz (Columbia, S.C.: University of South Carolina Press, 1973), pp. 253–82; and Hans Skei, *William Faulkner: The Short Story Career* (Oslo: Universitetsforlaget, 1981), especially Chapters 2 and 3.

5. *Selected Letters of William Faulkner*, ed. Joseph Blotner (New York: Random House, 1977), p. 17. To Mrs. M. C. Falkner, postmarked 6 September 1925.

6. *Sanctuary: The Original Text*, ed. Noel Polk. (New York: Random House, 1981); hereafter referred to as SO. *Sanctuary* (New York: Jonathan Cape and Harrison Smith, 1931); hereafter referred to as SR.

7. See Michel Gresset's important new book, *Faulkner ou la fascination* (Paris: Klincksieck, 1982), for cogent and useful discussions of these relationships.

8. Over 40 pages of a ribbon typescript version of the Quentin section of *The Sound and the Fury* are now on deposit in the Faulkner collection of the Alderman Library at the University of Virginia. These pages have been copy-edited, so it is clear that they were part of a novel that had been submitted for publication.

9. Sigmund Freud, *The Interpretation of Dreams*, in *The Standard Edition of the Complete Psychological Writings of Sigmund Freud*, vols. IV–V, trans. James Strachey (London: The Hogarth Press and the Institute of Psycho-analysis, 1953).

10. See Freud's "From the History of an Infantile Neurosis," in *The Standard Edition*, vol. XVII, pp. 7–122. This famous case was first published in English in 1925.

11. We have already noted the various mirror relationships between Horace and Temple, the extent to which Horace sympathetically *becomes* Temple in the vomiting scene described earlier. Temple makes a great deal out of the fact that her father is a judge; Horace not so much, but he is acutely sensitive when Clarence Snopes addresses him by his father's former title. Given the connection between Temple and Horace, there may be more than one implication when Temple calls Popeye "Daddy" (SO, p. 231; SR, p. 284).

12. John T. Irwin, *Doubling and Incest, Repetition and Revenge: A Speculative Reading of Faulkner* (Baltimore: Johns Hopkins University Press, 1975).

13. "'The Whole Burden of Man's History of His Impossible Heart's Desire': The Early Life of William Faulkner," *American Literature*, 53 (January 1982), pp. 607–29.

# "Cet affreux goût d'encre"
# Emma Bovary's Ghost in *Sanctuary*

## *André Bleikasten*

Il fallut soulever un peu la tête, et alors un flot de liquides noirs sortit, comme un vomissement, de sa bouche.[1]

He smells black, Benbow thought; he smells like that black stuff that ran out of Bovary's mouth and down upon her bridal veil when they raised her head.[2]

The first sentence is taken from *Madame Bovary*. It occurs toward the close of Flaubert's novel, in the ninth chapter of the third part—not, as one might assume in reading it out of context, *during* the scene of Emma's death, but *after* it, as Félicité, the maid, Madame Lefrançois and old Madame Bovary are dressing her corpse for the funeral.

The second excerpt comes from the sixth page of *Sanctuary*. It is quite clearly an allusion to the incident recounted in *Madame Bovary*, an allusion halfway between literal quotation (without quotation marks) and rephrasing (the "bridal veil" is inferred from the context). It is also worth noting that this is the only literary allusion to be found in Faulkner's novel and, as far as I know, the only reference to Flaubert's work in the whole Faulkner corpus.

Before examining the intertextual links between the two books, let us first turn back to *Madame Bovary* and take a closer look at the scene of Emma's macabre disgorgement. In Flaubert's narrative, the latter is the ultimate, posthumous occurrence in a whole series of vomitings, beginning at the time of Emma's long illness after the end of her first adulterous affair: "She started vomiting—and in that Charles thought he saw the first signs of cancer" (p. 222).[3] She vomits again—and more than

---

A version of this essay first appeared in *William Faulkner: Materials, Studies, Criticism* (Japan), 5 (May 1983), 1–25.

once—as she lies dying after the suicidal absorption of arsenic, convulsed with atrocious physical pain:

> And she vomited so suddenly that she barely had time to grab her handkerchief from under the pillow (p. 327).[4]

> At eight o'clock the vomiting began again (p. 327).[5]

> Not long afterwards she started vomiting blood (p. 330).[6]

Emma's is indeed a nauseous death, and in describing it in horrendous detail (groans and screams, writhing limbs, rolling eyes, chattering teeth, protruding tongue) with what most critics take to be "clinical detachment"—yet also, one suspects, with a measure of gothic glee—Flaubert does his best to make it nauseating to the reader. Nowhere else in *Madame Bovary* is his realism as meticulously brutal—except, perhaps, in the episode of Charles Bovary's botched operation on Hippolyte, the clubfoot. Five days after the operation, Hippolyte's foot has "swollen to an unrecognizable shape," and after another three days, "a livid tumour has spread right up the leg, with pustules here and there discharging a dark liquid" (p. 191).[7] Here too we are treated to the fulsome spectacle of physical corruption and extreme bodily pain, and in many ways the entire clubfoot episode might be seen as a grotesque anticipation or rehearsal of Emma's death throes: the operation, it should be recalled, was attempted by poor, inept Charles at Emma's (and Homais's) request, and its dire consequences—Hippolyte's agonies, climaxing in the "heart-rending shriek" (p. 197)[8] of his amputation—are further evidence of the "instantaneous decay" of "everything she leaned on" (cf. p. 295).[9] Remarkable, too, are the many verbal echoes linking the two scenes, and one can hardly fail to be struck by the occurrence, in both, of the same phrase, "liquide noir," the very phrase used in the sentence about Emma's corpse referred to in *Sanctuary*.

The intertextual encounter, then, involves much more than a fleeting reference, in *Sanctuary*, to a minor incident in *Madame Bovary*. For the sentence about Emma's final vomiting turns out to be a highly significant moment in the terminal phase of Flaubert's textual strategy. Coming as it does at the novel's close, it is here to convey the sense of an ending. It is a coda to the death scene, which is itself the ghastly dénouement and anti-climax of Emma's trivial and tumultuous career. Relating back beyond her dying to her first experience of nausea, after the fiasco of her first adulterous love, it is both her last revulsion and her final surrender, an epitome of the journey that has taken her from desire to death, or, to put it in more clinical terms, from neurosis to necrosis. Her first nauseas were symptoms of hysteria; the vomitings on her deathbed were the effects of poison. All spasms gone, her last discharge is a purely physical phenomenon: a regurgitation of dead matter by a dead body, an obscene postmortem belch. The process of liquidation or adult-eration, that had started with Emma's first adultery, has come to its predictable end.

At this point, it may be useful to recall that, as Charles Du Bos and Jean-Pierre Richard have brilliantly shown,[10] one of the major themes of Flaubert's "material imagination" is that of an ever threatening but also ever tempting self-dissolution in the steady flux of formless matter. *Madame Bovary* is perhaps above all a study in confusion, diffusion, and dissipation. Even the novel's landscapes are constantly melting away, with fogs, mists, or vapors blurring contours and suffusing all space with their mois-ture.[11] As to Emma, she has "a sort of fog in her head" (p. 122):[12] her being has neither substance nor identity, her mind is forever floating in a haze of languid revery, and to read her sad story is to follow the slow oozing away of her life into nothingness.[13]

Early in the novel, during one of his visits to Rouault's farm, Charles watches "little drops of perspiration" on Emma's bare shoulders (p. 35).[14] As she is dying, "drops of sweat [stand] on her blue-veined face, which [looks] as if it had been petrified by exposure to some metallic vapour" (p. 327).[15] And this is the last glimpse we get of her, as she lies dead in her room:

> The aromatic herbs still smoked; swirls of bluish vapour min-
> gled with the mist drifting in at the casement . . . On Emma's

satin dress, white as a moonbeam, the watering shimmered. She disappeared beneath it. It seemed to [Charles] as if she were escaping from herself and melting confusedly into everything about her, into the silence, the night, the passing wind, the damp odours rising. (p. 344).[16]

It should be clear by now that the "dark liquid" spewed forth by Emma's corpse is part of a richly modulated sequence of fluid matters running throughout Flaubert's novel, that it plays its role in a complex pattern of cumulative repetition, which in turn functions at once as a leitmotif in the novel's overall thematic configuration and as a trope in its overall rhetorical structure. In other words: it enfolds the whole volume of *Madame Bovary*'s "internal intertextuality."[17]

In being taken out of its original textual environment to be grafted onto another text, Flaubert's sentence is of course necessarily given a different status and a different relevance. Losing its immediate denotative function within a narrative sequence, it comes to serve as a pure connotator. What is connoted, however, is precisely the network of its relations to the totality of Flaubert's text; what is brought into play is *Madame Bovary* in its entirety as one of the intertexts of *Sanctuary*. The cited part, inasmuch as it stands for the noncited whole, functions as a kind of synecdoche. Yet, its relationship to its native place now no longer suffices to define it, as it is at present embedded in another text and therefore absorbed and transformed by another system of internal intertextuality, which is that of Faulkner's novel.

In *Sanctuary*, too, we discover repeated references to the outpouring of black liquid: "that black stuff that ran out of Bovary's mouth" foreshadows Horace Benbow's hallucinatory vision, in one of the novel's later chapters, of "something black and furious" (p. 268) streaming out of the pale and naked body of a woman (reminiscent of both Little Belle and Temple), and to readers of the first version of *Sanctuary* it will also bring to mind another of Benbow's fantasizings, in the course of which his own invalid mother appeared as an avatar of the dying Emma: "He saw her mouth open: a thick, black liquid welled in a bursting bubble that splayed out upon her fading chin. . . ."[18] In both novels, moreover, there are several scenes of vomiting,[19] and in both there is a great deal of bleeding, sweating, drooling, and spitting. The drops of sweat on dying Emma's blue-veined face are paralleled in *Sanctuary* by the feverish perspiration of Ruby's sick child, "its pinched face slick with faint moisture, its hair a damp whisper of shadow across its gaunt, veined skull, a thin crescent of white showing beneath its lead-colored eyelids" (p. 137). Examples of such parallels could be easily multiplied. In both books there is a steady concern with bodily excreta, with oozing or leaking flesh, and with all symptoms of organic corruption. Indeed, the theme of liquidity and liquefaction figures just as prominently in *Sanctuary* as in *Madame Bovary*, and each time its treatment points emphatically to a dual obsession with sex and death, a fascination with and revulsion from what comes to be felt as their common rankness. With Flaubert as with Faulkner, nausea is never far away.

What thus emerges is an intertext of intertexts. In this case at least, external and internal intertextuality are impossible to dissociate, since the encounter of Flaubert's and Faulkner's texts is beyond doubt also the encounter of two internal intertextualities. And not only their encounter, but also their embrace, their mutual enfolding. For their relationship might well be defined in terms of "metaphorical isotopy,"[20] the correlation between the two texts appearing to be one of semantic analogy very similar to that found at work in metaphors: Flaubert's text is to Faulkner's as vehicle to tenor—different from it, yet standing for it, replicating and representing it, paradigmatically, within the syntagmatic chain. Hence, the temptation to read one fiction in the light of the other, to read both in superimposition, to attempt what Philippe Lejeune has nicely called a "palimpsestuous reading."[21]

To read *Sanctuary* through *Madame Bovary* is first of all to discover their common ground, their common horizon, and from this discovery it would be easy to move on to a traditional discussion of the affinities in temper, imagination, and outlook of their authors. It should not be forgotten, though, that in the history of the novel, Faulkner came *after* Flaubert, that Flaubert was part of his literary heritage, and that he used that heritage for his own purposes. In Faulkner's text Flaubert's text ceases to be Flaubert's, and to determine to what extent it has been displaced and altered, one would perhaps do well to start with a close scrutiny of the *place* where the intertextual operation occurs.

It is interesting to note, for example, that while in *Madame Bovary* the "black liquid" incident takes the reader beyond the point where most novels end, i.e., beyond the protagonist's death, Faulkner's reference to it in *Sanctuary* comes fairly early, occurring as it does on the sixth page as a closure to Benbow's encounter with Popeye, which is the novel's first narrative sequence. (The sequence begins significantly with Popeye watching "the man drinking": the circuit from drinking to vomiting, from spring water to the "black stuff" already suggests a process of corruption.) In *Madame Bovary* the incident appears as a recapitulative moment in the novel's finale; in *Sanctuary* its function is, on the contrary, proleptic and programmatic: it offers a foretaste of foulness, a first hint of nausea, an intimation of dying and death. Another particularity to be considered is that in Faulkner's narrative the focus is at this point on Benbow: "[Popeye] smells black, Benbow *thought;* he smells like that black stuff . . ." (italics added). Naturally, but also ironically enough, Flaubert's heroine is brought in by the most bookish, most romantic, most Bovary-like character in the novel. Furthermore, the starting point is the visualization of an olfactive sensation, which is in its turn intellectualized by way of a comparison borrowed from Benbow's reading experience. The shift is typical of the character's strategies of evasion, but perhaps also suggestive of the writer's wiles: from odor to color to literary reminiscence; from the most primitive of all senses, and (as Freud has pointed out in his case history of Dora[22]) the one most likely to provoke disgust, to the inodorous pages of a book. Isn't *Sanctuary* also a nausea caught in words and turned into fiction?

Noteworthy too is the oblique connection established by Benbow's simile connecting Emma and Popeye, two figures belonging to radically different worlds, with nothing in common except their both being marked for decay and death. Emma, however, casts a shadow over other characters of Faulkner's novel: over Benbow, obviously, but even more (though less obviously) over Temple Drake, the central feminine presence in *Sanctuary*.

Admittedly, on the face of it, there is very little to suggest their affinities. Emma is a provincial bourgeois in nineteenth-century France, Temple a flapper, and, as such, representative of the American twenties. One is an adult woman in the triple role of frustrated wife, indifferent mother, and passionate adulteress; the other is little more than a pair of "long legs blonde with running" (p. 31), a slim girl still in her teens, "a small childish figure no longer quite a child, not yet quite a woman" (p. 106), bewildered by all that happens to her, yet seemingly emerging from what would have been, to most, a devastating experience as monstrously "innocent" as ever. Flaubert's Emma may be a shallow and silly sentimentalist, but her sensuousness, at least, is not without alertness and delicacy,[23] and as she loses her romantic illusions, she outgrows her mediocrity to become a pathetic victim figure. In many respects, she is still a fully realized nineteenth-century-fiction heroine. Temple, on the other hand, is at best a haunting silhouette. If, as Henry James complained, Madame Bovary is "too small an affair,"[24] Temple is assuredly an even smaller one.

What James objected to in Flaubert's novels was that their central characters—Emma in *Madame Bovary*, Frédéric Moreau in *L'Education sentimentale*—are "inferior" and "abject human specimens,"[25] characters with impoverished minds and stunted sensibilities lacking the fine quality of consciousness exhibited by the "reflectors" of his own fiction. James would have liked Flaubert's characters to be more Jamesian, and had he lived on to read Faulkner's novels, he would probably have condemned them for the same reasons. For what relates Emma to Temple is precisely a shrinkage of so-called "human substance," a narrowing of consciousness, a definite loss of the sense of depth and integrity we tend to associate with the traditional concept of self. As Leo Bersani has observed, "during much of the narrative,

[Emma] is nothing more than bodily surfaces and intense sensations,"[26] and as much could be said of course, with even greater relevance, of Temple Drake.

Both novelists, in describing their heroines, focus on the body rather than the mind (Emma no doubt thinks, but she thinks in clichés, and even her dreams are not her own) and less on the body as a whole than on its components. Emma and Temple are not portrayed; they are anatomized. Thus, Emma, after being first depicted in terms of clothing, setting, and activity, begins to emerge physically in the second chapter, and she does so under Charles's slow, methodical, all but medical gaze—item by item: first her hands (in turn itemized into fingers, nails, and knuckles), then her eyes, lips, neck, hair, ears, temples, and cheeks.[27] True, language being discontinuous, all descriptions are bound to be inventories; the disassembling of bodies just cannot be helped.[28] In Flaubert's as much as in Faulkner's novel, however, this linguistic necessity is pointed up by stylistic emphasis and given sharp thematic relevance. To borrow the term Tony Tanner uses in his fine discussion of Flaubert's book,[29] Emma is "morselized" in every possible way, and not only by the author, but also by the male characters in the novel. Taken apart, in the first description of her appearance, by the eyes of her future husband, she is so again, as Tanner shrewdly notes, on her deathbed, when the priest—another male—dips his thumb in the oil and successively touches her eyes, her nostrils, her mouth, her hands, and the soles of her feet.[30]

Consider now this arresting description of Temple in the trial scene of *Sanctuary*:

From beneath her black hat her hair escaped in tight red curls like clots of resin. The hat bore a rhinestone ornament. Upon her black satin lap lay a platinum bag. Her pale tan coat was open upon a shoulder knot of purple. Her hands lay motionless, palm-up on her lap. Her long blonde legs slanted, lax-ankled, her two motionless slippers with their glittering buckles lay on their sides as though empty. Above the ranked intent faces white and pallid as the floating bellies of dead fish, she sat in an attitude at once detached and cringing, her gaze

fixed on something at the back of the room. Her face was
quite pale, the two spots of rouge like paper discs pasted on
her cheek bones, her mouth painted into a savage and perfect
bow, also like something both symbolical and cryptic cut carefully from purple paper and pasted there. (p. 341)

Again a taking apart, a dismembering: clothing (hat, bag, coat,
slippers) and body (hair, face, hands, legs, eyes, cheeks, mouth)
are likewise itemized and displayed in a random arrangement of
inert fetish objects—a *nature morte*, a still life ritually offered to
the gaping crowd in the courtroom, its deadness matched by
their white cadaverous faces. The tableau is a fitting collective
apotheosis to the many scenes in which Temple has been "detailed" by the leering gaze of males, including the town boys
(p. 32), Tommy (p. 47), a schoolboy (p. 167), Clarence Snopes
(p. 251), and, of course, the rightly named Popeye. In *Sanctuary*,
even more than in *Madame Bovary*, the "morselization" of
woman's body points to the ravages of male fantasy and to the
perversions of fetishism, voyeurism, and sadism. Temple's rape
by Popeye is in a sense nothing else but the acting out of all the
"optical rapes"[31] that precede and follow it.

   Woman's gaze, however, has a deadliness of its own, the more
redoubtable as it begins with seduction, and in both novels lavish
attention is given to the heroine's *eyes*. As Charles watches Emma
for the first time, he is struck by the beauty of her eyes, ". . .
brown eyes, but made to look black by their dark lashes that
came to meet yours openly, with a bold candour" (p. 28).[32] Later,
Rodolphe exclaims: "It's her eyes, they pierce your heart"
(p. 144).[33] Later still, as Emma tries to goad Léon, her second
lover, into stealing:

   In her blazing eyes was a diabolical recklessness; their lids
   narrowed with sensual invitation. The young man felt himself
   succumbing to the mute will-power of this woman who was
   urging him to a crime. (pp. 308–09)[34]

As to Temple's eyes, they are, unlike Emma's, "cool" (p. 32) or
even "cold" (p. 42). Their look, however, is "predatory" (p. 32),

even as that of Emma's eyes impresses by its "boldness." With both women, then, eyes are instruments of erotic power, used for seduction and appropriation and capable of unmanning their fascinated preys. Surprisingly enough, they are also alike in the way they turn into gaps. Temple's eyes are repeatedly compared to "holes" (cf. pp. 82, 110, 194); Emma's become likewise "fixed, gaping," as, just before her death, she sits up "like a corpse galvanized" (p. 337).[35]

After her death, "her eyes [begin] to disappear in a viscous pallor, that [is] like a fine web, as though spiders had been spinning there" (p. 341).[36] At this point, nausea seeps in again: the repulsive spider is here its animal reminder, viscosity its material translation. By the way, "spider" and "viscid" are also words used in *Sanctuary* (cf. pp. 4 and 149), and, furthermore, Emma's "disappearing eyes" also remind one of the "two empty globes" of a dead child remembered by Benbow (p. 266). Blindness is indeed a conspicuous motif in both novels, one allowing us to uncover other patterns of internal and external intertextuality. In *Madame Bovary* Emma's gaping and fading eyes relate back to the two huge, oozing, empty eye sockets of *L'Aveugle,* the Blind Man, the repellent old beggar from Rouen (cf. pp. 277–78),[37] who appears three times at critical moments during the latter, increasingly dramatic, stages of Emma's life, and whose last appearance coincides, rather melodramatically, with the exact moment of her death (cf. p. 337).[38] Another blind old man, Pap, with "two clots of phlegm" (p. 12) where the eyes should be, appears likewise in *Sanctuary* at a crucial instant of the heroine's life: Temple meets him just before her rape and begs in vain for protection (cf. p. 122).[39] With regard to *Madame Bovary,* Tanner notes that the blind man is "the hole (or lack) made flesh, as well as the reverse, the body manifesting itself as a gap."[40] The symbolic role of his homologue in *Sanctuary* could be defined in identical terms.

Eyes, seeing, looking, and their negative, blindness, are given equal emphasis in *Madame Bovary* and in *Sanctuary*. As much could be said of *mouths* and the related motifs of eating, kissing, and vomiting. Revealingly, too, the sexual undertones in the two series are very similar. Eyes and mouths alike are weapons in the war of sexes, used for purposes of predatory appropriation; eyes and mouths alike are holes—devouring holes.[41]

*Madame Bovary:* among other things, the story of a woman's mouth. During Charles's first visit, Emma, while sewing, pricks her fingers and then puts them to her mouth to suck them (cf. p. 28),[42] and soon after we are told that she has the habit of biting (an inadequate translation of *mordillonner*) her full, fleshy lips in her silent moments (cf. p. 28).[43] In another early scene, Charles watches her drinking an almost empty glass of curaçao: "With her head back and her lips rounded and the skin of her neck stretched tight, she laughed at her own vain efforts, and slid the tip of her tongue between her fine teeth to lick, drop by drop, the bottom of the glass." (p. 35)[44] Again, the erotic suggestiveness of Emma's gestures is evident enough. Hints are given of her as yet dormant sensuality, with none of the sinister implications the same gestures will carry in the widely differing contexts of later scenes. Emma's is shown to be an active and voluptuously avid mouth, yet we should note as well that the glass is *empty,* as if to tell us beforehand that nothing will ever measure up to Emma's thirst and desire. Premonitory, too, is her nibbling of her own lips, a habit recalled several times in the course of the novel: Emma, as Roger Kempf remarks, "never stops biting and biting herself, devouring and devouring herself,"[45] in a series of increasingly frustrated attempts to fill up the gaps of her life. Not surprisingly, once she has embarked on her amorous career, she turns into a frantic, compulsive kisser, first "fastening" upon Rodolphe's lips (cf. p. 205),[46] and, during her second affair, vampirically "kissing Léon's soul away" (cf. p. 289).[47] All these kisses of love and lust will be echoed with stinging irony by her very last kiss, the one given in the last of her half-erotical, half-mystical élans to the crucifix before her death: "Reaching forward like one in thirst, she glued her lips to the body of the Man-God and laid upon it with all her failing strength the most mighty kiss of love she had ever given" (p. 335).[48] The gestures are familiar ones: so many times Emma had stretched out her neck, so many times she had pouted her lips for a kiss. And their pathos is the greater here, because, for the remainder of the scene, she lies on her back, "her mouth agape" (p. 332),[49] and, just before the end of her agonies, with "the whole of her tongue" protruding from it (p. 336).[50] This, however, is not yet the final glimpse, for, like the other parts of her body (namely her eyes), Emma's mouth will also be described in death, as it "[hangs] open, the corner of it showing like a black hole at the bottom of her face" (p. 341).[51]

Flaubert's description of Emma's corpse, or at any rate its English translation, has a definitely Faulknerian ring. It certainly would not be out of place in the gothic atmosphere of _Sanctuary_ and could be easily transferred to Red's corpse in the wake scene of Chapter XXV. Significant too are the many parallels in the treatment of the mouth motif. From Temple's first appearance to her last, _Sanctuary_ reverts time and again to her "bold painted mouth" (p. 32; see also pp. 42, 256), and even more frequent are the references to her gaping mouth (see pp. 44, 78, 164, 168, 169, 285, 287). Temple often opens her mouth in stupor or terror, to wail or to scream, yet with her as with Emma, it is also an aggressive sexual organ, as can be seen most plainly in the nightmarish "love-scene" between Temple and Red at the dance hall:

> When he touched her she sprang like a bow, hurling herself upon him, her mouth gaped and ugly like that of a dying fish as she writhed her loins against him. (p. 287)

> With her hips grinding against him, her mouth gaping in straining protrusion, bloodless, she began to speak. (p. 287)

> She strained her mouth toward him, dragging his head down, making a whimpering moan. (p. 288)

There is little of this lurid lasciviousness in _Madame Bovary_, yet in the novel's third part, in which Flaubert traces the insidious progress of Emma's corruption, there are unmistakable hints of it, especially in one of the scenes with Léon at the Hôtel de Bourgogne, when, "more ardent and more avid" than ever, she undresses "brutally," tearing off the thin lace of her corset, which [whistles] down over her hips like a slithering adder," and, once naked, sinks into Léon's arms "with a long shudder" (p. 293).[52] On "that cold-beaded brow," Flaubert adds, "on those stammering lips, in those wandering pupils, in the clasp of those arms, there was something extreme, mysterious, lugubrious . . ." (p. 293).[53] Fairly clinical again, the description points forward to Emma's condition on her deathbed: sexual ecstasy has become a deathlike trance.

In *Madame Bovary*, as in *Sanctuary*, the erotic and the macabre eventually run together—*se confondent*, to use one of Flaubert's favorite verbs. And not only that: the confusion of sex and death in both novels takes place on the same stage, which is none other than woman's body. Hence the maniacal, never-abating attention bestowed upon it by both novelists. True, the fates of their heroines could hardly be further apart, and one should not overlook that while in *Madame Bovary* the love scene at the hotel foreshadows Emma's own death, the Grotto scene in *Sanctuary* portends the imminent murder of Red. In Flaubert's novel a woman is the victim and, in point of fact, the only one to die;[54] in Faulkner it is the males who are killed off, and Temple, the victim turned victimizer, who survives. For all the differences in plotting and characterization, however, Emma and Temple are indeed sisters, and sisters they are, by and under the skin, as sexualized bodies.

Both novels register their bodily responses like seismographs, with particularly strong emphasis on coenesthesia.[55] Emma's life is an almost unbroken succession of *frissons*. To Rodolphe she surrenders "swooning, weeping, with a long shudder, hiding her face" (p. 173), just as Temple, in the Grotto scene, feels "long shuddering waves of physical desire going over her" and eventually succumbs to "a shuddering swoon" (p. 286). In both, extreme erotic excitement combines with extreme dizziness: the awakening of Emma's sensuality begins revealingly during her waltz with the vicomte at the Vaubyessard ball, and it is perhaps not fortuitous either that Temple, whom we have seen so many times swirling and spinning, breaks into nymphomaniac frenzy in a dance hall. Consciousness is with both a very volatile prop-

erty: Emma has numberless fits of faintness; Temple, in the
Grotto scene, seldom emerges from her voluptuous daze. From
intense sensations and thrilling emotions it is always a short step
to numbness and drowsiness: Emma, between her spells of
fevered, romantic exaltation, languishes away in tedium and tor-
por, and her *engourdissements* have their counterpart in Temple's
state of bemusement and benumbment after her rape, as she
"[sways] limply to the lurching of [Popeye's] car" (p. 162), or,
later, in the courtroom, where she is depicted like a lifeless doll,
or again, at the novel's close, as she yawns in the Luxembourg
Gardens, under a "sky lying prone and vanquished in the embrace of the season of rain and death" (p. 380).

Shuddering, swooning, giddiness, agitation alternating with
apathy—all of these disturbances in bodily response indicate a
pathological condition and could be related, more specifically, to
what has come to be identified as *hysteria*. This is not to say, of
course, that Emma's and Temple's behavior conforms to the
symptomatology of this supposedly feminine neurosis and that
we should read their stories as case histories. The matter, however, deserves closer examination, for it turns out that if the two
characters can be credited with any consistent personality, it is
precisely the concept of hysteria that provides the unifying pattern. Among the features commonly ascribed to hysterics, we
find egocentricity, a strong penchant for histrionics, deceit-
fulness, emotional dearth and imbalance, a compulsive need to
please, tease, and seduce, and a tendency to eroticize all personal
relationships, often paired with sexual frigidity. Apart from the
latter, all these features are clearly shared, in varying degrees, by
Emma and Temple. Both are incurable narcissists (in both
novels they appear in several deliberately spaced mirror
scenes[56]); both are coquettes and seducers, fond of playing roles;
both deceive and lie without any scruples; both are rich in sensations and poor in feeling. Even more interestingly, their hysterical character also comes out in the strange, paradoxical way in
which they combine hyperfemininity and bisexuality.[57] Ever
since Baudelaire, Emma's masculinity has often been remarked
upon. When Charles sees her for the first time, she wears "a pair

of tortoise-shell eyeglasses attached, *in masculine fashion,* to two buttonholes of her bodice" (p. 29).[58] Later, we are told that she parts her hair on one side and rolls it under "like a man" (p. 137).[59] Moreover, with at least two of the three men in her life, she appears to have reversed sexual roles: after the wedding night, Charles is "the one you would have taken for yesterday's virgin" (p. 43),[60] and during her second affair, it is Léon who plays the submissive part: "he had become her mistress rather than she his" (p. 289).[61] A similar sexual ambiguity attaches to Temple in *Sanctuary,* even though her type of androgyny is that of the "epicene" girl, so often encountered in Faulkner's early fiction, rather than that of the masculinized woman. And remarkably enough, she too, after her brutal and sordid initiation into sex at Reba's brothel, eventually turns into a phallic aggressor, with Red cast in Léon's passive role.

Why should Flaubert and Faulkner have been so much interested in portraying hysterics? Perhaps because, like the witch in former times, the hysterical woman has become in our culture the most troubling embodiment of the enigma of femininity. Needless to say that she has become so in the eyes of men, hysteria being above all *their* creation, a way of rearticulating the immemorial question of what it means to be a woman, yet also a way of answering it or, rather, evading it by explaining it away, by fixing it in a discourse of knowledge and codifying it in an authoritative text. The text has been rewritten many times; its latest and most sophisticated version is psychoanalysis, probably the finest triumph, so far, of male expertise on woman and the riddles of her sex. And the text is with us, in us, whether we are writers or readers: but for Charcot, Breuer, and Freud, we surely would not read Flaubert's and Faulkner's novels as we do. Which brings us back, after a few detours, to our subject: intertextuality. And also to its unlocatable, undefinable boundaries. Do as we will, we won't be able to restrict ourselves to *Madame Bovary* and *Sanctuary,* nor can the discussion be limited to the field of literature. For if the two novels never cease to echo each other, even seem on occasion to quote each other, it is clearly also because they incorporate identical fragments of the large, anonymous, all-pervasive subtexts of a common culture and a common ideology—texts which, to all appearances, have barely changed from Flaubert's time to Faulkner's. The likeness between Emma and Temple, then, is not simply a matter of chance encounter, no more than it is one of influence. It has much to do, however, with established modes of perception and interpretation, very much to do, in particular, with the amazingly long-lived myths of womanhood. In *La volonté de savoir*, Michel Foucault comments upon what he calls "the hysterization of woman's body," a cultural process that, he argues, started in the eighteenth century and in the course of which the "nervous woman," as she was first called, came to be seen as the negative of the Mother.[62] The process can be easily traced through the development of medical discourse, but it is hardly surprising that it should also be reflected in literature, especially in fiction. *Madame Bovary* and *Sanctuary* are cases in point. In the former, the "nervous woman" appears in the guise of a provincial adulteress; in the latter, we encounter one of her debased, cheapened early twentieth-century avatars: the sexless and sexy *demi-vierge*, less repressed, less neurotic perhaps than her predecessors, yet all the more perverse.

This is not to say that Flaubert's and Faulkner's novels were wholly programmed by their cultural environments, and even if they were, the highly personal investments at stake should certainly not be ignored. "Madame Bovary, c'est moi. . . ," Flaubert exclaimed, and we know from his correspondence how much he borrowed from his own experience to create Emma and how much he projected himself into her. What his correspondence also reveals is that this self-projection is nowhere as evident as in the scene of Emma's poisoning and dying. On July 12, 1853, he wrote to Louise Colet: "The vulgarity of my subject sometimes fills me with nausea."[63] Three months later: "This book tortures me so much (if I could find a stronger word, I would use it) as to make me *physically* sick. For three weeks now, I have often felt pain to the point of fainting. At other times, I suffer from weights on my chest or feel sick at table. Everything disgusts me."[64] No doubt about it: Emma's nausea is Fláubert's, and so are, as biographical evidence fully bears out, most of the somatic symptoms of her neurosis. In this novel, as Sartre has persuasively shown,[65] Flaubert sought an aesthetic metamorphosis into femininity. *Madame Bovary* is the portrait of the artist as an hysterical woman.

Not so *Sanctuary*. For one thing, Temple is exempt from nausea, Temple never vomits. She is not the subject, but—nearly as much as Popeye—the object and cause of revulsion. The one who experiences nausea, the one who vomits (after listening to Temple's tale of ignominy) is Horace Benbow, and if Faulkner has empathized with anyone in the novel, it is with him.[66] We might note, however, that even though he is a male, Horace belongs with the novelist's "sick heroes," the ones whom, according to sexual stereotypes, one would call effeminate. While Flaubert projected and discovered himself as a masculinized woman, Faulkner identified in some measure (and not only in *Sanctuary*) with the feminized male.

Bisexuality was to both writers a besetting concern, one closely related to their puzzlement about the "dark continent" of feminine sexuality as well as to their anxieties about their own sexual identity. Faulkner's neurosis still awaits its Sartre, and Faulkner having been far more reticent about his private life than Flaubert, its analysis is likely to prove much more hazardous. There is no evidence at hand that in writing *Sanctuary* Faulkner went through the terrible stress and struggle that Flaubert described in his letters to Louise Colet, and if we are to believe his notorious preface to the Modern Library issue, the book was conceived in cold blood, with the cynical intention of pandering to the public rather than out of some personal urgency. But are we to believe it? For, whatever Faulkner's deeper motivations may have been, the fact remains that his novel conveys a sense of nausea at least as intense as Flaubert's.

From Flaubert, probably more than from any other writer, Faulkner learned how to raise "vulgar subjects" to art, and in Flaubert, too, he discovered the supreme model of total commitment to writing, the writer for whom writing had been a matter of life and death. On August 14, 1853, Flaubert wrote: "Ink is my natural element. A fine liquid, besides, this dark liquid! And dangerous! How easy to drown in it! How attractive it is!"[67] In *Madame Bovary,* as Starobinski remarks,[68] this *danger* becomes "that dreadful inky taste,"[69] which Emma felt in her mouth after taking arsenic. So the "black liquid" running out of Emma's mouth, the ultimate nauseous reminder of all the bodily liquids running through Flaubert's text, also brings to mind the liquid flowing from pen to page, the writer's liquid, his delight and torment, his drug and poison, that without which there would be no writing, no literature at all: *ink,* the only liquid to come and stay alive after it has dried. Faulkner's allusion to *Madame Bovary* might then be seen as well as a token of recognition, a fraternal salute from one writer to another writer, who had lived at another time, in another place, but whose pen had dipped in the same dark ink.

---

NOTES

1. *Madame Bovary,* in *Oeuvres de Flaubert,* I, ed. A. Thibaudet and R. Dumesnil (Paris: Gallimard, Bibliothèque de la Pléiade, 1951), p. 628. For a translation, see *Madame Bovary,* trans. Alan Russel (Harmondsworth, Middlesex: Penguin, 1950), p. 342: "They had to lift her head a little, and as they did a stream of dark liquid poured from her mouth, as though she were vomiting." All subsequent references to the original text are to the Pléiade edition and will be made in the notes; all subsequent references to the translation are to the Penguin edition and will be made parenthetically within the text.
2. *Sanctuary* (New York: Modern Library, 1932), p. 6. All subsequent references are to this issue and will be made parenthetically within the text.
3. "Il lui survint des vomissements où Charles crut apercevoir les premiers symptômes d'un cancer" (p. 517).
4. "Et elle fut prise d'une nausée si soudaine qu'elle eut à peine le temps de saisir son mouchoir sous l'oreiller" (p. 614). This sentence is the only one in the novel where the word "nausée" occurs.
5. "A huit heures, les vomissements reparurent" (p. 614).
6. "Elle ne tarda pas à vomir du sang" (p. 617).
7. ". . . par où suintait un liquide noir" (p. 489).
8. "Un cri déchirant" (p. 494). Hippolyte's is one in a long series of cries heard from a distance.
9. ". . . cette pourriture instantanée des choses où elle s'appuyait" (p. 584).
10. See Charles Du Bos, "Sur le milieu intérieur chez Flaubert" (1921), in *Approximations,* new ed. (Paris: Fayard, 1965), pp. 165–82; Jean-Pierre Richard, "La création de la forme chez Flaubert," in *Littérature et sensation* (Paris: Editions du Seuil, 1954), pp. 118–219.
11. See, for example, p. 171: "A mist lay over the land, swirling away to the horizon between the folds of the hills, or tearing asunder and drifting up into

nothingness . . . From where they were, high up, the whole valley was like a vast white lake melting into the air." For the original text, see pp. 469–70.

12. ". . . une manière de brouillard qu'elle avait dans la tête" (pp. 424–25).

13. Emma herself comes eventually to realize her inner liquefaction: ". . . she felt her soul escape from her as a wounded man in his last agony feels life flow out through his bleeding gashes" (p. 327). For the original text, see p. 611.

14. ". . . on voyait sur ses épaules nues de petites gouttes de sueur" (p. 345).

15. "Des gouttes suintaient sur sa figure bleuâtre, qui semblait comme figée dans l'exhalaison d'une vapeur métallique" (p. 614). The adjective "bleuâtre" occurs repeatedly in *Madame Bovary;* so does "bluish" in *Sanctuary,* used twice in descriptions of Ruby's sick child (cf. pp. 73 and 142), and once with reference to Popeye (cf. p. 191).

16. ". . . il lui semblait que, s'épandant au dehors d'elle-même, elle se perdait confusément dans l'entourage des choses, dans le silence, dans la nuit, dans le vent qui passait, dans les senteurs humides qui montaient" (p. 630). The French "S'épandant au dehors d'elle-même" is far more suggestive of liquefaction than the translator's "escaping from herself."

17. The phrase is Jean Ricardou's in *Pour une théorie du nouveau roman* (Paris: Editions du Seuil, 1971), p. 162. Ricardou opposes "external intertextuality," i.e., the relationship of one text to another, to "internal intertextuality," i.e., the relationship of a text to itself.

18. *Sanctuary: The Original Text,* ed. N. Polk (New York: Random House, 1981), p. 60. It is interesting to note that in this version of the novel, the sentence about Emma Bovary appears twice and that its second occurrence comes right after the passage just quoted.

19. See pp. 39 (Gowan), 182 (a coed), 268 (Horace), 312 ("Uncle Bud").

20. The phrase is Laurent Jenny's in "La Stratégie de la forme," *Poétique,* 27 (1976), p. 274.

21. Quoted by Gérard Genette in *Palimpsestes* (Paris: Editions du Seuil, 1982), p. 452.

22. See "A Case of Hysteria," in *The Standard Edition of the Complete Psychological Works of Sigmund Freud,* ed. and trans. James Strachey (London: The Hogarth Press, 1964), vol. VII, p. 31.

23. Ferdinand Brunetière already praised her "finesse des sens." See *Le Roman naturaliste* (Paris: Calmann-Lévy, 1883), p. 195.

24. "Gustave Flaubert," in *The House of Fiction,* ed. Leon Edel (London: Rupert Hart-Davis, 1957), p. 199.

25. *Ibid.*

26. "Flaubert and Emma Bovary: The Hazards of Literary Fusion," *Novel,* VIII (Fall 1974), p. 17.

27. See *Madame Bovary,* Penguin, pp. 28–29; Pléiade, pp. 338–39.

28. As Roland Barthes put it: "Malice du langage: une fois rassemblé, pour se *dire,* le corps total doit retourner à la poussière des mots, à l'égrenage des détails, à l'inventaire monotone des parties, à l'émiettement: le langage défait le corps, le renvoie au fétiche." S/Z (Paris: Editions du Seuil, 1970), p. 120.

29. *Adultery in the Novel: Contract and Transgression* (Baltimore and London: Johns Hopkins University Press, 1979), pp. 349–65.

30. See *Madame Bovary,* Penguin, p. 335; Pléiade, p. 622.

31. The phrase is Michel Gresset's in *Faulkner ou la fascination: Poétique du regard* (Paris: Klincksieck, 1982), p. 199.

32. ". . . son regard arrivait franchement à vous avec une hardiesse candide" (p. 339).

33. "C'est qu'elle a des yeux qui vous entrent au coeur comme des vrilles" (p. 445).

34. "Une hardiesse infernale s'échappait de ses prunelles enflammées, et les paupières se rapprochaient d'une façon lascive et encourageante;—si bien que le jeune homme se sentit faiblir sous la muette volonté de cette femme qui lui conseillait un crime" (p. 596).

35. "Emma se releva comme un cadavre que l'on galvanise, les cheveux dénoués, la prunelle fixe, béante" (p. 623).

36. ". . . ses yeux commençaient à disparaître dans une pâleur visqueuse qui ressemblait à une toile mince, comme si des araignées avaient filé dessus" (p. 627).

37. For the original text, see p. 568.

38. For the original text, see p. 623.

39. This parallel has already been pointed out by Margaret Yonce in "'His True Penelope Was Flaubert': *Madame Bovary* and *Sanctuary*," *Mississippi Quarterly*, XXIX (Summer 1976), pp. 440–41. Margaret Yonce also notes the similarity between the repulsive eating habits of the old *duc de Laverdière*, whom Emma watches with fascination during the dinner party at La Vaubyessard, and those of "Pap."

40. *Adultery in the Novel*, p. 303.

41. Needless to say that a psychoanalytical discussion of the matter would emphasize the dual theme of orality and castration, or more precisely castration in terms of orality.

42. In his early scenarios of the novel Flaubert has Emma suck Léon's wounded finger—a gesture plainly intended to suggest the progress of her sexual frenzy. See *Madame Bovary: Nouvelle version précédée des scénarios inédits*, ed. J. Pommier and G. Leleu (Paris: José Corti, 1949), p. 106.

43. For the original text, see p. 339.

44. ". . . la tête en arrière, les lèvres avancées, le cou tendu, elle riait de ne rien sentir, tandis que le bout de sa langue, passant entre ses dents fines, léchait à petits coups le fond du verre" (p. 345).

45. *Sur le corps romanesque* (Paris: Editions du Seuil, 1968), p. 104. My translation.

46. "Et elle se précipita sur sa bouche. . . " (p. 502).

47. "Elle avait des paroles tendres avec des baisers qui lui emportaient l'âme" (p. 578). Variant: ". . . des baisers *dévorateurs* qui lui emportaient l'âme" (p. 1063; italics added).

48. ". . . alors elle allongea le cou comme quelqu'un qui a soif [cf. the curaçao scene], et, collant ses lèvres sur le corps de l'Homme-Dieu, elle y déposa de toute sa force expirante le plus grand baiser d'amour qu'elle eût jamais donné" (pp. 621–22).

49. ". . . la bouche ouverte" (p. 618).

50. "La langue tout entière lui sortit hors de la bouche" (p. 622).

51. "Le coin de sa bouche, qui se tenait ouverte, faisait comme un trou noir au bas de son visage" (p. 627).

52. "Elle se déshabillait brutalement, arrachant le lacet mince de son corset, qui sifflait autour de ses hanches comme une couleuvre qui glisse. . . puis elle faisait d'un seul geste tomber ensemble tous ses vêtements;—et, pâle, sans parler, sérieuse, elle s'abattait contre sa poitrine, avec un long soupir" (p. 583).

53. ". . . il y avait sur ce front couvert de gouttes froides, sur ces lèvres balbutiantes, dans ces prunelles égarées, dans l'étreinte de ces bras, quelque chose d'extrême, de vague et de lugubre. . ." (p. 583). I have changed the

## 56   André Bleikasten

translator's "mournful" to the more literal and also more suggestive "lugubrious."

54. With the exception of Charles, her husband, who dies of grief, and so may be seen as Emma's victim after her own death.

55. For a subtle study of coenesthesia in *Madame Bovary*, see Jean Starobinski, "L'échelle des températures: lecture du corps dans *Madame Bovary*," in *Le Temps de la réflexion, 1980*, the first issue of the annual journal published by Gallimard, pp. 145–83.

56. There are three important mirror scenes in *Madame Bovary*. The first is prior to Emma's adultery, when she takes joy in saying, "I am a virtuous woman," and in contemplating her own attitudes of resignation in the mirror (cf. Penguin, p. 121; Pléiade, p. 423); the second is after her first act of adultery, when she revels in the thought of having a lover and muses about all the heroines and adulteresses in fiction to whom she feels related (cf. Penguin, p. 175; Pléiade, p. 473); the third and last is shortly before her death: "In a clear voice she asked for her mirror, and remained bowed over it for some time, until big tears began to trickle out of her eyes" (Penguin, p. 336; Pléiade, p. 622). Temple watches herself in the tiny mirror of her compact at Old Frenchman Place (cf. p. 83). After the rape, in Popeye's car, she again peers into it, "whimpering a little" (p. 165). She also examines her face in the mirror of the washroom in the Grotto (cf. p. 280). The last reference to the mirror occurs in the final scene: "Temple yawned behind her hand, then she took out a compact and opened it upon a face in miniature sullen and discontented and sad" (p. 379). In *Madame Bovary* mirrors reflect change; in *Sanctuary* they point to Temple's inalterable futility.

57. See Freud, "Hysterical Phantasies and Their Relation to Bisexuality," in *Standard Edition*, vol. IX, pp. 155–66.

58. "Elle portait, comme un homme, passé entre deux boutons de son corsage, un lorgnon d'écaille" (p. 339).

59. "Elle se fit une raie sur le côté de la tête et roula ses cheveux en dessous, comme un homme" (p. 439).

60. "C'est lui plutôt que l'on eût pris pour la vierge de la veille. . ." (p. 352).

61. "Il devenait sa maîtresse plutôt qu'elle n'était la sienne" (p. 578).

62. See *La volonté de savoir* (Paris: Gallimard, 1976), p. 137.

63. *Correspondance*, II, ed. J. Bruneau (Paris: Gallimard, Bibliothèque de la Pléiade, 1980), p. 382: "La vulgarité de mon sujet me donne parfois des nausées. . . ." My translation.

64. *Ibid.*, p. 452: "Ce livre, au point où j'en suis, me torture tellement (et si je trouvais un mot plus fort, je l'emploierais) que j'en suis parfois malade *physiquement*. Voilà trois semaines que j'ai souvent des douleurs à défaillir. D'autres fois, ce sont des oppressions ou bien des envies de vomir à table. Tout me dégoûte." My translation.

65. See his *Critique de la raison dialectique* (Paris: Gallimard, 1960), pp. 89–94.

66. The hypothesis is strengthened by the novel's original version, in which Horace plays a much more prominent role and appears much more as one of the author's fictional doubles.

67 .*Correspondance*, II, p. 395: "L'encre est mon élément naturel. Beau liquide, du reste, que ce liquide sombre! Et dangereux! Comme on s'y noie! Comme il attire!"

68. See "L'échelle des températures," p. 172.

69. "Cet affreux goût d'encre. . ." (p. 613).

# Of Sailboats and Kites:
# The "Dying Fall" in Faulkner's *Sanctuary*
# and Beckett's *Murphy*

## Michel Gresset

If intertextuality is to be understood in the rather strict sense of "a mosaic of quotations,"[1] if, in other words, one should be able to prove that a text inserts, or incorporates, direct identifiable borrowings from another text before calling it "intertextual," admittedly my topic lies outside the scope of these proceedings.

Even within this narrow field, however, I would like to mention, as in a preamble, the existence in the canon of Faulkner's original titles of at least two direct quotations from the Bible: *Absalom, Absalom!* and *If I Forget Thee, Jerusalem* (the original title of *The Wild Palms*), to which can be added the title of the biblical hymn (after Exodus 19:21) *Go Down, Moses.* In the case of the first title, it occurred to me recently that the exclamation mark, coming after a repetition of the name called, precludes any other interpretation of the interjection than as a fragment of reported speech, which in turn implies that, even before he opens the book, the reader hears the voice of David, the bereft father. We may even generalize about these quotes-as-titles by saying that the interjection, the supposition, and the injunction are all cases of enunciation and therefore that they presuppose some communication between "I" and "Thou"—the interpersonal relationship which, as we know since Benveniste,[2] excludes the third-person pronoun. Regardless of the question as to who is the implicit "Thou," it may be a clue to Faulkner's growing ambition that he should have thus successively implied King David, the whole people of Israel, and finally no less than God Himself in the titles of three of his most powerful novels.

But there are other kinds of intertextuality, one of which—let us call it "external"—involves no quotation at all (be it with or without quotation marks) and "clearly cannot be reduced to a

problem of sources and influences."[3] Indeed, it "comes to take
the place of intersubjectivity."[4] I am definitely not going to raise
the question of influence in comparing texts by Faulkner and by
Beckett because, although *Sanctuary* is dated 1931 and *Murphy*
1938 (publication dates, that is), I have, and I suspect there is, no
proof whatever of any kind of deliberate borrowing by the latter. Although Beckett lived away from France from the spring
of 1932 to the fall of 1937, it is highly unlikely that the omnivo-
rous reader that he was never read *Sanctuary,* particularly after
André Malraux hailed it in his well-known preface in 1933. But
this probability must remain hypothetical until we have more
than Deirdre Bair's highly selective quotation from Beckett's
correspondence in her biography.[5]

Be that as it may, however, biography would certainly not
have been my concern if, by a stroke of luck which I should
perhaps consider as a case of "interreadability," I had not received the "shock of recognition" in finding that the final scenes
of *Sanctuary* and *Murphy* had exactly the same roots in the
writers' lives. What clinches the argument is that this is attested
not by their biographers only, but indeed by their own letters.
Thus, the rooting of the scenes in the authors' own experiences
can hardly be doubted and must be considered as autobiography
rather than biography, which in turn enables me to suggest that
we are dealing here with two cases of "autobiografiction," however refined or "spiritualized," as Hawthorne might have put it.

It is no more than commonplace to say that all novels have at
least three things in common: a title, a beginning, and an end (or
an ending, as the case may be, and as we shall see). But while we
are all familiar with what has been written on beginnings—I am
referring here both to an article entitled "Audacity," in which
Rex Warner studied such opening lines as "Call me Ishmael,"
and to what Lucien Goldman has written on first paragraphs as
"microstructures"—it does not seem that much has been done
(except in a few cases like the well-known controversy over the
ending [or the end] of *Huckleberry Finn,* or on Hemingway's
trouble bringing *A Farewell to Arms* to a close) on the way novels
end, and perhaps even less on what I suggest we consider as the

novelist's last rather than first word on his own work, namely the title. In other terms, what I am addressing here is what I may perhaps call the problem of "interstructurality"—of which there can hardly be a better illustration than the "dying fall."

I doubt whether it is necessary to quote the context in which the phrase first appeared:

> If music be the food of love, play on;
> Give me excess of it, that, surfeiting,
> The appetite may sicken, and so die.—
> That strain again!—it had a dying fall.[6]

Thus, originally, as used by Shakespeare, the phrase referred to music. But it may be that, to take up Michel Butor's recent suggestion, music should be considered as a parameter in any landscape. It was through T. S. Eliot, however, that the generation of American writers who were 20 at the time of World War I got interested in the image of the "dying fall" and in the idea of finishing a novel "on a fade-away instead of a staccato," to quote from a letter by Scott Fitzgerald to John O'Hara.[7] And again, I doubt whether it is necessary to quote the relevant, haunting lines in "The Love Song of J. Alfred Prufrock," except perhaps to recall that it was published in 1917—the very year of *The End of American Innocence*,[8] as Henry May called it:

> For I have known them all already, known them all—
> Have known the evenings, mornings, afternoons,
> I have measured out my life with coffee spoons;
> I know the voices dying with a dying fall
> Beneath the music from a farther room.
> So how should I presume?[9]

Here the motif of the dying fall, although still associated with music, no longer connotes surfeit, as in Shakespeare, but rather wistfulness, in the sense of "longing with little hope," which, I suggest, is common to all dying falls in modern literature, and most certainly, in Faulkner's case, to the ending of all of his early novels except two: *Mosquitoes* and *As I Lay Dying*. Here are the last words of *Soldiers' Pay* (Faulkner's addition on the ts. is italicized):

> The voices rose full and soft. There was no organ; no organ was needed as above the harmonic passion of bass and baritone soared a clear soprano of women's voices like a flight of gold and heavenly birds. They [the Rector Mahon and Joe Gilligan] stood together in the dust . . . listening, seeing the shabby church become beautiful with mellow longing, passionate and sad. Then the singing died, *fading away along the mooned land inevitable with to-morrow and sweat, with sex and death and damnation;* and they turned townward under the moon, feeling dust in their shoes.[10]

Even regardless of its intrinsic, mellow, moving beauty, this is an interesting passage as a link between the end of "The Hill" (certainly the first visible sign of Faulkner's *apocrypha*)[11] and later, better-known endings, such as that of *The Sound and the Fury.* And it does have both music and wistfulness.

At this stage, however, one cannot but evoke the beautiful, though certainly romantic (but why should it not be so?) last lines of both *Flags in the Dust* and *Sartoris,* in which indeed the very words "dying fall" are to be found literally embedded in the best possible illustration of an aesthetic theory:

> The music went on in the dusk; the dusk was peopled with ghosts of glamorous and old disastrous things . . . For there is death in the sound of it [Sartoris] and a glamorous fatality, like silver pennons downrushing at sunset, or a dying fall along the road to Roncevaux.
> . . . beyond the window evening was a windless lilac dream, foster-dam of quietude and peace.[12]

In the very last words, of course, Keats may be found to prevail over Eliot. No longer so in *The Sound and the Fury,* in which again sound (if not music) and the final landscape (or "novelscape") are finely interwoven:

> Ben's voice roared and roared. Queenie moved again, her feet began to clop-clop steadily again, and at once Ben

hushed. Luster looked quickly back over his shoulder, then he drove on. The broken flower drooped over Ben's fist and his eyes were empty and blue and serene again as cornice and façade flowed smoothly once more from left to right; post and tree, window and doorway, and signboard, each in its ordered place.[13]

No wonder, then, if the end of *Sanctuary,* which I think we may call the paradigm of all dying falls, is also found to associate—as of necessity—the theme of death (and its traditional objective correlative, the Fall—of a gray year, of a gray summer, of a gray day), and the motif of music. It need not necessarily be music: a voice may suffice, or even a bellowing—as in *The Sound and the Fury*—or "only the sound of the idiot negro,"[14] as in *Absalom, Absalom!;* but it seems as though for Faulkner *there is no finishing a novel without somehow appealing to the ear.* Particularly interesting is the triple ending of *Light in August:*

1) Chapter XIX (Joe Christmas): "Again from the town, deadened a little by the walls, the scream of the siren mounted toward its unbelievable crescendo, passing out of the realm of hearing."

2) Chapter XX (Gail Hightower): " . . . it seems to him that he still hears them: the wild bugles and the clashing sabres and the dying thunder of hooves."

3) Chapter XXI (Lena Grove: her voice): "My, my. A body does get around. Here we aint been coming from Alabama but two months, and now it's already Tennessee."[15]

So music, or at least a voice, or a sound, at the end of a Faulkner novel is definitely not an ornament; it is not only an integral part of, but the very means of a return to time—which is exactly what, in the well-known passage following his enumeration of his dead friends, Proust's narrator finds at the end of *La Recherche du temps perdu;* and for the first time the author, Proust, can write Time with a capital "T."

The case for the ending of *Sanctuary* is very special:

I have just written such a beautiful thing that I am about to bust—2000 words about the Luxembourg gardens and death.

It has a thin thread of plot, about a young woman, and it is poetry though written in prose form. I have worked on it for two whole days and every word is perfect.[16]

We can always regret that we can never compare the 344 remaining words of the two final paragraphs of the novel with the original "2000" as announced in this letter to his mother dated September 6, 1925, since these have apparently been lost. But we can compare the ending of the definitive version with that of the first. From the point of view of this paper, it is clear that the change evinces a typical shift from staccato to fade-away, since in the first version, the last line ran in italics:

*Sure, the sheriff said, I'll fix it for you; springing the trap.*[17]

This is a line which, in the final version, can be found immediately before the "dying fall" as a reply to Popeye's Eichmann-like: "Fix my hair, Jack."[18] One can only admire Faulkner's ultimate choice away from the "tough guy" stand, since rather than simply putting an end to Popeye's career, it provides a timely closure to the whole space of the novel.

So, and very deliberately so, did Beckett in his first novel, *Murphy.* And in his case as in Faulkner's, it is quite possible, if not even likely, that the end was conceived, if not even written down, before the rest of the novel, or at least somehow independently from it, as a scene in itself, but a scene so pregnant or so meaningful for the writer as to impose itself as the only possible ending to the novel in the making. We have not only Deirdre Bair's paraphrase of Beckett's letters to McGreevy, but also a fragment of his letter dated September 8, 1935, quoted in her biography, which bears a striking similarity to Faulkner's letter to Mrs. McLean ten years before almost day for day:

*Samuel Beckett:* "My next old man, or old young man, not of the big world, but of the little world [i.e. fiction?] must be a kite flyer. So absolutely disinterested, like a poem, or useful in the depths where demand and supply coincide, and the

prayer is the god. Yes, prayer rather than the poem, in order
to be quite clear."[19]
*William Faulkner:* "There is an old bent man who sails a toy
boat on the pool, with the most beautiful rapt face you ever
saw. When I am old enough to no longer have to make excuses for not working, I shall have a weathered derby hat like
his and spend my days sailing a toy boat in the Luxembourg
Gardens."[20]

After recalling that they have the same roots in the lives of two
young writers (both in their late 20s) during a prolonged stay in
a foreign capital (Paris, London), let us now compare the two
scenes. They have in common most of the elements of their
extremely careful composition:
PLACE: a public garden or a park, with a pool and (a) statue(s)
TIME: an evening in the fall of the year
CHARACTERS: in the foreground, a young woman and an old
man; city people in the background
PRESENCE OF SYMBOLIC OBJECTS (sailboats and kites):
each implying an element equally symbolic, since both water and
air may be said to represent a means of escape from the biblical
association of death with dust.

   Above all, however, the two scenes have in common the (typically romantic) "Death and the Maiden" motif. Of course, the
maidens are modern, and no virgins: Celia is a professional
prostitute (so professional indeed that in the midst of the "dying
fall" scene she "paused for a second to clinch the client"), and we
need not expatiate on Temple's "progress," which is perhaps
best described in Baudelaire's viciously puritanical words: "The
young girl—what she is in fact. A little ninny, a little bitch: the
greatest imbecility wedded with the greatest depravity."[21] However, they are young women all the same.

   As to Death, it is (omni)present in a triple way. First, and quite
explicitly, it is present under the guise of the two old men, Judge
Drake and Mr. Kelly, Celia's grandfather, both widowers (or at
least probably so, since in neither novel is there the least allusion
to their wives). The former is seen to be sitting, "his hands

crossed on the head of his stick, the rigid bar of his moustache beaded with moisture like frosted silver."[22] The combination of rigidity and moisture is evocative of both the *rigor mortis* and putrefaction.[23] As to Mr. Kelly, who is first seen sitting "bolt upright, with one gloved hand clutching the winch, with the other the kite furled and in its sheath, and his blue eyes blazed in the depths of their sockets."[24] Here, too, the image of the corpse is unmistakable.

Second and even more important, the presence of death is felt implicitly, owing to the fact that in both cases the central character is a young woman who, even though officially unmarried, has just become a widow. One might even go so far as to say, since ultimately both are seen in movement again, i.e. walking after being arrested (one with "her smart new hat," the other with her "yellow hair [falling] across her face"), that the endings of both novels close a man's career, and open on a widowed whore's progress. Granted, neither Temple nor Celia is literally a "veuve joyeuse"; they are wistful widows, to whom some future remains opened. And, provided one takes up the suggestion that in the "Compson Appendix" to *The Sound and the Fury* what we attend, in fact, is a somewhat collocated reappearance of both Caddy Compson and Temple Drake, in Faulkner's case this future was to be materialized and corroborated fifteen years later in the extraordinary vignette of Caddy on the Canebière:

> . . . the woman's face hatless between a rich scarf and a seal coat, ageless and beautiful, cold serene and damned; beside her . . . a German staffgeneral.[25]

On a third level, of course, death is present everywhere in texts literally steeped in the symbolism of autumn, and very consistently so; just as in Faulkner's sailboat and pool scene, water is ultimately echoed by the rain in the last sentence,

> . . . and on into the sky lying prone and vanquished in the embrace of the season of rain and death,

so in Beckett's kiting scene, the wind has the last say: "Celia toiled along the narrow path into the teeth of the wind."[26] Not quite, though: "*All out,*" repeated only once for the third time, is Beckett's lovely ironic way of bidding adieu to his characters. It is as if one read: "*Exeunt omnes.* Light fades, and disappears. Curtain. You may all go back home." However, let us not forget that, for Celia, there is "no shorter way home" than "fac[ing] north up the wide hill." In other terms, or rather in the terms of another,

> All breathing human passions far above,
> That leaves a heart high-sorrowful and cloy'd,
> A burning forehead, and a parching tongue.[27]

This leads me to my last point. Insofar as both *Sanctuary* and *Murphy* can be described as inverted quest novels (which can equally be said of Sartre's *La Nausée* and of Camus's *L'Etranger,* published in 1938 and in 1942, respectively), as they draw toward their ends, the writers can be seen to have brought a human experience so far as to be left with only one of two possibilities: either escape into the nonhuman (which was John Cowper Powys's choice at the end of *A Glastonbury Romance* [1932]) or revert to the scene of "all breathing human passions"—only, this time, with a pervading awareness of what Faulkner, in *Mosquitoes,* called "the imminence of dark and death."[28] Not only was the latter clearly Faulkner's and Beckett's choice, but it seems to me that, in both cases, their ending functions as the objective correlative of what Freud called "the work of mourning," or the psychic process that takes place after the loss of an object of attachment, and by which the subject (the heroine) progressively succeeds in detaching herself from it. According to Freud, the proof of this work of mourning lies in the well-known fact of the subject's indifference to reality after the loss of the object. Daniel Lagache even went so far as to say that the work of mourning consists in "killing the dead."[29] And this, I submit, is precisely what takes place at the end, or rather perhaps in the *ending,* of both novels.

The English language provides us with a distinction that French does not allow, at least not directly (which is one more reason why Maurice Edgar Coindreau translated *As I Lay Dying* as *Tandis que j'agonise*). This distinction was already present in the text of "Adolescence," an early Faulkner story in which, in Sherwood Anderson's manner, he described a young girl at the moment when she is about to leave home forever:

> At last she, too, was frankly crying because everything seemed so transient and pointless, so futile. That every effort, every impulse she had toward the attainment of happiness was thwarted by blind circumstance, that even trying to break away from the family she hated was frustrated by something from within herself. Even dying couldn't help her: death being nothing but that state those left behind are cast into.[30]

At this point, we may not even be surprised to find that the same idea is expressed in Chapter Eight of Beckett's novel. Murphy is trying to comfort Celia after the violent death of their next-door neighbor:

> Murphy spent most of that night and the next day and the next night expounding by way of comfort to Celia, on and off, angrily, the unutterable benefits that would accrue, were already accruing, to the old boy from his demise. This was quite beside the point, for Celia was mourning, like all honest survivors, quite frankly for herself.[31]

Mourning involves narcissism as well as the interplay of innocence and guilt. Mourning indeed becomes Elektra. As Freud put it in *Death and Melancholy* (1915), "the ego must decide if it will share the destiny of the lost object; and, considering the narcissistic gratifications lying in not doing so, it decides to break its ties with the annihilated object. But in order to be able to accomplish this breaking away, a psychic work is necessary, which involves the presentification and the introversion of each of the memories that used to tie the libido with the object, and upon each of which the detachment of the libido must be accomplished."[32]

Some of this is shown at the end of *Sanctuary,* in which Temple can be seen as the mourning widow of both Popeye, whom she called "Daddy," and Red, her lover. Indifference to reality and narcissism are both explicit: "Temple yawned behind her hand, then she took out a compact and opened it upon a face in miniature sullen discontented and sad." The triad of highly subjective adjectives here echoes the one read earlier: "that quality of autumn gallant and evanescent and forlorn." In both cases the dominant feeling is one of loss—as of a paradise radically and forever lost. So it is with Beckett's ending, focused as it is on Murphy's common-law widow, and also overwhelmingly elegaic.

Both Faulkner's and Beckett's dying falls, or scenes of mourning, can thus be found to rest on the technique, well-known to movie directors, of the fadeaway. But what is remarkable about them is that the focus of male observation (a young woman confronted with death) should gradually be blurred into a vanishing point where, by dint of the added dimension of voice or music, time becomes the qualifier of space. Therein, to me, lies the secret of the potent, though wistful, charm worked upon the reader by such endings.

In order to manage my own dying fall, I shall finish on yet another intertextual note by using one or two quotations from Beckett's remarkable study on *Proust* (1931), which, as Mayoux has observed, may tell us more about Beckett than about Proust. Just before recalling Proust's definition of love as "Time and Space made perceptible to the heart," Beckett quotes from Proust's admirable analysis of the relationship between the object of desire and the categories of time and space:

> We imagine that the object of our desire is a being that can be laid down before us, enclosed within a body. Alas! it is the extension of that being to all the points of space and time that it has occupied and will occupy. If we do not possess contact with such a place and with such an hour we do not possess that being. But we cannot touch all these points.

And again:

A being scattered in space and time is no longer a woman but a series of events on which we can throw no light, a series of problems that cannot be solved.[33]

My final comment, then, will simply be this: Temple Drake and Celia Kelly disappear from our sight, only to be replaced in our desire by heroines who do indeed illustrate Proust's point that "a being scattered in space and time is no longer a woman but a series of events on which we can throw no light." Here is one well-known later ending:

> . . . and then I knew that the hopelessly poignant thing was not Lolita's absence from my side, but the absence of her voice from that concord.[34]

And another, equally well-known:

> The auctioneer cleared his throat. Oedipa settled back, to await the crying of lot 49.[35]

No symbolically orchestrated dying falls there, but postmodern heroines who, instead of fading away, are stolen from our sights by authors who no longer, even halfheartedly, believe in the pathetic fallacy upon which, after all, all symbolist literature is based. *Watt,* the second novel of the last of the symbolists, ends on these words: "Honni soit qui symboles y voit." ["No symbols where none intended."][36] And his third, *Molloy:*

> Then I went back into the house and wrote, It is midnight. The rain is beating on the windows. It was not midnight. It was not raining.[37]

---

Appendixes

**I (a)    (Auto)biographical circumstances behind the final scene of *Sanctuary***

In the fall of 1925, Faulkner lived in Paris, 26 rue Servandoni, where he wrote to his mother the following:

August 18. "I am moving today. I have a nice room just around the corner from the Luxembourg gardens, where I can sit and write and watch the children."

August 30. "I wrote you, didn't I, about the old man who sails his boat in the pool in the Luxembourg gardens? He was there bright and early this morning when I came back from breakfast. It was a lovely day— (Paris weather is overcast and grey, as a rule)—the sun was out and it was crisp and cool. I saw him right away, hobbling along at top speed with his stick, sailing his boat while people watched him in a sort of jolly friendliness . . . Then I went on and stopped to watch two old gray haired men, a middle-aged man and a young boy play croquet."

September 10, to his great-aunt, Mrs. Alabama McLean. "I live just around the corner form the Luxembourg Gardens, where I spend all my time. I write there, and play with the children, help them sail their boats, etc. There is an old bent man who sails a toy boat on the pool, with the most beautiful rapt face you ever saw. When I am old enough to no longer have to make excuses for not working, I shall have a weathered derby hat like his and spend my days sailing a toy boat in the Luxembourg Gardens."[38]

## I (b)  (Auto)biographical circumstances behind the final scene of *Murphy*

1. Most of the years 1934 and 1935, Beckett lived in London, where he wrote *Murphy*. Deirdre Bair writes: "The weather was so beautiful in London that fall that Beckett spent long afternoons at Round Pond in Hyde Park, where legions of elderly kite flyers gathered each day. He was moved to declare that he wanted to live his entire life in a haze of perpetual Septembers [letter to Thomas McGreevy, September 8, 1935]. *Murphy* was still stalled. He tried to inspire himself by watching the shabby old men who arrived with their kites dismantled in separate pieces, each carefully wrapped. The old men lovingly assembled the kites in time for the first gust of wind to carry them so high above the roof tops of London that birds often were sighted flying far below them. Every so often the men tugged gently on the strings, as if to keep the kites from losing height, and when the afternoon light began to fade, they pulled them gently in, dismantled the kites, and left the park as the guide called, 'All out, all out.'"

The sight so moved Beckett that, no matter what happened within the pages of his novel, he knew it would end at Round Pond with one or several old men flying kites:

My next old man, or old young man, not of the big world, but of the little world, must be a kite flyer. So absolutely disinterested, like a poem, or useful in the depths where demand and supply coincide, and the prayer is the god. Yes, prayer rather than poem, in order to be quite clear. [Same letter to T. McGreevy]

2. On July 17, 1936, Beckett wrote to McGreevy:

> The point you raise is one that I have given a good deal of thought to. Very early on, when the mortuary and the Round Pond scenes were in my mind as the necessary end, I saw the difficulty and danger of so much following Murphy's own "end." There seemed two ways out. One was to let the death have its head in a frank climax and the rest be definitely epilogue . . . And the other, which I chose, and tried to act on, was to keep the death subdued and go on as coolly and finish as briefly as possible. I chose this because it seemed to me to consist better with the treatment of Murphy throughout, with the mixture of compassion, patience, mockery and 'tat twam asi' that I seem to have directed on him throughout . . . The last section is just the length and speed I hoped, but the actual end doesn't satisfy me very well.[39]

## II  The 'dying fall' in *Sanctuary* and in *Murphy: A Comparative Analysis*

| *SANCTUARY* | *MURPHY* |
|---|---|
| **TIME:** | |
| "It had been a gray day, a gray summer, a gray year" | "Late afternoon, Saturday, October the 26th." |
| **PLACE:** | |
| "the Luxembourg Gardens," "the circle with its spurious Greek balustrade" | Hyde Park, "the plot between the Round Pond and the Broad Walk". |

**SETTING:**

**A. Visual Elements**

| | |
|---|---|
| "in the sad gloom of the chestnut trees . . . that quality of autumn, gallant and evanescent and forlorn. From beyond the circle . . . filled with a gray light of the same color and texture as the water which the fountain played into the pool . . . the twilight dissolved in wet gleams from the branches." | "A mild, clear, sunless day, sudden gentle eddies of rotting leaves, branches still against the still sky, from a chimney a pine of smoke." "The leaves began to lift and scatter, the higher branches to complain, the sky broke and curdled over flecks of skim blue, the pine of smoke toppled into the east and vanished, the pond was suddenly a little panic of grey and white, of water and gulls and sails." |
| "the opposite semicircle of trees where at sombre intervals the dead tranquil queens in stained marble mused" | "he brought himself smoothly to rest level with the statue of Queen Victoria, whom he greatly admired, as a woman and as a queen" |

## B. Auditory Elements

"the dry click of balls, the random shouts of children," "a steady crash of music"

"The wail of the rangers came faintly out of the east against the wind. *All out. All out. All out.*"

## CHARACTERS AND THEIR ACTIVITIES
### A. Foreground

A young woman: Temple Drake walking/sitting/walking . . .

Celia, a prostitute, walking/sitting/walking . . .

An old man, her father, sitting rigidly . . .

Kelly Willoughby, her paternal grandfather, sitting in his wheelchair and flying a kite . . .

### B. Background

Woman knitting, men playing croquet, children and an old man sailing toy boats . . .

A weekend lecher, a child flying a tandem kite . . .

"an old woman came with decrepit promptitude and collected four sous."

The rangers crying "*All out.*"

---

NOTES

1. Julia Kristeva, *Semeiotike: Recherches pour une sémanalyse* (Paris: Seuil, 1969), p. 146.
2. Emile Benveniste, *Problèmes de linguistique générale* (Paris: Gallimard, 1966), Chapter XX: "La Nature des pronoms."
3. Roland Barthes, "Texte [Théorie du]," in *Encyclopaedia universalis*, vol. XV (Paris, 1973).
4. Julia Kristeva, *Semeiotike*, p. 146.
5. Deirdre Bair, *Beckett: A Biography* (New York: Harcourt Brace Jovanovich, 1978), Chapters IX ("1935") and X ("Murphy").
6. *The Tempest*, I, i.
7. Andrew Turnbull, ed., *The Letters of F. Scott Fitzgerald* (London: The Bodley Head, 1964), p. 538 (the letter is dated July 25, 1936).
8. New York: Knopf, 1959; Chicago: Quadrangle Books, 1964.
9. T. S. Eliot, *Collected Poems, 1909–1962* (New York: Harcourt, Brace & World, 1963), pp. 4–5.
10. *Soldiers' Pay* (New York: Boni & Liveright, 1926), p. 319.
11. William Faulkner, *Early Prose and Poetry*, ed. Carvel Collins (Boston: Little, Brown & Co., 1962), pp. 90–92; see my "Faulkner's 'The Hill,'" *Southern Literary Journal*, vol. VI, 2 (1974), pp. 3–18.
12. *Sartoris* (New York: Harcourt, Brace & Co., 1929), p. 380; *Flags in the Dust*, ed. Douglas Day (New York: Random House, 1973), pp. 369–70.
13. *The Sound and the Fury* (New York: J. Cape and H. Smith, 1929), p. 401.
14. *Absalom, Absalom!* (New York: Random House, 1936), p. 376.
15. *Light in August* (New York: H. Smith and R. Haas, 1932), pp. 440, 467, 480.
16. Joseph Blotner, ed., *Selected Letters of William Faulkner* (New York: Random House, 1981), p. 17.

17. William Faulkner, *Sanctuary: The Original Text*, ed. Noel Polk (New York: Random House, 1981), p. 291.

18. *Sanctuary* (New York: J. Cape and H. Smith, 1931), p. 378. On the parallel Popeye/Eichmann, see my *Faulkner ou la fascination* (Paris: Klincksieck, 1982), p. 212.

19. *Beckett: A Biography*, p. 207.

20. *Selected Letters of William Faulkner*, pp. 19–20.

21. Charles Baudelaire, *De l'amour* (Paris: Société anonyme d'édition et de librairie, 1919), p. 134.

22. *Sanctuary* (1931), pp. 379–80; *Sanctuary* (1981), p. 291.

23. Quite worthy of notice is the fact that in both the manuscript and the typescript of *Flags in the Dust*, Faulkner wrote of Nature "flouting that illusion of purifaction [sic] which he [man] has foisted upon himself and calls his soul." *Flags in the Dust*, p. 289, 1. 2.

24. *Murphy* (London: Routledge & Co., 1938; Pan Books, "Picador," 1973), p. 155.

25. Malcolm Cowley, ed., *The Portable Faulkner* (New York: Viking, 1946), p. 746.

26. *Murphy*, p. 158.

27. John Keats, "Ode on a Grecian Urn," 11. pp. 28–30.

28. *Mosquitoes* (New York: Boni & Liveright, 1927), p. 30.

29. Jean Laplanche & J.-B. Pontalis, *Vocabulaire de la psychanalyse* (Paris: Presses universitaires de France; second edition, revised, 1968), p. 504.

30. Joseph Blotner, ed., *Uncollected Stories of William Faulkner* (New York: Random House, 1979), p. 472.

31. *Murphy*, p. 79.

32. Quoted in *Vocabulaire de la psychanalyse*, p. 504.

33. *Proust* (New York: Grove Press, 1957), pp. 41–42.

34. Vladimir Nabokov, *Lolita* (London: Corgi Books, 1973), p. 324.

35. Thomas Pynchon, *The Crying of Lot 49* (Philadelphia: J. B. Lippincott, "Bantam Books," 1967), p. 268.

36. *Watt* (Paris: Minuit, 1968), p. 268.

37. *Molloy* (Paris: Minuit, 1951), p. 272.

38. *Selected Letters of William Faulkner*, pp. 13, 15, 19–20.

39. *Beckett: A Biography*, pp. 206–07, 228–29.

# Oratory and the Dialogical in *Absalom, Absalom!*

## Stephen M. Ross

One difficulty faced by Faulkner studies, at least as they have been proceeding in America, arises in just how to infuse our concern with Faulkner as a Southerner, as an American writer situated in history, with the insights into the nature of discourse provided by continental semiotic theory. Faulkner's texts do interrogate discourse in compelling ways; but they do so from a highly historicized grounding. The questions about the nature of language and linguistic relationships raised by Faulkner's texts grow out of a cultural discourse that forms part of the "mosaic of citations" imbedded within specific texts.

My intent, therefore, is to discuss, within a limited scope, Southern oratory as a context for the discourse in *Absalom, Absalom!* In doing so, I will draw upon Mikhail Bakhtin's fundamental distinction between single-voiced and double-voiced narration, between what he calls the monological and the dialogical.[1] A brief examination of the role played by oratory as a discursive context can give us insight into the struggle within the novel between the monological and the dialogical, for from this struggle comes much of the novel's tremendous verbal energy.

On the surface level of its style, *Absalom, Absalom!* speaks from within a clearly oratorical tradition. Much of the novel's highly ornate rhetoric so closely resembles oratory as to seem not merely a deliberate stylization—which I believe it to be—but even at times a parody of the entire heritage. We hear, in all the narrators' voices and in the authorial discourse, those rhythms of celebratory exhortation typical of all American—especially of Southern—oratory.

In speaking of "oratory," I am not speaking of classical Ciceronian oratory, of course, but of colloquial oratory—the speechmaking practiced by politicians and revivalist preachers what-

ever their level of "classical" education. I am referring to the
oratory practiced by "stump orators" or "word slingers" as they
were sometimes called—the kind of oratory heard at Fourth of
July picnics or camp meetings, at those huge "oratorical feasts"
where speech-making (like the drinking and the eating) would
go on for days, even weeks, at a time.[2] This is the kind of oratory
derided by one historian as "the folk art of the South—the
spread-eagle, ornate oratory, superfluous in verbiage and all but
barren of thought."[3]

*Absalom's* discourse is neither superfluous nor barren of
thought, but it does share oratory's essential discursive movement toward ever greater *amplification,* that constant expansion
of the simple into the elaborate, the brief into the extended, so
typical of oratory. The rhythms of oratory are cumulative: a
building up and piling on of words and images, a gathering of
speed and momentum. The expansive *ore rotundo* typical of the
colloquial orator in Faulkner's Southern heritage bears little re-
semblance to Ciceronian balance and structural completeness. If
for Aristotle the period had in itself a beginning and an end, for
the colloquial orator there can be no closure, for there is no end
to what he has to say. What mattered was the ability to add to
what was said, not to construct completed periods. What mattered was the relentless movement forward—like a boy crossing
a stream on slippery stones, the stump orator kept his balance by
ceaselessly moving forward.

It is possible to examine oratory's accumulating rhythm in
various ways. The syntax, for example, is such as to allow endless
addition or qualification: conjunctive patterns predominate,
with few embedded clauses. We can also examine oratorical
prose under the categories of classical rhetorical devices, and
while this is not the time to explore such matters in detail, I will
mention one example because it so clearly illustrates that on-
rushing power of oratorical rhetoric. Probably the most compulsive mannerism of American stump orators was their use of
*anaphora,* the repetition of a word or phrase at the beginning of
successive clauses or sentences. Anaphora creates a mechanical
parallelism that permits constant variation—one merely has to

repeat the triggering word or phrase to add another clause on the same topic. Anaphora—and it would be hard to overstate this—is the prevalent pattern in colloquial oratory. It amounted to an obsessive habit in which clause after clause would begin with the same word or words. Here is a typical example, from a speech by Senator John T. Morgan of Alabama, opposing the use of bank notes instead of silver as money:

> Another leading reason why I have so earnestly favored the full and free coinage of silver is that it is gathered by the toil of man in the deep and dangerous mines; it is converted into coin by the highest art of the chemist; it is the gift of God, who made silver and gold alone for use as money in their functions of real value, and it is the reward in money, not in promises to pay, of the laborer; the reward of each day's work when the night shuts in. It is the fruit of the pick and the shovel, and it is not the product of some artful brain in a bank parlor that is busy with contrivances to deceive the world into the belief that his credit is better for the people than this gift from heaven and that his wisdom has made a back number of the omniscience of God.[4]

Faulkner turns this mechanical rhythm into expansive images that start with some specific detail and move toward a crescendo full of rhetorical emotion. Rosa Coldfield's narration contains many of these, as might be expected, though all the narrators, even the authorial voice, use anaphora. One of my favorites is in the first chapter, a passage I call "Rosa's Briefs," in which she tells Quentin all the excuses she does *not* plead for what happened between her and Sutpen: after saying, "No, I hold no brief for myself," she begins successive sentences with "I dont plead . . . ," leading to the climatic, "and most of all I do not plead myself: a young woman emerging from a holocaust which had taken parents, security, and all from her, who had seen all that living meant to her fall into ruins about the feet of a few figures with the shapes of men but with the names and statures of heroes—a young woman, I say, thrown into daily contact with one of those men. . . ."[5]

Certainly one of the most striking examples is the marvelous

opening passage of Chapter Five, when Rosa describes riding
out to Sutpen's Hundred beside Wash Jones, whom she
anaphorically describes as "that brute":

> *I had only to lock the house and take my place in the buggy and
> traverse those twelve miles which I had not done since Ellen died,
> beside that brute who until Ellen died was not even permitted to
> approach the house from the front—that brute progenitor of brutes
> whose granddaughter was to supplant me . . . that brute who (brute
> instrument of that justice which presides over human events . . .) brute
> who was not only to preside upon the various shapes and avatars of
> Thomas Sutpen's devil's fate but was to provide at the last the female
> flesh in which his name and lineage should be sepulchered—that brute
> who appeared to believe that he had served and performed his ap-
> pointed end by yelling of blood and pistols in the street before my house
> . . . . (pp. 134–35)*

Examples of such oratorical mannerisms could be multiplied,
for *Absalom, Absalom!* is Faulkner's most sustained performance
in the high, ornate style. Faulkner himself spoke of Southern
oratory as an influence on his style in an interesting letter to
Malcolm Cowley. The letter is interesting, not just because it
acknowledges the evident similarities between oratory and the
novel's style, but also because of the way Faulkner refers to the
influence as an inherited and unavoidable curse. Cowley had
suggested that solitude was the reason for Faulkner's elaborate
style; Faulkner answered:

> I'll go further than you in the harsh criticism [of *Absalom's*
> style]. The style, as you divine, is a result of the solitude, and
> granted a bad one. It was further complicated by an inherited
> regional or geographical (Hawthorne would say, racial) curse.
> You might say, studbook style: "by Southern Rhetoric out of
> Solitude" or "Oratory out of Solitude."[6]

But my central purpose here is not to establish an influence.
Rather, I want to explore certain effects of the oratorical heritage as it is absorbed into and transformed by Faulkner's discourse. The assimilation of an oratorical rhetoric into this fiction

text affects the relationships among the voices within the text—those crucial dialogical relationships Bakhtin describes.

We should recall that by "monological" Bakhtin means discourse that is simply assertive of claimed truth; he means an object-oriented discourse uttered with no mind to any other speaker, a discourse expressive of the full semantic authority of the speaker. By "dialogical" Bakhtin means discourse that by its nature takes other speech, other voices, into account. The dialogical is discourse that is "warped" or "bent" by the presence of another's voice as light is bent by gravity. The clearest examples are stylization or parody, where we detect a voice that is being parodied, and a voice that is parodying—indeed, without our awareness of the dialogical quality of parody, we could not detect it at all. The most complex dialogical relationships exist in prose fiction, in what Bakhtin calls the "polyphonic novel" where many voices, named and unnamed, vie with each other and affect each other from within the discourse.[7]

Regarded as a speech act, oratory (we might logically assume) is a highly dialogical mode of discourse. Rhetoric, by definition, is the art of persuasion and must therefore take an audience into account. The listener's "word" (in Bakhtin's sense) may be silent, but it still warps oratory's discourse toward it. There is always in oratorical rhetoric what Bakhtin calls the "sideward glance" at the listener.[8] The implied discourse of the silent listener lurks just over the horizon of the oratorical act; though in this rhetorical relationship the silent listener is not permitted to speak, nonetheless that listener's implied discourse exerts its influence on the orator.

*Absalom, Absalom!* overtly dramatizes the implied dialogical relationship inherent in oratory in the many listening scenes—that is, those scenes of narration when someone, usually Quentin Compson, listens to the discourse of another (a discourse that later becomes his own). We remember that Quentin "was not a being, an entity," but "an empty hall echoing with sonorous defeated names" (p. 12).

But although oratory is dialogical in that it presupposes an

audience, it is also in the nature of oratorical discourse to dis-
simulate its dialogical relationship with the audience. Colloquial
oratory with its relentless movement forward, its accretion of
layer upon layer of assertion, its affirmation of and its appeal to
accepted values—in these ways oratory adopts the pose of *monological* discourse. It feigns what Bakhtin calls the expression of a
speaker's "ultimate semantic *authority.*"[9] The monological is a
discourse of certainty and claimed truth; an object-oriented discourse that does not question itself—all the questions an orator
asks are *rhetorical* questions, not meant to be answered. Thus, it
is in the nature of the oratorical to mask itself as monological
even within a dialogical circumstance.

The southern writer and critic Allen Tate has described perfectly, though in different terminology, the relationship created
by rhetoric in what he calls the "Southern mode of discourse":

> The traditional Southern mode of discourse presupposes
> somebody at the other end silently listening: it is the rhetorical
> mode. Its historical rival is the dialectical mode, or the give
> and take between two minds, even if one mind prevail at the
> end. The Southerner has never been a dialectician. . . . The
> Southerner always talks to somebody else, and this somebody
> else, after varying intervals, [may be] given his turn; but the
> conversation is always among rhetoricians.[10]

In his theory of the polyphonic text, Bakhtin wants to generate a
kind of analysis that goes far beyond merely distinguishing between the monological and the dialogical, or what Tate calls the
rhetorical and the dialectic. But this simple duality is a crucial
beginning point in Bakhtin's theory and, I would argue, in any
analysis of *Absalom's* discourse. As Bakhtin describes, any discourse can change; that is, it can move from dialogical status to
monological, or vice versa. So a complete analysis of the relationships among the voices in *Absalom* must begin with a recognition
of just how great the pressure is to transform all the discourse in
the text into the monological. All voices are driven inexorably
toward one voice; all narrators merge into one narrative voice.
This pressure stems in part from the oratorical heritage or cul-

tural text embedded in the novel's discourse; it stems in part from the nature of the novel's subject. The pressure to reduce all the discourse to one monological kind generates a violence within the text's discourse, a violence created by the attempted but unsuccessful blurring of dialogical differences. Just as Sutpen seeks to create a perfect unified "design" in his land and lineage, so too the novel's discourse seeks to become single-voiced. It is this tendency, this pressure, that we need to examine further.

The highly charged oratorical style of *Absalom, Absalom!*, a style Faulkner called a "regional curse," drives all the text's voices toward a single voice. All listeners, all speakers, all events are taken up into a monological "overvoice" generated by the overdetermined, cumulative rhetoric. The result is an excess, a plentitude of voice. Even when assigned to a particular character-narrator, voice is too rich or too dense, too resistant to variation to be considered the possession of any one character. The dramatic illusion in *Absalom* that we are hearing different characters narrate the story is often clouded by the text's dense figural rhetoric. Indeed, as I have argued elsewhere, the novel's mimetic power, its very referentiality, is threatened by this over-voice. It is a voice that overpowers the represented world.[11] The "Oratory out of Solitude" becomes its own brooding celebration, a kind of monument to itself that overwhelms differentiation among speakers. In Bakhtin's terms, we might say that the monological overwhelms the dialogical. While many commentators have emphasized the differences among the narrators and the high level of speculation in their stories, I would argue that the narrative discourse with its monological overvoice creates tremendous *authority*, an implied and truth-uttering presence. The oratorical discourse, *as discourse,* re-presents Sutpen's authority as "father" in the novel: Quentin may tell us that all the narrators (Shreve, himself, even Rosa) "sound just like father" (p. 181), but the word "father" means a principle of authority far greater than Mr. Compson. This is not to say that the overvoice is Sutpen's voice in any literal or realistic or even rhetorical sense; rather the overvoice is a discursive re-presentation of Sutpen's symbolic role. In *Absalom, Absalom!* discourse does not merely present symbol, it represents symbol and even becomes symbol itself.

The overvoice in *Absalom, Absalom!* is excessively motivated; it is overdetermined in the Freudian sense, as if emanating from sources insufficient to account for the intensity of feeling it conveys. Also, the text abounds in images of voice that make it seem something palpable, something all voices are trapped in, unable to escape. Voice is a space one occupies, as Sutpen "haunts" Rosa's voice "where a more fortunate one would have had a house" (p. 8), or as Quentin walks "out of his father's talking at last" (p. 174).

Quentin especially wants to escape this voice he has heard, in its various forms, all his life. To truly *see* Sutpen, Quentin must try to escape "behind and above the voice" (p. 14). But the overvoice never disappears, even when Quentin is not listening. Rosa's voice is "not ceasing but vanishing into and then out of the long intervals like a stream, a trickle running from patch to patch of dried sand" (p. 8). Or Quentin "hears without listening" his father's voice reading the letter from Bon to Judith. Shreve and Quentin most obviously participate in a single voice when they share speculations between them, when they think as "one, the voice which happened to be speaking the thought only the thinking become audible, vocal" (p. 303). The overvoice energizes even the written. The few documents that play a role in the text are subverted into voice even as they function as writings inserted into the talking; the written is infused with rhetoric and gives over its hardened permanence to voice: the inscriptions on the tombstones, for example, those "bombastic and inert carven rocks" seem impermanent, "momentary and legible in the faint light" (p. 188). Bon's letter to Judith is called a "voice," and "a dead tongue speaking," its script "not like something impressed upon the paper by a once-living hand but like a shadow cast upon it . . . which might fade, vanish, at any instant while he still read" (p. 129). And indeed the letter has the same rhetorical excesses that most of the novel's discourse has.

The consistency of what I have been calling the overvoice, the pervasive oratorical quality of the rhetoric, exerts pressure within the discourse to reduce all dialogical relationships to one—that between the orator's authoritarian word and the silent word of the listener. And because it is the essence of oratorical discourse to feign univocality, to pretend to ignore all other voices, *Absalom's* discourse tends to hide the complicated dialogical relationships within the novel. The text's narration, in other words, is always close to what Bakhtin identifies as the boundary between monological and dialogical discourse. Bakhtin describes the tendency, inherent in certain discourse such as stylization or narration by characters, to become monological when "the objectification . . . is decreased."[12] That is, where we have discourse such as stylization or character narration and when the differentiation between the stylizer and the stylized, or between the authorial and the character's voices, is blurred, then dialogical differences are reduced so that the speakers merge into one voice. Relationships among speakers and listeners, between narrators and author, among various discourses within a polyphonic text—these become masked and difficult to articulate. Just as oratory tries to hide that dialogical "slant" or angle at which it approaches a listener's implied discourse, so the oratorical rhetoric of *Absalom, Absalom!* pushes the text's voices toward the boundary where the dialogical becomes (or seems to become) the monological—with all the univocal semantic authority that implies.

I am not, of course, arguing that *Absalom* in fact becomes monological, or that it loses it polyphonic complexity. The pressure exerted by oratorical discourse actually makes the interweaving of various voices in the novel all the more complicated, all the more dialogical. What we have is a polyphonic text, one traversed by many voices, that is made more difficult to explicate because of a discursive rhetorical gesture—the gesture of masking voices within a single oratorically derived overvoice.

But there is resistance to the authority of the overvoice, to the principle of the father as it manifests itself in the discourse. The polyphonic voices of the novel's discourse reassert themselves in various ways—and it is here, in the reassertion, that the violence

I spoke of earlier arises within the discourse. We might speak of this process as a countergesture in which the mask of the mono-logical word is torn away and the dialogical reasserts itself— almost with a vengence. The sign of this reassertion is found in the novel's dialogue, or, to be more precise, in certain special dialogues that recur throughout the novel. *e - g . —*

In the context of oratorical discourse, dialogue is a violence, for by its nature, dialogue does violence to oratory's dissimulated monological certainty: dialogue strips the mask of univocality behind which the orator hides. Historically the collo-quial southern oratory Faulkner was heir to reflected that violence I am describing. Orators were often challenged physically to come down off the stump and engage in "dialogue": one historian describes how, during oratorical festivities in Kentucky, a political orator with the appropriate name of Cassius Marcellus Clay was shot and wounded by a member of the audience. Clay came off the podium with "his bowie knife, cleaved his antagonist's skull, gouged out an eye, cut off an ear, and tossed his mangled body over a nearby cliff. Surprisingly," the commentator adds, "both lived to testify to the hazards of political speaking in the south."[13]

But more importantly, at the level of discourse, *Absalom* crystallizes this dialogical violence in remarkable moments when dialogue becomes objectified as symbol for violence and death in the story. Inserted within the narration, or coming within the extended rhetoric, are moments when the overvoice vanishes and speech emerges with a startling simplicity and clarity. We can call these moments "dialogical scenes" when the *principle* of dialogue is in fact acted out.

These "dialogic scenes" are moments of dramatic visualized clarity that emerge from the turgid narration as in the momentary and sudden lifting of a fog. They are scenes of speech. They appear suddenly from longer narrative segments as climactic condensations of the story. As we listen to the overvoice, it vanishes and speech appears—and "appears" is the right word because the represented dialogic confrontation is usually italicized to differentiate it from the narrative text. At the close of chapter five, Rosa's long tirade suddenly ends (we are told that "Quentin was not listening"), and Quentin imagines the confrontation between Judith and Henry:

> *Now you cant marry him.*
> *Why cant I marry him?*
> *Because he's dead.*
> *Dead?*
> *Yes. I killed him.* (p. 172)

This dialogical scene, like all such scenes, is one of assault, violence, even murder. Judith and Henry speak "in short brief staccato sentences like slaps, as if they stood breast to breast striking one another in turn neither making any attempt to guard against the blows" (p. 172). Dialogue does not merely accompany assault, it *is* assault: "the two of them slashing at one another with words" (p. 174). Dialogue is paradigmatic of all confrontations, of all the violence underlying the Sutpen design. Chapter one coalesces into the scene in Sutpen's barn where he fights with his slaves "both naked to the waist gouging at one another" (p. 29), a scene that includes the only dialogue between Sutpen and Ellen in which (according to Rosa) the true horror of the marriage is spoken. Chapter four ends with Quentin imagining Bon's murder, the ultimately violent confrontation between Charles and Henry in which "the voices [are] not even raised: *Dont you pass the shadow of this post, this branch, Charles;* and *I am going to pass it, Henry*" (p. 133). In Chapter Seven, Sutpen's death is rendered as a dialogue overheard by the midwife: ". . . *the old negress squatted there and heard them, in voices, he and Jones: 'Stand back. Dont you touch me, Wash'—'I'm going to tech you, Kernel'"* (p. 185).

Two of these dialogical scenes deserve particular mention because they capture perfectly the struggle occurring within the discourse: Sutpen's meeting with Henry at the bivouac, and Quentin's meeting with Henry.

When Quentin and Shreve render Henry's meeting with his father, they render the secret power of the word—of the orator's monological, and monomaniacal, word. The dialogue between father and son and the relationship this dialogue expresses run headlong against Sutpen's oratorical word. Sutpen, whenever he has spoken in the novel, has spoken univocally; he proclaims or pontificates like an orator, creating the Sutpen's Hundred "like the oldentime *Be Light*," proclaiming his marriage to Rosa, even using "bombastic phrases" to ask for a match (p. 240). He is the personification of the principle of the monological. He is even described as oratorical at various times in the novel, with his "swaggering gestures" and "forensic verbiage" (p. 246), or his "forensic anecdotal manner," "the very sober quality of his gestures and the set of his shoulders forensic, oratorical" (p. 275). In his meeting with Henry at the bivouac, Sutpen tells Henry that Bon is a Negro. Sutpen, the very principle of "semantic authority," speaks a word to his son, and death follows. Sutpen enters into a dialogue for one of the few moments in the novel— in Sutpen's life—but no dialogical relationship is thereby established except Sutpen's own univocal authority to speak the death of his son Charles. In this gesture of semantic authority, Sutpen *represents* Bon as a Negro; he is given voice in dialogue so that the true horror can be called forth, his disregard of Bon's humanity. And the irony is compounded still further when Sutpen speaks to Henry in words that echo King David's cry at the death of Absalom:

> —*Henry . . . his father holds his face between both hands, looking at it.*
> —*Henry, Sutpen says—My son.* (p. 355)

Sutpen, in other words, has been inserted into a dialogical relationship only once, and then virtually to speak the novel's title (as Addie, in *As I Lay Dying*, "speaks" that novel's title). Even when he sounds least like an orator, least bombastic, he still plays at being one, denying any relationship except that of semantic authority, unable to transcend oratory's limited dialogical relationship to speak to his son. Sutpen is orator. Henry is audience, as the name "negro" is given univocally to Bon.

The second dialogical scene I would point to occurs when Quentin climbs over the sill at Sutpen's Hundred and comes face to face with the dying Henry Sutpen. The italicized exchange between them feels little like an exchange between two speakers. Rather the dialogue becomes a discursive object, a symbol for the death of dialogue—a death perpetrated by Sutpen and enforced on the level of discourse by the overvoice. The phrases, on the page, form a virtual palindrome, a symmetrical image turning on the words "to die":

> *And you are———?*
> *Henry Sutpen.*
> *And you have been here———?*
> *Four years.*
> *And you came home———?*
> *To die. Yes.*
> *To die?*
> *Yes. To die.*
> *And you have been here———?*
> *Four years.*
> *And you are———?*
> *Henry Sutpen.* (p. 373)

Talk, voices, language itself freeze symmetrically above the flesh of the dying Henry Sutpen. Discourse is removed from voice. Speech is transformed into a symbolic object marking the violence within the discourse of *Absalom, Absalom!*. A strange and silent writing is erected as a monument, a memorial, a tombstone if you will, to the dialogical word that oratory and Sutpen would banish. Here and there, as in Quentin's meeting with Henry, the monological overvoice reneges momentarily to allow dialogical speech to appear—literally *appear*—as a struggle between speakers. *Absalom, Absalom!* thus depicts a history and its constituting narrative as a violence within the narrative's discourse itself, an eruption of the dialogical within the monological oratorical discourse behind which Sutpen's history would hide itself.

---

NOTES

1. Mikhail Bakhtin, *Problems of Dostoevsky's Poetics,* trans. Caryl Emerson (Minneapolis: Univ. of Minnesota Press, 1984); see also *The Dialogic Imagination,* ed. Michael Holquist, trans. Caryl Emerson and Michael Holquist (Austin: Univ. of Texas Press, 1981).
2. See William Garrett Brown, *The Lower South in American History* (New

York: Peter Smith Reprint, 1930; original publication 1902), p. 127. For excellent discussions of the history of Southern oratory, see Waldo W. Braden, ed., *Oratory in the Old South, 1828–1860* (Baton Rouge: Louisiana State University Press, 1970). See also Francis Gaines, *Southern Oratory: A Study in Idealism* (University, Alabama: Univ. of Alabama Press, 1946).

3. Gaines, p. 4.

4. Reprinted in the Atlanta *Constitution*, February 16, 1900, p. 5, col. 2. The Atlanta *Constitution* is an excellent source for the study of Southern oratory because nearly every issue includes one or more reprinted speeches and because it had a high reputation and a wide circulation.

5. *Absalom, Absalom!* (New York: Modern Library, 1951), pp. 19–20. All page references are to this issue.

6. Malcolm Cowley, *The Faulkner-Cowley File: Letters and Memoirs, 1944–1962* (New York: Viking Press, 1966), p. 78.

7. See Bakhtin, *Problems of Dostoevsky's Poetics*, pp. 181–204 generally.

8. Bakhtin, *Problems*, p. 163.

9. Bakhtin, p. 188; my emphasis.

10. "A Southern Mode of the Imagination," *Essays of Four Decades* (Chicago: Swallow Press, 1968), pp. 583–84.

11. See "The Evocation of Voice in *Absalom, Absalom!*," *Essays in Literature*, 8 (Fall 1981), p. 135–50.

12. Bakhtin, p. 198.

13. See Robert G. Gunderson, "The Southern Whigs," in *Oratory in the Old South*, pp. 125–26.

# *The Wild Palms:* Degraded Culture, Devalued Texts

## Pamela Rhodes and Richard Godden

"That raggledy palm tree in the middle of the court was more
raggledy & forlorn than ever. Nothing looks any more forlorn
in the rain than a Hollywood palm tree . . ."
HORACE MCCOY[1]

### I.

*The Wild Palms* was written between September 1937 and June
1938.[2] Faulkner had just spent about a year and a half in California, returning home in September 1937. His contract with
Twentieth Century-Fox had been his lengthiest to date, and he
had made only intermittent visits back to Mississippi. It is a commonplace that Faulkner never felt at ease with the work or in the
life of the motion-picture business, but though the anecdotage
about the "Hollywood Years" continues to multiply, Faulkner's
literary response to the machinery of mass culture is still largely
ignored. Critics who have touched upon the issue have, like
Bruce Kawin, written about his "cinematic" technique,[3] or like
Tom Dardis and Thomas McHaney, have suggested that the
post-Hollywood works are exorcisms, containing vestigial moments that are the aftertaste of despair.[4] We would argue that
*The Wild Palms* came out of Hollywood, but as more than a wail
of self-pity, a submerged biography, or a tribute to Hawks or
Eisenstein; instead, we suggest that, although Faulkner could
have gathered his insights elsewhere, southern California provided him with a textbook on commodity. Lukács has said that
the commodity "can be only understood in its undistorted essence when it becomes the universal category of society as a
whole;"[5] arguably, like Fitzgerald, West, McCoy, Wilson, Hux-
ley, Mann, and Adorno, among others, Faulkner found such a
phenomenon in Hollywood.

---

A version of this essay first appeared as *"The Wild Palms:* Faulkner's Hollywood
Novel," in *Amerikastudien/American Studies,* 28 (1983), 449–466.

Hollywood novels[6] seem to produce voices which can only go in circles, which are heard from inside institutions, or which are reabsorbed by publicity or authority when they try to get out. In *The Wild Palms,* Harry's voice works best when he "could say it to himself"[7] and comes from inside a cell. Other Hollywood artists use the image of the speaker in a locked room because it provides a figure for the ineffectuality of the voice raised against the market's invasion of every aspect of life. This oppression is driven home to us by the authorial sleight-of-hand that produces the first-person "manuscript" and simultaneously shows the closed room it comes from. Only on the penultimate page of *The Postman Always Rings Twice,* for example, does James M. Cain finally let Frank let us know where his "voice" is coming from: "So I'm in the death house, now, writing the last of this, so Father McConnell can look it over and show me the places where maybe it ought to be fixed up a little, for punctuation and all that."[8] Fitzgerald's room was notional: in *The Last Tycoon* he planned that we should find Celia's voice in a sanitorium. West's sudden dislocation of the final chapter of *The Day of the Locust* is a more complex trick: he offers us a potentially liberating moment in the form of a riot on a preview night, but the crowd remains effectively silent, permitted only to "roar" when the publicity mechanism requires. The artist is equally subservient. Tod Hackett's record of the event, a canvas entitled "The Burning of Los Angeles," is less art work than film poster. Not surprisingly, the painter's voice is finally heard imitating a police siren.[9]

With the exception of *The Postman Always Rings Twice,* these novels were published after Faulkner had finished *The Wild Palms;* in choosing them, we wish merely to mark out certain areas where the manner of Faulkner's oppressive pessimism is endorsed by other writers. However, it is likely that *The Wild Palms* has a nearer Hollywood neighbor, which not only acts as a paradigm for the species, but precedes Faulkner's novel, and which may have helped to focus his approach.

Much to Horace McCoy's annoyance, since he had completed a draft in 1933, his first novel, *They Shoot Horses, Don't They?* (1935), was generally taken to be a derivation from James M.

Cain's *The Postman Always Rings Twice* (1934). Certainly, Cain's death-house line might stand as the *locus classicus* for the sudden revelation of voice and manuscript from within the punitive institution. Frank's story is a "confession" in its crudest form and, in its attempt finally to implicate the reader, performs like much pulp, by absorbing its public through empathy. As Joyce Carol Oates writes: "Frank, begging the reader to pray for him and Cora, is the very voice of mass man. There is no doubt but that brutality brutalizes, and sentimentality is but one form of brutality."[10] Given its reputation, Faulkner might well have read *Postman*, but McCoy's is the more complex and more analytical novel, and even if McCoy did not use Cain, there is enough in the way he pursued and organized the "Hollywood" lines of thought to suggest that Faulkner might have used McCoy.

*They Shoot Horses, Don't They?* was published in 1935; in December of that year, Faulkner arrived in southern California to take up his new contract. Joseph Blotner makes no reference to McCoy, but it seems possible that they could have met through Nathanael West, with whom Faulkner now renewed an earlier acquaintanceship. West was then working with Republic, where, according to Tom Dardis, McCoy "was probably the best-known writer on the payroll." Both McCoy and West frequented Stanley Rose's book store, and West introduced Faulkner there.[11] Even given Faulkner's own reticence about literature, and discounting actual conversations or acquaintance, Faulkner may well have heard McCoy in discussions, and as Rose was well-known for his enthusiastic promotion of the writers who were "regulars" at his shop, it would seem likely that McCoy's recent novel would have been much in evidence, at least in Faulkner's visits early in 1936. Faulkner had a 1935 paperback copy of the novel in his library,[12] and it seems not unreasonable to assume that he bought and read it in California in the year before he wrote *The Wild Palms*.

There are several aspects of *They Shoot Horses, Don't They?* in which Faulkner might have been interested and which may have been assimilated in *The Wild Palms* for his own purposes, providing him with more specific ways to focus his ideas on the "prison" of society than he would have found, for instance, in *An American Tragedy* (1925), which exemplifies a more general treatment of a similar theme without the Hollywood connection. It is, perhaps, less than fortuitous that Harry's journalist friend is named McCord and that Harry himself discovers a propensity for writing pulp fictions—even as the Tall Convict goes to prison for reading them. There are, however, more substantial points of reference.

From the beginning of *They Shoot Horses,* man overtly stands condemned: "The prisoner will stand"[13] acts almost as an epigraph to a novel dominated by a judge's voice. McCoy contains the narrator's story within the trial, letting us hear his narrative only within the interrupting cadences of the death sentence. Moreover, it soon becomes clear that the juxtaposition does not simply contrast the trial with "freedom" and "innocence," but that McCoy intercuts two forms of prison, to argue that the one is the logical conclusion of the other. In McCoy's Dance Marathon, Faulkner read a perfect representation of the prison of commodity-exchange, where every aspect of life is exploited as novelty for the "customers" (*TSH,* p. 33). The image of the dance focuses the use of mass culture as a mediating agent of domination. The public dance hall is an arena and the "marathon dance" is like "a bull fight" (*TSH,* p. 51), a commercialised ritual. On this floor McCoy drew in miniature the features of Hollywood that Faulkner experienced as ubiquitous: "Hollywood . . . is no longer in Hollywood but is stippled by a billion feet of burning colored gas across the face of the American earth" (p. 209).

The Derby event, especially, sums up both the rootlessness and the mobility of the characters and the structures of free enterprise of which they are a symptom. Like Faulkner's Tall Convict, McCoy's contestants, Robert and Gloria, are sold their fantasies by the magazines, read in Gloria's case during her hospital convalescence after a suicide bid. Detective magazines lead to the arrest of another contestant, Mario, and the fifty-year sentence he gets becomes "the best break" the promoters ever had (*TSH,* p. 96). This anticipates Robert's own trial and execu-

tion for murder, which will become publicity, promising customers more excitement at future contests.

If death serves the profit motive, so too does conception. In
looking at the way the culture industry has used up all real
experience, Faulkner might have been struck by Gloria's final
statements. As she asks Robert to kill her, she speaks of her own
refusal of reproduction. It took him a few sentences, Robert tells
us, before "it dawned on" him what she was talking about. Then
she asked, ". . . suppose I get caught?" He goes on:

> "You're not just thinking of that, are you?" I asked.
> "Yes, I am. Always before this time I was able to take care of
> myself. Suppose I do have a kid?" she said.
> "You know what it'll grow up to be, don't you. Just like us."
> "She's right," I said to myself, "she's exactly right. It'll grow
> up to be just like us—"
> "I don't want that," she said. "Anyway, I'm finished. I think
> it's a lousy world and I'm finished." (*TSH*, pp. 227–8)

The sentiment is echoed in *The Wild Palms* where Faulkner's
couple agonize about the benefits of abortion as opposed to the
problems of parenthood. For Charlotte, children "hurt too
much" (p. 217). It takes Harry, as it does Robert, a while to
follow what she is saying: "Then he understood, knew what she
meant . . . He was about to say, 'But this will be ours,' when he
realised that this was it, this was exactly it". Faulkner, like
McCoy, gives the aggression and force of dissent to the female.
These women's protest finds theoretical expression in Lukács's
question: "How far is commodity exchange together with its
structural consequences able to influence the *total* outer and inner life of society?" (p. 84)[14] *The Wild Palms* is Faulkner's answer,
as he displays the condition of a world where man appears as
just an instrument of passage for the circulation of commodities.

Basic to this argument is Faulkner's transformation of society
into a prison and of each half of his novel into an escape story.
Faulkner's escapees, like McCoy's, search for an exit from commodity, in a quest for a form of authentic experience. The
sphere of freedom is the realm beyond the market, where man

might be restored to wholeness and to his own authority. There is a particularly suggestive paragraph in *They Shoot Horses* when Robert first meets Gloria and offers her the movies or the park:

> I was glad she wanted to go to the park. It was always nice there. It was a fine place to sit. It was very small, only one block square, but it was very dark and very quiet and filled with dense shrubbery. All around it palm trees grew up, fifty, sixty feet tall, suddenly tufted at the top. Once you entered the park you had the illusion of security. I often imagined they were sentries wearing grotesque helmets: my own private sentries standing guard over my own private island. (*TSH*, pp. 12-13)

Its elements, the need for self-enclosure and for the safe retreat, find their echoes throughout *The Wild Palms* in the locations Faulkner chooses for Harry's dreaming; he is sealed finally in a real cell—a private island shadowed by the significant presence of a palm tree. While palms may be a commonplace on the Gulf Coast, Faulkner goes to some length to grant this specimen a singular and spectral energy. When Harry reaches the jail, Faulkner writes: "there were no oleanders. But the palm was there. It was just outside his window, bigger, more shabby; when he and the officer passed beneath it to enter, with no wind to cause it it had set up a sudden frenzied clashing . . ." (p. 307).

The "clashing" may be "inexplicable" (p. 307) to Harry, but Faulkner, with Twentieth Century-Fox fresh in his mind, knows that the cell and the palm are essentially Californian. If "Holly-wood . . . is no longer in Hollywood" (p. 209), then references to California, specific and oblique, are merely signs that the whole social metabolism has been invaded by the dominant commodity form.

## II.

In *Marxism and Form*, Frederic Jameson offers an analysis of the condition that usefully sets the terms of our account.

> Little by little, in the commercial age, matter as such has ceased to exist, and has given place to commodities, which are

intellectual forms, or the forms of intellectualized satisfactions: this is to say that in the commodity age, need as a purely material and physical impulse (as something "natural") has given way to a structure of artificial stimuli, artificial longings, such that it is no longer possible to separate the true from the false, the primary from the luxury-satisfaction, in them.[15]

In *The Wild Palms* Faulkner shows man as having lost touch with "matter." He has lost sight of his relations with his own objects and his own kind and is reduced to yet another item of merchandise in the market that appears to control him. When we are formally introduced to Harry, one of the novel's main samples, Faulkner swiftly presents the condition (p. 31). What begins as almost a *Who's Who* biography ("the youngest of the three children") quickly reveals the oddities, as it becomes clear that to be "born" now means to be produced explicitly as a commercial prospect. Although we are told that Harry "was left an orphan at the age of two," there is no mention of the mother's death (a second wife of the father's old age), and it is clear that she has been acquired solely to manufacture the male child. Faulkner allows Harry very little "innocence": at "two days" old, he not only has a name but is stamped and certified in his father's will as an investment for a sliding class. With money built in to every tissue, small wonder that he grows up able to taste only cash, not food (p. 104), that his emotions turn into "currency" (p. 136), and that even his ethics change into capital and start accruing interest—after his initial refusal to perform the abortion on the manager's wife, he finds his stock as a doctor increases and his price goes up (p. 191).

Faulkner is insistent that all "natural" impulse has nearly evaporated and that spontaneity has turned into habit, or atrophied altogether. When "genuine experience" is lost, one of the problems we have in identifying it again is, as Jameson says, that "a degraded culture intervenes between us and our objects."[16] A good part of the criticism of *The Wild Palms* has devoted itself, quite justifiably, to tracing Faulkner's allusions, but for the most part the critical research has not addressed the problematic meaning of the intertextual form itself. Despite the

presence of the Bible and, inevitably, Mark Twain in "Old Man,"
the allusions come most conspicuously in "Wild Palms," where
reading forms part of the characters' biographies. The story is
cluttered with chewed-over bits of the cultural objects that the
characters need in order to define themselves, but which simultaneously get in their way, and actually prevent the achievement
of "real" feeling. At the lake, when McCord describes Harry's
effusions as "ninth-rate Teasdale" (p. 100), we may feel that
there is some truth in the abreviation: after all, Harry seems
unable to experience sensation until he has struck it off against
his reading. His activity when Charlotte is dying is no exception.
He needs literary voices to tell him what is happening. The
wind's "whisper" turns to the "sound" of the lamp, which begins
to "rustle and murmur" on Charlotte's flesh (p. 284). They speak
in Elizabethan imagery as Harry tries, and fails, to realize his
own "cuckolding" and "horning" by death (p. 284). Then, a few
minutes later, he snatches at Owen Wister, characteristically at a
scene of a woman as an object, fêted and dying, "the whore in
the pink ball dress . . . remembering and forgetting it in the
same instant since it would not help him" (p. 287). In the hospital, he filters his wait through *A Farewell to Arms,* using Frederic
Henry's atomized perception to help him see what is happening
(pp. 303–04).

Faulkner's presentation of Harry as being possessed by
artificial constructs, measuring himself by them, unable to liberate any authentic feeling, acts as a perfect image of the problems
of a reified existence. Such moments show the behavior of all
"artificial stimuli," which by their very nature as commodities
dehumanize the consumer, deliberately leaving him unsatisfied,
making him dependent on them and eliminating any power of
resistance. There may, however, be some danger in drawing an
equation between artificial longing and textual profligacy. A de-
constructionist, certainly, would feel no qualm: arguing for the
radical nature of the released signifier, his case might run—once
freed from stultifying and singular meaning the intertextual
reference undercuts the givenness both of the main text and of

the reality towards which that text points. As Derrida has argued:

> . . . language will substitute itself for that living self-presence of the proper, which, as language, already supplanted things in themselves. Language *adds itself* to presence and supplants it, defers it within the indestructible desire to rejoin it.[17]

John T. Matthews, for whom this is one of Derrida's "most fruitful observations,"[18] chooses, specifically, to read Faulkner's fictions through "the rich array of languages . . . all of which make their meaning through the play of difference, the deferring of conclusive truth, the pure pleasure of making marks."[19] But in *The Wild Palms,* the play is less than pleasurable. In the context of the novel, the intertextual, if pursued to its esoteric and self-referentially eccentric extremes, acquires meaning and becomes a synecdoche for overproduction. At which point, the cultural blight that is the novel's subject infects the text itself. Thomas McHaney has done much to trace the ramifications of the parodic network, but for all his helpful annotations, he has not touched on the meaning of the literary form.[20] The more the artificial longings expand their own artificiality through deepening layers of parody, the more an excess of artifice comes to signify only its own falsity, leaving the novel in danger of collapsing upon itself, as fabricated as the fabric it sought to comprehend.

A brief detour through theory may prove helpful. Paul Ricoeur summarizes the consequences of systematic intertextuality in terms that apply both to "the ideology of the absolute text" and to the ideology of commodity as "the universal category of society as a whole" (Lukács):

> The suspense which defers the reference merely leaves the text, as it were, "in the air," outside or without a world. In virtue of this obliteration of the relation of the world, each text is free to enter into relation with all the other texts which come to take the place of circumstantial reality referred to by living speech. This relation of text to text, within the efface-

ment of the world about which we speak, engenders the quasi-world of texts or *literature*.[21]

In *The Pleasure of the Text* Roland Barthes celebrates the efface-ment of reference. Reading Flaubert "according to Proust," Barthes says,

> I savor the sway of formulas, the reversal of origins, the ease which brings the anterior text out of the subsequent one . . . Proust is what comes to me, not what I summon; not an "au-thority" simply a *circular memory*. Which is what inter-text is: the impossibility of living outside the infinite text—whether this be Proust or the daily newspaper or the television screen: the book creates the meaning, the meaning creates life.[22]

Intertextuality with its systematic suspension of reference and its appeal to "the infinite text" might well be the literary form for a mode of production that atomizes objects and alienates per-sons, only to reintegrate its anomic particles through the prom-ise of "abstract value" as a universal equivalent. "Abstract value," realized through money, is effectively the means to social syn-thesis under capital.[23] Like Barthes's "infinite text," "value" acts as a missing promise of reintegration: both provide a measure of cohesion at the cost of particularity of reference—either by the text to its world or by men to their immediate needs. Nonetheless, intertextuality is divisive (Barthes cuts "Sarrasine" into 561 "lexia"); it appears most frequently under the banner of subversion:

> Let us first posit the image of triumphant plural, unimpover-ished by any constraint of representation (or imitation). In this ideal text, the networks are many and interact, without any one of them being able to surpass the rest; this text is a galaxy of signifiers, not a structure of signifieds; it has no beginning; it is reversible; we gain access to it by several entrances, none of which can be authoritatively declared to be the main one; the codes it mobilizes extend as far *as the eye can read*, they are interminable . . .[24]

The "triumph" is in reality modest, since it most resembles the triumphant workings of the money form. Witness Barthes's reading of "Sarrasine." Balzac's story is to the lexia of *S/Z* as "abstract value" is to money and to its exchange—just as the fiction is the entity that guarantees the worth of Barthes's many subdivisions, so "value" is the

> integral whole in every single incident of exchange, and in order to be able to serve all incidents in this capacity it must, on the contrary, allow for any degree of divisibility, or as the corresponding philosophical term has it, for sheer atomicity.[25]

Put more generally, "value" is a nondescriptive substance, which, materialized in money, provides for the interrelation of an endless number of entities. Likewise, intertextuality (and its parental Derridean "differance") is a contentless principle of structure that allows all literature, indeed all discourse, to intersect. Intertextuality could be read as literary criticism for advanced capitalism.

Our digression through the broad implications of a critical method suggests that in form it is political. To return to its use in "Wild Palms" is to find something of that political meaning affirmed. Faulkner's awareness of intertextuality as a commercial venture becomes plain if we consider one of the significant difficulties of the story: the problem of where the voice is coming from. The narrative is in the third person but apart from the Doctor's passages, it approximates to Harry's consciousness. We cannot, however, accept the narrative voice as a simple one. Increasingly, as we read, we recognize that Harry's voice is capable of disrupting the authorial frame. Indeed, there are fairly frequent anticipatory moments that posit a real location for the speaker—that location can only be the prison cell:

> Then for the first of the two times in their lives he saw her cry. (p. 50)
>
> Later he was to recall. . . . (p. 60)
>
> He approached the bed (it was now that Wilbourne seemed to

remember him putting the pistol into the bag). . . . (pp. 293–
94)

These examples demonstrate the care for exactitude of someone
going over the episodes, trying to fix the details, to get the story
right. Effectively, at these points, Faulkner's voice is interrupted
by Harry's, so that the author's authority quite suddenly coincides with that of the character. The implications of the coincidence are troubling. At the point where we see Harry's writing
hand before his author's—that is, at the turning of the narrative
trick—the issue ceases to be one of coexisting worlds, realized
through vocal polyphony. Rather, the shock of recognition involves the submission of one voice to another. We learn, not that
a third-person narrative is really a first-person narrative (though
this is technically the case), but that "persons," whom we might
have treated discretely, have elided embarrassingly. Where,
prior to the trick, we had one author, we now have two: one, an
experimental novelist, the other, a hack for the pulps. Stated less
divisively, the case for authority might run: Faulkner finds in the
consciousness of another an aspect of himself—an aspect that
troubles and at times dominates him.[26] Certainly, the various
elements of self-parody and the literary cross-referencing within
"Wild Palms" serve not only to present the afflictions of the
characters, but set on display Faulkner's own moral problems as
a producer for the market, as he seems ingeniously to introduce
himself into the narrative. It is not unimportant, for example,
that an author who, as a young man, wrote out in meticulous
hand six copies of *Marionettes,* should show puppets "almost as
large as small children" (p. 91), already blasted with syphilis,
being bred for magazine covers. Biographically the contradiction of his work in Hollywood may have sharpened his concern,
but his anxiety extended beyond the personal to comprehend
the wider fate of the artist in the age of accelerating mass "enter-
tainment." Faulkner's original title for his novel came from a
Psalm that asked, "How shall we sing the Lord's song in a
strange land?"[27] By implication the "strange land" might well be
Hollywood, since Hollywood has spread "across the face of the

American earth" (p. 209). If so, the singer in Babylon must learn the language of commodity, and be prepared to cut out his tongue by ravaging his own earliest and most "precious" art work.

The idea that "Wild Palms" is a retrospective narrative, composed by Harry, finds support in "Old Man," which has a similar form and, too, is told from the penitentiary. There, however, it is an oral tale, with the short convict being used, as Faulkner said,[28] to draw out the performance, whereas Harry is his own audience. We know that Harry has a propensity for mental home movies. He sits in the park playing out the domestic scene of the Rittenmeyer parting—for a screen, "he watched against his eyelids" (p. 221). For Harry to use projection like this is for him to substitute for failed wholeness another artificial satisfaction, a motion that Adorno has analyzed:

> The pronouncement . . . that memories are the only possessions which no-one can take from us, belongs in the storehouse of impotently sentimental consolations that the subject, resignedly withdrawing into inwardness, would like to believe the very fulfillment that he has given up. In setting up his own archives, the subject seizes his own stock of experience as property, so making it something wholly external to himself.[29]

Harry ingests his past, as another commodity for his own consumption, turning his narrative, not into archives, but into a pulp novel written over the grave of Charlotte.

Joseph Moldenhauer sees Harry's pulp writing as masochistic self-indulgence and "exhibitionist self-degradation,"[30] an observation that catches the way the activity both arouses and frustrates (pp. 121–23). Given the presentation of the previous stories, his final "confession" of guilt, from the penal cell, becomes another "sexual gumdrop" (p. 123), bought with "emotional currency" to "titillate" (p. 136). In analyzing his thoughts about Francis's pink cheque (played with like an "opium pipe," p. 94), Harry diagnosed a "form of masturbation" (p. 94). The memories of Charlotte seem to be another version of the same habit. His imaginative behavior finds, possibly, its appropriate physical counterpart as he stands at the window of his cell, watching Venus, the evening star. Thomas McHaney (*WFWP*, pp. 172–74) goes into very useful detail about the furtive lexicon of masturbation in these final passages. Once we have been alerted, it is very difficult not to read this section in the light of innuendo, which gives more force to Harry's sexualization of vocabulary and his enfleshment of memory: " . . . it would stand to his hand" (p. 324), for example, or " . . . so there was just memory, forever and inescapable, so long as there was flesh to titillate" (p. 323).

Harry adds the laurel to the palm. Having recalled his experiences, he effectively prepares to exchange them in pulp form. Even as Harry stands "about to get it, think it into words" (p. 323), Faulkner shows how there is no release, no authentic memory and how the most heroic dissent turns in on itself and leaves the sphere of reification unharmed. His last phrase— "*between grief and nothing I will take grief*" (p. 324)—has come a long way from his pulp juvenilia—"If I had only had a mother's love to guard me on that fatal day" (p. 121)—but not far enough. By telling his own story in the third person, Harry generalizes his grief as McCoy's Robert and Cain's Frank could not. But he does so in terms that manifest his literary training. Skillfully, he keeps himself (and his readers) quiet with the reconciliation of a fake catharsis. A synopsis of "Wild Palms" might read: "Brief spells of happiness, paid for by woman's death. Unhappy ending, used to affirm indestructibility of life." The culture industry would approve. As he was in Chicago, so he is in New Orleans— a ghost writer for the pulps. To follow Harry in turning Harry into a tragic hero is to accede to the degraded consolation that a maimed life is better than nothing. Such aphorisms, as Adorno and Horkheimer suggest, are the prescriptions of the market place: "The pathos of composure justifies the world which makes (composure) necessary. . . . Tragedy . . . comforts all with the thought that a tough, genuine human fate is still possible" (*D of E*, pp. 151–53). Harry is neither "genuine" nor "tragic," he is "tough" after the manner of hard-boiled heroes. His final fiction enables him to face life in Parchman, but only by means of brutalizing sentimentality. Between "grief" and "nothing," Harry takes "grief," and Faulkner takes "nothing." The fictions of McCoy and Cain allow him to focus his resentment of commercial production while acknowledging his own complicity: they do not provide him with ways of disrupting what he sees.

### III.

Having tried to establish a working analogy between intertextuality and the artificial forms that characterize commercial production, we'd like to turn now from "Wild Palms" to "Old Man," in order to suggest that intratextuality further dramatizes Faulkner's preoccupation with commodity. At a schematic level in "Old Man," a drive to pretextual intensity (the flood), moves through intratextual reference towards that intertextual networking, which, in "Wild Palms," is one aspect of an overwhelming reification of experience. Such a survey is formulaic but may give greater direction to what follows.

Faulkner repeatedly insisted that he wrote the stories as they appear, that "Wild Palms" was the primary one, and that he moved to "Old Man" whenever he needed "counterpoint."[31] Taken alone, Harry's sealed onanistic chamber typifies the closed and rigid thought forms of commodity production, presenting themselves as immovable and eternal, a pretension that "Old Man" seems at pains to deny. Marx suggests that

> The whole mystery of commodities, all the magic and necromancy that surrounds the products of labour as long as they take the form of commodities, vanishes therefore, so soon as we come to other forms of production.[32]

It is a recommendation that Jameson appears to have in mind when describing the Surrealist opposition to the amnesia of the commercial age:

> Surrealism presents itself . . . as a reaction against the intellectualized . . . The Surrealist image is thus a convulsive effort to split open the commodity forms of the objective universe by striking them against each other with immense force.[33]

Striking against the inert blocks of "Wild Palms," "Old Man" attempts through a violent intensity—stylistic, thematic, and comic—to smash open the forms of reification. In its subject matter, Faulkner is testing the hypothesis, framed here by Lukács as an absolute, that "Only the consciousness of the pro-letariat can point to the way that leads out of the impasse of capitalism" (*H & CC*, p. 76). Taking the Tall Convict as his sample, Faulkner submits him to a process that examines this claim. The convict's role as representative of the proletariat was noted by one of the earliest reviewers, Edwin Berry Burgum, writing in *New Masses* in 1939. His reading is perhaps overly optimistic, but it allows a greater effort to "Old Man" than do many later interpretations, which dissolve it somewhat bizarrely into a version of pastoral, making the world of the Tall Convict an "idyllic one, cut off from civilization's time and receding into the dim past."[34] The Tall Convict is hardly an Arcadian shepherd, and he is certainly no primitive. Unlike the Noble Savage, the convict is carried towards class consciousness. The flood is a process of undoing that brings him to culture's very edge and to the chance of the first economic insight that would allow him to escape domination and to invent himself as a man.

Once out on the water, the convict is exposed to a systematic derangement that cleanses and abrades his body and senses. The often synesthesic purgation expresses Faulkner's realization that the coefficient of commodity fetishism and of man's disas-sociation from his own labor is a flattening of perception itself.[35] However, to be outside reification almost defies description, as-saulting consciousness "like the notion of a rifle bullet the width of a cotton field" (p. 145). The reader undergoes the active physiotherapy of facing "something which the intelligence, rea-son, simply refuse[s] to harbor" (p. 145). At the peak of the Mississippi's histrionic decision to flow backwards, the Convict, too, "waiting his chance to scream" (p. 157), has his perception rehabilitated. The darkness acquires tactile powers, behaving energetically to stretch and tauten his slack muscles, and in battl-ing with it, he begins "wrenching almost physically at his eyes as if they were two of those suction-tipped rubber arrows shot from the toy gun of a child . . ." (p. 164). The startling comparison turns eyesight almost inside out, in a retinal engagement with matter, making the Convict anything now but a passive spectator, receiving only the manufactured images of a One-Dimensional world. As perception falls apart, all logical categories vanish too. If to end reification it is necessary first to be seen to dissolve facts into process, as Lukács prescribes, then "Old Man's" ludic parentheses take the injunction to its extreme, as the entire objective world, Harry's parks included, "leaped and played about him like fish" (p. 161).

Given the general unhealthiness of flesh in the novel, it is essential that Faulkner batters and wrings the Tall Convict into feeling. He suffers multiple lacerations, itches, burns, and blisters, as matter which has been forgotten rises up and hits him on the back of the head to remind him—by making his nose bleed. Faulkner's precise motivation for the Convict's hemophilia is elusive. In part, perhaps, it is another form of purging. With such strenuous therapy the body does indeed seem to gain access to a new kind of life. Reading that "he seemed to hear the roar of his own saliva" (p. 232), it is almost possible to believe again in "primary needs." Perhaps after all, Lukács and Hegel are right in arguing that "It is easier to bring movement into sensuous existence than into fixed ideas,"[36] at least it certainly seems so when the Convict, having seen a deer only on a Christmas card, is restored through instinct to swimming as it did (p. 234).

While still reconditioning his subject, Faulkner deposits him on an Indian mound, the earliest specimen he can offer of land known to man through its uses. Here the Convict begins to be conscious of himself as economic man. Faulkner gives him, virtually all at once, the activities through which man comes into being. Critics have noted how the Tall Convict races through a condensed evolutionary history;[37] as he does so, his hands are restored to their material. The mound is essential as a training place for "infant" man, teaching him midwifery, hunting, tool-making, and cooking; but Faulkner does not let him linger there too long. With the Convict primed and practiced, Faulkner at last brings him to the swamp.

Like the Mound, the swamp lies on society's very periphery, not outside or before it. The Cajan's wilderness is a fully functioning economic system in the first stages of its working into which the Tall Convict makes his entry. Faulkner saves this moment until he has told us that he "was in partnership now with his host" (p. 255), hunting on "halvers." Percentages retain their links with the objects of labor, which are there to be divided, and "truth" can be learned from a close observation of phenomena. The Convict is sure that, "*even if he cant tell me how I reckon I can watch him and find out*" (p. 257). Newly energized as it is, his gaze works actively, "going here and there constantly" (p. 257), teaching him that he must make his own world through his perception of it, possessing it by description: "*What? What? I not only dont know what I am looking for, I dont even know where to look for it*" (p. 257). The two sentences that follow are the crucial ones.

First, Faulkner makes the reader participate in the Convict's activity, through a syntactic strenuosity extreme even for "Old Man":

> Then he felt the motion of the pirogue as the Cajan moved and then the tense gobbl*ing* hiss*ing* actually, hot rapid and repressed, against his neck and ear, and glanc*ing* downward saw project*ing* between his own arm and body from behind the Cajan's hand hold*ing* the knife, and glar*ing* up again saw the flat thick spit of mud . . . . (p. 257; emphasis added)

Faulkner demands a sequence of decisions, forcing the reader to assign the designated words to their status as substantive, qualifier, and participle, and so to sort out the ownership of the limbs, the Convict meanwhile being similarly preoccupied. Then, having galvanized perception, Faulkner takes both sets of eyeballs, the Convict's and ours, to the alligator. It is the most exciting moment in the novel. The "mud" turns to "log," then, "still immobile," seems to "leap suddenly against his retinae" (p. 258)—and at this instant, it seems as if the reified "spectacle," already badly bruised, bursts open, as Adorno said, "irradiated by the light of its own self-determination." The alligator takes form in "three—no, four—dimensions," and the fourth, it turns out, is "pure and intense speculation" (p. 258). The phrase explodes with meanings, perceptual, judgmental, and economic, purging them of appropriation. The Convict gathers his whole self together, concentrating all his experience on the logistics of the task. It is the crucial chance for transition. That he kills the animal, surface to surface, using a knife not a gun, is essential to make this moment of phenomenological impact with matter and the ultimate abrasion of the husk of commodity, the instant of interchange between man and nature that makes life. There is a quick here that allows complete knowledge, and apparently the "speculation" pays off, bringing the Convict the full value of his own labor, the plenteous moment: "Tout l'argent sous le ciel de Dieu!" (p. 259), the Cajan cries, admitting him to the oral history of the swamp, as a legendary hero. It is no surprise when Faulkner turns him into the "*matador*" surrounded by his "*aficionados*" (p. 263), using Hemingway as index to the intensity of experience, as he was to its debasement. In rejecting the gun, the Tall Convict becomes the stylist, insisting upon a material engagement with his objects, learning from his relationship with them a sense of his own alterability. "*Will have to get on back*" (p. 261), no longer looks like a plain statement once the Convict sees that the "last seven years had sunk like so many trivial pebbles into a pool" (p. 261): the convict's imperative recalls the early thought that is now about to know itself—the difference between "toil" and "work" (p. 264) that the prisoners expressed in their observation that "it could have been pebbles they put into the ground" (p. 30). The Tall Convict is poised on the edge of seeing himself as subject rather than object, controlling his own market, with the meaning of his work returned to memory: "*I had forgot how good it is to work*" (p. 264). With the hide pegged out like "a mahogany board table," and himself a member of a "corporation" (p. 261), the relations are all on the surface for the Convict to understand and act upon. Even his sweat is now measurable, so that he can make the choice between investing his efforts in one tedious night carving up the paddle or in a few energetic minutes carving up an alligator. Having seen himself as economic man, he is in a position to move on through the hierarchy.

Yet, Faulkner turns him back at the threshold. From the start we know that the sojourn in the swamp is just a nine days' wonder (pp. 252, 264); we suspect that the percentage will never acquire a denomination (p. 261) and that plenitude will stay in a foreign language. We do not really need the mordant, "Damn your hides" (p. 272), to know that the skins will never enter the market. The work finally has little more status than the "hunkies'" pleasure in dynamiting rock for the money that will never arrive ("Wild Palms")—and we are led to increasingly pessimistic conclusions—conclusions that are dangerously reminiscent of the position of the more eccentric Agrarians. (John Crowe Ransom in 1933 requested that fertilizers should be highly taxed so that subsistence farmers might better enjoy the delights of their subsistence.[38])

Faulkner's point is not to advocate work for work's sake, but to situate the experience of labor within the market, through the juxtaposition of the two stories. However, any dialectical "but" between the chapters must work two ways. In cross-referencing the sections, then, it is not enough to stop at such labels as "ironic parallel" or "counterpoint." There are parallels in this chapter with moments in the "Wild Palms" which, certainly, have two edges, but they make an unmusical point. The intratextual network of the novel is part of Faulkner's argument about commodity. The previous section of "Wild Palms" was the end of a movement begun at the party in Chapter Three, where Harry's perception was jolted for a moment by the pictures, "which . . . impacted" upon him, making "the very eyeballs seem to start violently back in consternation" (p. 37). Moreover, Harry is cast as "a yokel" who, having seen "a drawing of a dinosaur," "was looking at the monster itself" (p. 38), while Charlotte materializes behind him to personify new possibilities. The terms are the same as the "alligator" passage—a dislocation of vision, a glimpse of a different reality, and the introduction of a means of exit. But the process ends in Harry's action with the knife in Chapter Seven. When the next chapter of "Old Man" begins with "When the woman asked him if he had a knife" (p. 229), Faulkner is clearly encouraging the after-image. The knowledge of the abortion lingers when we see the birth of the child, swaddled at once in the private's tunic, marked from the start by the institutions it will grow up to occupy; but worse, and more horribly, it mediates our reading of the "birth" of the Tall Convict. The movement is telescoped as the break in the reified vision, the means for transition and their own negation surface together in one moment, in the killing of the alligator. As Charlotte turned the operation into a parodic sexual penetration,[39] so, too, "straddling" the "thrashing" beast (pp. 258–59), the Convict engages in a grotesque variant of the bid for "true" carnal knowledge. In allowing the Convict the knife, Faulkner was intent on awaking the echoes of the abortion, showing the Convict "probing for the life and finding it, the hot fierce gush" (p. 259); in so doing Faulkner, like Charlotte, identifies the moment of coming to life (conception/birth) with the moment of its ruin. Charlotte needed the immolation of the seed and the termination of the embryo to prevent their "fall" into commodity exchange, a movement Faulkner carried out here to show that the very instant of the origins of labor is shadowed by its consequences at the extreme end of the market. With its "temperature close to blood heat" (p. 262) and its miniature gestatory cycle (everything happens in nines) the swamp has itself been seen as a womb.[40] In aborting the Convict, Faulkner is making it grimly clear that new social dynamics will not arise spontaneously in the power of the proletariat to see "from the centre" (Lukács). The swamp for all its energies remains as Lukács's "mire of immediacy" (*H & CC*, pp. 163, 164) from which man cannot extricate himself.

For a time the convict is oblivious; delighting in his own singleness, he is content to ignore even the evacuation of the swamp since it affirms that singleness. Temporarily released from prison and no longer the direct guardian of his female charge, he is the self-employed paddler of his own pirogue. But the solitude quite suddenly reverses itself. What was positive is negative—in a passage of some difficulty:

> . . . he departed too with his knotted rope and mace . . . as though not only not content with refusing to quit the place he had been warned against, he must establish and affirm the irrevocable finality of his refusal by penetrating even further and deeper into it. And then and without warning the high fierce drowsing of his solitude gathered itself and struck at him. . . . it was his very solitude, his desolation which was now his alone and in full since he had elected to remain; the sudden cessation of the paddle, the skiff shooting on for a moment yet while he thought, *What? What?* Then, *No. No. No,* as the silence and solitude and emptiness roared down upon him in a jeering bellow: and now reversed, the skiff spun violently on its heel, he the betrayed driving furiously back toward the platform where he knew it was already too late, that citadel where the very crux and dear breath of his life—the being allowed to work and earn money, that right and privilege which he believed he had earned to himself unaided . . . was being threatened, driving the home-made paddle in grim fury, coming in sight of the platform at last and seeing the motor launch lying alongside it with no surprise at all but actually with a kind of pleasure as though at a visible justification of his outrage and fear, the privilege of saying *I told you so* to his own affronting . . . . (pp. 269–70)

What has flowed in with the motor launch are the workings of the Mississippi, the authority's efforts to control those workings and even perhaps the bureaucratic process that elects to flood Cajan territory rather than a New Orleans suburb. It is all of this and more that the convict's solitude has silenced. Despite Faulkner's assertion that his character "could not have told this if he had tried" (p. 269), the consciousness is not solely Faulkner's. The Convict's negative bolt from the blue is the moment of dialectical reversal that characterizes the historical imagination. The Convict sees with his mind's eye a motor boat standing where once there was vacancy and the odd "sauric protagonist" (p. 270). What matters is not the content but the structure of the image, which allows him to recognize what his isolation is through a simultaneous awareness of what it is not.[41] For a moment he is no longer a comfortable prisoner of the swamp's ☞ immediacy; his singleness is ruptured by itself.

The negative cry is long and threefold because it contains the pain of self-dissolution. The launch is "no surprise"; it does not intrude because it has always been present in the mind of the Convict. Its arrival is a visible materialization of that suppressed spectre—the money form. The Convict may have thought he was in a "citadel" of his own making, but even the gratifications of innocent labor pleased him only because he playfully "computed" (p. 269) them against what the market would give him on the final day of reckoning. It is a reckoning that he hardly thinks about—he hardly needs to, since he is doing it all the time. When he declines the Cajan's paddle (p. 269), he sets up elaborate equivalences, translating an evening, a sapling, a quantity of alligator skin and some of his own sweat into "something" sufficiently "embracing and abstractional" (p. 268) to include volume, weight, number, time, and energy. Money fits the bill. Though alligator hides are a primitive money form, their computer understands their rewards and is plainly at home in the system of exchange that measures Cajan swamps against civic suburbs and sends a launch.

If the "citadel" has always been insubstantial, the "crux" is equally delusive. The Convict persuades himself that he can experience directly and labor immediately and as a result at last feels truly potent. In "penetrating even further and deeper," he closes his ears to the voices of the market in himself and so enters a place that, for all its labors, gives his self-knowledge a holiday. A voice makes itself heard: "*No. No. No.*" The shock of self-consciousness negates his potency, and "he strove dreamily with a weightless oar, with muscles without strength or resiliency" (p. 270). What he triply refuses is the choice to return to "the silence and solitude and emptiness," the preverbal and presocial. Instead, his acceptance of the penitentiary is the compromise of a half-life. Like Harry, he is caught inescapably in the fact of his reified consciousness.

To return to the structural level of Faulkner's argument—if the intertextual style of "Wild Palms" is a hypothesis about how the world is under capital, and if the improvisatory language of "Old Man" briefly inaugurates an unreified world, then the intratextual relation of the stories ensures that escape is short-lived. After all, our last glimpse of the Tall Convict is of a man whose anecdotal powers are improving; his cigar has become a prop, underlining innuendo as he pauses significantly over women. Even as Faulkner's voice became Harry's, so, during "Old Man," the Convict's interruptions of the third-person narrator grow more frequent and more sustained. Plainly he has not forgotten the *Detectives' Gazette*, and is working towards a future in which he will give his Parchman public what it wants—a verbal peep show delivered by the man who has lived the censored pages of "the impossible pulp-printed fables" (p. 149). Despite the Convict's momentary recognition, "Old Man," as we have it, leaves the oral tale of the proletariat as confined and impotent as Harry's reverie.

---

NOTES

1. Horace McCoy, *I Should Have Stayed Home* (London: Arthur Barker Ltd., 1938), p. 92.

2. The first page of the surviving holograph manuscript is dated September 13, 1937 (see William Faulkner, *Helen: A Courtship and Mississippi Poems* [Oxford, Miss., and New Orleans: Yoknapatawpha Press and Tulane, 1981], introduction by Carvel Collins, pp. 88–89).

3. Bruce Kawin, "The Montage Element in Faulkner's Film," in *Faulkner, Modernism and Film: Faulkner and Yoknapatawpha 1978*, ed. Evans Harrington and Ann Abadie (Jackson: University Press of Mississippi, 1979), pp. 103–26; and "Faulkner's Film Career: The Years with Hawks," pp. 163–81; and *Faulkner and Film* (New York: Frederick Ungar Publishing Company, 1977). See also David Minter, *William Faulkner, His Life and Work* (Baltimore and London: Johns Hopkins University Press, 1980), Chs. 7 and 8, particularly pp. 171–176.

4. Tom Dardis, *Some Time in the Sun* (London: André Deutsch, 1976), pp. 98, 99, 113. Thomas McHaney, *William Faulkner's "The Wild Palms"* (Jackson: University Press of Mississippi, 1975), p. 54. Subsequent page references will be to these editions. McHaney's work will be cited as *WFWP*.

5. Georg Lukács, *History and Class Consciousness* (London: Merlin Press, 1968), p. 86. Subsequent page references will be to this edition, which will be cited as *H & CC*.

6. A genre has been critically mapped. See especially: Walter Wells, *Tycoons and Locusts: A Regional Look at Hollywood Fiction of the 1930s* (Carbondale and Edwardsville: Southern Illinois University Press, 1973). Carolyn See, "The

Hollywood Novel: The American Dream Cheat," in *Tough Guy Writers of the Thirties,* ed. David Madden (Carbondale and Edwardsville: Southern Illinois University Press, 1968).

7. William Faulkner, *The Wild Palms* (New York: Random House, 1939), p. 217. Subsequent page references will be to this edition.

8. James M. Cain, *The Postman Always Rings Twice* (London: Cape, 1934), p. 189.

9. For further examples of voices stultified by Hollywood, see Horace McCoy's *I Should Have Stayed Home* (1938), where the motif is used extensively.

10. Joyce Carol Oates, "Man Under Sentence of Death: The Novels of James M. Cain," in *Tough Guy Writers of the Thirties,* p. 124.

11. Tom Dardis, *Some Time in the Sun,* p. 198, p. 111. Blotner, *A Biography* (New York: Random House, 1974), p. 934 also mentions the book store, but not McCoy, whom Dardis places, without comment, in a general list of people Faulkner may have heard there.

12. Joseph Blotner, *William Faulkner's Library—A Catalogue* (Charlottesville: University Press of Virginia, 1964), p. 41.

13. Horace McCoy, *They Shoot Horses, Don't They?* (London: Arthur Barker Ltd., 1935), p. 1. Subsequent page references will be to this edition, which will be cited as *TSH*.

14. The relevance of a question from a Hungarian Marxist to a disgruntled Southerner, exiled in Hollywood, may seem tenuous—but even as Faulkner wrote *The Wild Palms,* a group of anxious Jewish philosophers, soon to be exiled from Germany, were considering the problem of commodity: their work was also to take its final and focused form in Hollywood, where Adorno and Horkheimer were writing during the 40s. See particularly *Dialectic of Enlightenment* (London: Verso Books, 1979), first published in 1947. Subsequent references will be to the 1979 edition, which will be cited as *D of E.* The Frankfurt School were the first thinkers to take seriously the need to analyze mass culture from a radical perspective: it is our general contention that Faulkner shared this perspective.

15. Frederic Jameson, *Marxism and Form* (Princeton: Princeton University Press, 1971), p. 96. Subsequent page references will be to this edition. Jameson offers what is effectively a paraphrase of Marx, *Capital,* Volume 1, Chapter 1, "The Commodity." The terms "true/primary" and "false/luxury" repeat Marx's distinction between "use" and "exchange" values. The work of Jean Baudrillard calls this distinction into question (see particularly, "Beyond Use Value" in *For a Critique of The Political Economy of the Sign* (St. Louis: Telos Press, 1981), pp. 130–42). However, the quotation remains strategically useful in its application to a novel written in the South in the late 30s. The Agrarian flight from the marketplace rested firmly on a faith in "use value," though other names were used (see particularly Andrew Nelson Lytle, "The Hind Tit," in *I'll Take My Stand* (New York: Harper, 1962), pp. 201–45). Faulkner never espoused the agrarian politics of the 30s, but his account of the MacCallums (*Sartoris,* 1929), his antipathy to the Snopeses (*The Hamlet,* 1940) and his preoccupation with labor ("Old Man"), suggest a continuing, though not uncritical, concern with the issues focused by the term "use value."

16. Frederic Jameson, *Fables of Aggression* (Berkeley: University of California Press, 1979), p. 73.

17. Jacques Derrida, *Of Grammatology* (Baltimore: Johns Hopkins University Press, 1976), p. 280.

18. John T. Matthews, *The Play of Faulkner's Language* (New York: Cornell University Press, 1982), p. 24.

19. Matthews, p. 31.

20. At one level this claim is too abrasive: McHaney appeals to Schopenhauer's systems as a stabilizing point of reference. Jung is also used to fix the parodic deferrals. Our analysis of textual redundancy is heavily dependent on Terry Eagleton, *Walter Benjamin or Towards a Revolutionary Criticism* (London: Verso, 1981), particularly Chapter 2.

21. Paul Ricoeur, *Hermeneutics and the Human Sciences*, ed. J. B. Thompson (London: Cambridge University Press, 1981), pp. 148–49.

22. Roland Barthes, *The Pleasure of the Text* (London: Cape, 1976), p. 36.

23. To exchange commodities is to equalize and to abstract: various kinds of labor, ranges of need, and qualities of material are declared comparable by the setting up of a price. "The effect of the world of commodities on real men . . . has factually separated or *abstracted* from man his 'subjectivity', i.e. his 'physical and mental energies,' his capacity for work and has transformed it into a separate essence. It has fixed human energy *as such* in the 'crystal' or 'congelation' of labor which is *value*, turning it into a distinct entity, an entity which is not only independent of man, but which also dominates him." (Lucio Colletti, *From Rousseau to Lenin* (London: New Left Books, 1972), pp. 86–87. See also Alfred Sohn-Rethel, *Intellectual and Manual Labor* (London: Macmillan, 1978), pp. 29–34, for a discussion of commodity exchange as a means to social coherence.

24. Roland Barthes, *S/Z* (London: Cape, 1975), pp. 5–6.

25. Alfred Sohn-Rethel, *Intellectual and Manual Labour*, p. 21.

26. The idea that an author's world may experience resistance from the world of his character belongs essentially to Mikhail Bakhtin: the distinction that he draws between "polyphonic" and "monologic" novels is rooted in a wider conviction that any voice, even one striving to utter a monologue, is a point of intersection among many voices. "The problem of the orientation of speech toward another utterance has a sociological significance of the highest order. The speech act by its nature is social. The word is not a tangible object, but an always shifting, always changing means of social communication. . . . Through it all the word does not forget its path of transfer. . . . The word enters his [the speaker's] context from another context, permeated with the intentions of other speakers. His own intention finds the word already occupied. Thus the orientation of word among words, the various perceptions of other speech acts, and the various means of reacting to them are perhaps the most crucial problems of the sociology of language usage, any kind of language usage, including the artistic." Cited by I. R. Titunc in his appendix to V. N. Vološinov's *Marxism and the Philosophy of Language* (London: Seminar Press, 1973). Titunc's translation of the passage is preferred to T. W. Rotsel's in Mikhail Bakhtin, *Problems of Dostoevsky's Poetics* (Ardis, 1973), p. 167. What we are suggesting is that the submission of the author's voice to that of his character, though not conclusive, inserts an awkward and continuing strand into Faulkner's voice: the memory of that submission remains important because it implies that, in a commercial world, voices, too, are standardized.

27. Psalms 137:4.

28. F. L. Gwynn and J. L. Blotner (eds.), *Faulkner in the University* (New York: Random House, 1959), p. 179.

29. T. W. Adorno, *Minima Moralia* (London: New Left Books, 1974), p. 166. Subsequent page references will be to this edition.

30. Joseph Moldenhauer, "Unity of Theme and Structure in *The Wild Palms*," in *William Faulkner: Three Decades of Criticism*, ed. F. J. Hoffman and O. L. Vickery (New York: Harcourt, Brace, 1963), p. 311.

31. See *Faulkner in the University* (pp. 171–84) and *Lion in the Garden*, ed.

James B. Meriwether and Michael Millgate (New York: Random House, 1968), pp. 54, 132, 247. McHaney (p. xv) argues that the manuscript bears out Faulkner's claims that the stories were written in the sequence in which they are read.

32. Karl Marx, *Capital*, vol. 1 (London: Lawrence & Wishart, 1976), pp. 80–81.

33. Frederic Jameson, *Marxism and Form*, p. 96.

34. Melvin Backman, *Faulkner: The Major Years* (London: Indiana University Press, 1966), p. 130.

35. Harry's color blindness is a symptom of his debilitation as a consumer, accompanying the way he views the world as a two-dimensional spectacle. The external forms of his environment, the glare, the neon, and the glitter, all collude with the market and conspire to help him forget materiality.

36. Cited by Lukács, *H & CC*, p. 171.

37. See Olga Vickery, *The Novels of William Faulkner* (Baton Rouge: Louisiana State University Press, 1961), and Arthur F. Kinney, *Faulkner's Narrative Poetics* (Amherst: University of Massachusetts Press, 1978), pp. 79–80.

38. See A. Karinikas, *Tillers of a Myth* (Madison: University of Wisconsin Press, 1966), particularly ch. 3.

39. In entering the abortion, Charlotte presents herself as one of the most exploited of all female bodies: "What was it you told me nigger women say? Ride me down, Harry" (p. 221). Faulkner precedes it with another suggestion, "We've done this lots of ways but not with knives, have we?" (p. 221)—a joke echoed by the officer who arrests Harry—thus turning the operation into the ultimate refinement in the couple's search for new stimuli, as they try to avoid the tired "preprandial . . . relieving of the ten years' married" (p. 129). Where the slackened muscles can be tautened only with the knife, sexuality does not overthrow the structures of domination, but introverts them to achieve a kind of satiety as victim. (See Zoltan Tar, *The Frankfurt School* (New York: John Wiley, 1977), pp. 87–89, for a summary of the thesis). In which case Harry is no "innocent," rather, he is the fount of final excitement: Charlotte has always known him as such, he is introduced to her as an abortionist, with scalpel up his sleeve, and blank cheque ready for would-be clients (p. 37). Adorno offers comments that could stand as a summary of the commercial structure of Charlotte's desire: "Today the appeal to newness, of no matter what kind . . . has become universal. . . . The decomposition of the subject is consummated in his self-abandonment to an ever-changing sameness . . . which as a mere stimulus, no longer simulates. Perhaps in this lassitude, mankind's renunciation of the wish for children is declared. . . . Baudelaire had reason to extol infertile beauty. Mankind, despairing of its reproduction, unconsciously projects its wish for survival into the chimera of the thing never known [in the instance of "Wild Palms" the embryo], but this resembles death" (*Minima Moralia*, p. 238).

40. See particularly John Feaster, "Faulkner's 'Old Man': A Psychoanalytic Approach," *Modern Fiction Studies*, vol. XIII, no. 1 (Spring 1967), pp. 92–93.

41. At this point we are paraphrasing Frederic Jameson, *Marxism and Form*, p. 311, and are more generally indebted to chapter 5.

# Forgetting Jerusalem:
## An Ironical Chart for *The Wild Palms*

### François Pitavy

The interview Faulkner gave to Jean Stein in 1956 seems to have become such a necessary reference for criticism that the discourse on Faulkner sometimes tends to be an intertext itself, through which run scraps or formulas from that interview—an instance of obvious intertextuality, as Faulkner's own words retain their status of more or less recognizable quotations. The title of this essay is a case in point, where the word "chart" appears in connection with a phrase ("forgetting Jerusalem") that is clearly a Biblical image, or what Faulkner himself calls an "allegory":

> [The] various allegories [of Christianity] are the charts against which [man] measures himself and learns to know what he is. It cannot teach man to be good as the text book teaches him mathemetics. It shows him how to discover himself, evolve for himself a moral code and standard within his capacities and aspirations, by giving him a matchless example of suffering and sacrifice and the promise of hope.[1]

The Bible so permeates Faulkner's fiction that its dissemination in it may very well provide the most profound—though not necessarily the most obvious—instance of intertextuality in his novels. To a man of Faulkner's time and place, and to Faulkner himself,[2] the Bible was so much a part of the culture and of the environment (the "Bible belt") that some of the words that now, to the critic, have a decidedly Faulknerian ring, such as "travail," "labor," "burden," or even "shibboleth" (these instances taken at random all seem to point to the Old Testament, as verily they should), were certainly perceived if not as specific Biblical quotations, at least as unmistakable borrowings. Nowadays, these words, absorbed into Faulkner's texts as they are, can no longer be recognized for what they are—or were—by readers who are hardly conversant with the Bible.

Attempting to uncover the fading, or faded, Biblical connotations in Faulkner's vocabulary is not the purpose of this essay, and it may now be a well-nigh impossible task, unless, possibly, attempted by computerized research. On the other hand, the presence in Faulkner's texts of such names as "Golgotha" or "Moses" (as in *The Wild Palms*), or of the phrase "Passion Week," immediately points to one of those Christian charts, so inescapable that they are liable to take command of the fiction in an obtrusive and belabored way instead of being absorbed into it and redistributed in it[3]—which may be one of the reasons why *A Fable* is not so much a most splendid failure as, in some respects, what might be called an intertextual monster. However, when the Passion Week becomes "of the heart" (as in *Mosquitoes*), or when we read in *The Wild Palms* that with the birth of the child the Tall Convict had "reached and crossed the crest of his Golgotha,"[4] the metaphorical or parodical use of the Bible breaks up the Christian charts to the status of allusions or images that do not inform the structure of the text. Unless he be perverse, the critic cannot see the Tall Convict as a Christ figure. So the functioning of the Bible in *The Wild Palms,* its emergence as an intertext, is not to be found primarily in the vocabulary itself or even in some of the images.

Yet, even with the accepted premise that there is no pure discourse, unrelated to what precedes and environs it, that language is never "innocent" (as Faulkner himself would agree), in other words that "every text is an intertext,"[5] *The Wild Palms* appears as one of Faulkner's densest and richest intertexts. Not only must the ideals of Charlotte Rittenmeyer and the attitudes of Harry Wilbourne towards love be understood in the context of the Western tradition of romantic love, as exemplified in Denis de Rougemont's *Love in the Western World,*[6] and not only do the "invincible" (p. 149) dreams of love and success of the Tall Convict derive from the same "borrowed" ideals (to take up René Girard's remarkably operative concept), crossed by the clichés of

popular literature he absorbs from the *Detectives' Gazette* which
he peddles "among his pinehill neighbors" (p. 25),[7] but, even
more significantly, the original title of the novel, *If I Forget Thee,
Jerusalem,* provides one of those Christian allegories that seems
here the better absorbed and distributed into the text as this title
was cancelled. So the critic may be led to think that, in a way, the
decision of Saxe Commins[8] or Robert Haas[9] to do without the
novel's original title was profoundly, albeit unwittingly, a wise
one, though it was evidently made for the wrong reasons—
commercial reasons—and though the confusion between the title of the whole novel and that of the story of Charlotte and
Harry would lead not only to misreadings of the novel, but to
separate publications of "Wild Palms" and "Old Man," the two
narrative segments making up a one and same novel, a structured whole, *The Wild Palms.*

Faulkner's title for the novel, visible on what is extant of the
typescript at the University of Virginia, *If I Forget Thee, Jerusalem,*
is an almost verbatim quotation from Psalm 137, telling of the
captivity of the Jews in Babylon and urging them not to forget
Jerusalem, their chief joy. The time in Babylon, away from
home and familiar, effortless patterns of living and thinking,
was marked not only by instances of straying away from God's
law, but, more importantly, by an intense intellectual and religious activity, setting the beginning of a religious restoration, a
deepening and refinement of religion. Thus, the motif of the
Babylonian captivity in the Bible is associated at once with an
eschatological reflection and with the theme of memory—that is,
with a new awareness of the significance of one's experience
(which already points to the retrospective structure of *The Wild
Palms,* as both Wilbourne and the Tall Convict, though with different modes, retrospectively try to come to terms with their
analogous experiences).

> By the rivers of Babylon, there we sat down, yea, we wept,
> when we remembered Zion.
> We hanged our harps upon the willows in the midst thereof.
> For they that carried us away captive required of us a song;

and they that wasted us *required of us* mirth, *saying,* Sing us one
of the songs of Zion.

How shall we sing the Lord's song in a strange land?

If I forget thee, O Jerusalem, let my right hand forget *her
cunning.*

If I do not remember thee, let my tongue cleave to the roof
of my mouth; if I prefer not Jerusalem above my chief joy.
(Ps. 137: 1-6)

To English-speaking persons, second to Psalm 23, "The Lord
is my shepherd," Psalm 137 is possibly the best-known psalm (as
it was also familiar to Blaise Pascal, who made it the text for one
of his *Pensées*[10]). And the psalm is echoed in other texts familiar
to readers of the Bible, for instance in Jeremiah and Ezekiel—
which shows that the spiritual meaning of the Babylonian captivity and the themes associated with it were certainly widely known
and readily perceived.

Ye that have escaped the sword, go away, stand not still:
remember the Lord afar off, and let Jerusalem come into
your mind. (Jer. 51:50)

Then I came to them of the captivity at Tel-abib, that dwelt
by the river of Chebar, and I sat where they sat, and remained
there astonished among them seven days. (Ezek. 3:15)

The change of title, the disappearance of this too visible
marker of intertextuality, prevents the presence of the Biblical
chart in *The Wild Palms* from being first of all a matter of quotation or reminiscence, and prevents the reader from looking
primarily for specific analogies with the Bible: it sets him free to
trace intertextuality at work in the novel and eventually to perceive that the Christian "chart" functions here in an ironical way.

Some specific analogies do exist however, which have already
been recognized.[11] The verse that Faulkner used for his original
title ("If I forget thee, O Jerusalem, let my right hand forget her
cunning") may indeed exemplify a decisive moment in the lives
of the two lovers and the cleavage in their respective attitudes
toward the adventure for which they are "embarked," as Pascal
would say. Harry bungles the operation he attempts upon Char-

lotte (his hand trembles, forgetting its professional cunning), and he is bound to do so because he is unworthy of his Jerusalem—the ideal conception of love propounded by Charlotte, however mediated and degraded her desire may be.

Remarking that the story of the Tall Convict takes place by or on the great American river has no real relevance in the search for Biblical analogies, but a taste, an odor, of the Biblical Babylon may be perceived in the atmosphere of the richly rotting New Orleans by the river. In the striking description of Crowe's courtyard (the place where Harry and Charlotte meet), all the images tend to emphasize the sense of heaviness, closure, imprisonment, and of decay and death:

> . . . a court paved with the same soft, quietly rotting brick. There was a stagnant pool with a terra-cotta figure, a mass of lantana, the single palm, the thick rich leaves and the heavy white stars of the jasmine bush where light fell upon it through open French doors, the court balcony—overhung too on three sides, the walls of that same annealing brick lifting a rampart broken and nowhere level against the glare of the city on the low eternally overcast sky, and over all, brittle, dissonant and ephemeral, the spurious sophistication of the piano like symbols scrawled by adolescent boys upon an ancient decayed rodent-scavengered tomb. (pp. 36–37)

It is from such a prison that Harry and Charlotte decide to escape toward what they think will be freedom and love: the true life they both seemed to have forgotten in their respective prisons of family respectability or hospital routine, prisons they never really escape as they come back to New Orleans, full circle, acknowledging the failure of their flight to freedom.

Such remarks already make it clear that the Bible does not function here as a text within the text, as the Word among words, but rather as a pattern—a chart—*informing* the circular, regressive structure of the novel, as it shapes the desires (conscious or repressed), the behaviors, and thus the journeys of both Harry and the convict.

For the Jews in captivity by the Euphrates, Jerusalem meant not just freedom, the familiar, secure environment they had known, or dreamed of, but, more importantly, the true life, the mode of thinking that they had forsaken and hoped to recover, idealized for its being distant. Is it not, too, the "idyllic" life in the penitentiary to which the convict tries furiously, undeviatingly, to go back, a life meaning not just physical security, but dignity, honor, pride, compassion, to take up a well-known verbal series of Faulkner's? Here are indeed the convict's thoughts while the monstrous Mississippi flood toys with him and he is ironically prevented by shotguns (and later by actual gunshots) from giving himself up to the secure world of shotguns—Parchman:

> He thought of home, the place where he had lived almost since childhood, his friends of years whose ways he knew and who knew his ways, the familiar fields where he did work he had learned to do well and to like, the mules with characters he knew and respected as he knew and respected the characters of certain men; he thought of the barracks at night, with screens against the bugs in summer and good stoves in winter and someone to supply the fuel and the food too; the Sunday ball games and the picture shows—things which, with the exception of the ball games, he had never known before. But most of all, his own character . . . his good name, his responsibility not only toward those who were responsible toward him but to himself, his own honor in the doing of what was asked of him, his pride in being able to do it, no matter what it was. (pp. 165–66)

Such is the convict's Jerusalem while he is retained captive by the "Old Man," literally out of itself, the pregnant woman, and then the child—the family triad cutting him off from life as a "free" man, that is, life in Parchman—to him, the true life. A sign of his dogged determination to return to it is his attachment to "the known, the desired" uniform (p. 337) he never discards, wearing it at first, then, during his stay at the Cajan's, keeping it behind a rafter carefully wrapped in a newspaper after the woman has washed it (restored it as much as possible to its pristine condition); and he puts it on again when he is about to go back to his former life, ironically retrieving the symbol of his lost Jerusalem.

Similarly, Wilbourne has been in spite of himself dragged away from the serene routine of his "monastic" life in the hospital (p. 32)—however dull and grey and empty—dragged and drowned in the yellow liquidity of Charlotte's stare:

> . . . he seemed to be drowning, volition and will, in the yellow stare. (p. 39)

> . . . the unwinking yellow stare in which he seemed to blunder and fumble like a moth, a rabbit caught in the glare of a torch; an envelopment almost like a liquid. (p. 87)

He drowns in the furious waters of love and sex—truly the "rivers of Babylon" of the psalm, where, as is expressed in Pascal's meditation, no security and stability, no fixed point to anchor one's hopes, can be found. His life with Charlotte is a succession of what he calls "eclipses," followed by returns into time, that is, to his sense of guilt: each return marks the beginning of a more difficult and perilous journey, undertaken out of no social pressure or financial need, but of his own will, or suicidal desire, through narrower and narrower gates—leaving Chicago for the lake, where life should have been idyllic but soon becomes still as death—then coming back from the lake to Chicago in winter, to "iron" cold, to the canyonlike streets and the "infernal inverted life" of the store, a "chromium glass and synethetic marble cavern" (p. 120), and then plunging into the even narrower and deadlier Utah canyon. Notwithstanding the self-justifying rhetoric of his long speech to McCord (pp. 131–41), all of those moves manifest his masochistic desire to punish himself for his original sin, that is, having forgotten his Jersualem—the "monastic" life in the hospital and the rectilinear, accidentless career, conforming to morality, which his father had chosen for him. He has indeed strayed away from the Law of God and of his father, or rather from its degraded form: bourgeois morality. That is why, rather than escaping from the prison, jumping the bail, or committing suicide—the temptations proferred by the fiend-husband—he chooses life in the penitentiary, which most resembles the former life that he cannot or will not forget: the dormitory in Parchman is no different from the "barracks-like room" in the hospital, "furnished with steel army cots" (p. 33). This same penitentiary is also—but Harry does not know it yet— the convict's Jerusalem, where the journeys of the two men eventually converge, since the convict gets an extra ten years' sentence.

So the ideal places which the convict and Harry have unwillingly left and to which they yearn to return are a prisonlike hospital and an aseptic prison, places where they can, and will, forget even the meaning of the word "freedom," places where they will have no initiative, no responsibility, no woman, places "sans anything." Harry Wilbourne's and the convict's constricted and empty Jerusalems are thus ironical inversions of the one that kept the Jews sitting by the rivers of Babylon, weeping.

The irony is compounded by sexual inversion. The two poles of the Jews' life and thinking in captivity are clearly differentiated sexually: Babylon—the prison—is a whore, hence feminine, whereas there has never been any doubt as to God's sex in the Old Testament; and Jerusalem is the place with which God is much pleased, the place of the privileged allegiance with His people. In addition, there are numerous references in the Bible to the house of the Father—the agency of the Law: it never is a mother's place.

In _The Wild Palms,_ the pattern is clearly reversed: the convict's and Harry's journeys—that is, the time they spend away from "home"—are dominated by masculine figures. The "Old Man" is really the one father figure in the novel, or rather the forefather, the creator of the American land, whose "original stream," "following undisturbed and unaware its appointed course," can still be perceived beneath "the rush and fury of the flood itself" (p. 62–63). On the surface, the monstrous tidal wave, an expression of the cosmic joker's might, is perceived as the Beast, the monster of all the terrors and myths—here again a masculine figure: a beast with crest and fangs (p. 171), or a feline creature, or an ophidian, with its "iron-like and shifting convolutions like an anaconda" (p. 145).

In "Wild Palms," the relation between Harry and Charlotte is

sexually inverted, as Harry is dominated by the masculine Charlotte (who has nothing of the epicene Faulknerian figure). Her
masculinity is stressed from their first encounter: she stares at
him "with a speculative sobriety like a man might" (p. 39). She
dresses with a "ruthless indifference," wearing her garments as
if they were overalls (p. 42). She takes the initiative at once, leads
Harry by the hand at Crowe's party, and later in the train to
Chicago she undresses and almost rapes him. There are constant references to her hard blunt hands, to her hard gestures
and arms:

> She held him hard against her, leaning back, her hips against
> him and moving faintly while she stared at him, the yellow
> stare inscrutable and derisive and with that quality which he
> had come to recognise—that ruthless and almost unbearable
> honesty. . . . "Come on. That's right. That's better. That's fine
> now." She freed one hand and began to unfasten his shirt.
> (pp. 108–09)

When they make love, she is constantly in the superior position,
jabbing her hard elbows in his stomach.

Conversely, though they are all-male places, the penitentiary
(in spite of or, rather, because of the shotguns) and the hospital
are safe, maternal places, where the sense of security and comfort are compounded by the expected duties and the reassuring
routine. "*I've got to make . . . everything last,*" Harry thinks after the
aborted encounter with Charlotte at the hospital, "*so there wont be
any gaps between now and six oclock when I can hide behind my white
jacket again, draw the old routine up over my head and face like niggers
do the quilt when they go to bed*" (p. 51). The sense of the word
"routine" here is unambiguous in its double suggestion of maternal protection and *overcoming* sense of guilt ("blackness" is
covered up by "the old routine"), which is confirmed by the next
occurrence of the word, when Harry in Chicago has settled in to
a regular sex life: "*the routine even of sinning, an absolution even for
adultery*" (p. 126).

To complete the picture, the convict, back in Parchman where he is telling his story, and Harry in prison waiting for the trial that will take him to that same Parchman, are seen in similar positions, fœtuslike—the convict bunched up between two bunks, holding and nursing his rich cigar, Harry sitting on the cot's edge, "crouching, hovering" above the coffee he cannot drink and the cigarette he cannot even roll with his trembling hands, making a mess of it, as with his scalpel he had made a mess of Charlotte's body (pp. 309–10).

The fœtus images are not connected only with the inverted Jerusalems of Harry and the convict, they also recur throughout their journeys, telling the obsessive desire of each protagonist to regain his secure, maternal Jerusalem. The convict is ironically barred from such regression by the pregnant woman, and then the woman with the child: the place he desires phantasmatically is already taken. That is why he wishes to get rid of "the woman, the belly"—to him a useless belly. The boat he never forsakes is clearly a substitute womb: it keeps him afloat through that fabulous flood, it shelters him effectively from danger and death; and at the climax of his voyage, when the wave at last catches him up, it raises him out of reach of its deadly masculine power, as in a "*bower* of new-leafed boughs and branches," as if he were "a bird in its *nest*": the skiff then "soared on above the *licking* crest itself and hung *cradled* into the high actual air" (p. 157; my emphasis). These almost too obvious maternal images make the link between the convict and his boat a real umbilical[12]: indeed he will never sever it until he gives up the boat and himself, at last surrendering in the "desired" uniform to the womb-prison, which renders the boat useless.[13]

"Wild Palms" is even more densely strewn with fœtal or maternal images. On the morning of his twenty-seventh birthday, Harry wakes up and looks back to his past years, as if his life "were to lie passively on his back as though he floated effortless and without volition upon an unreturning stream" (p. 34). In an inverted way, this comparison also applies aptly to the convict's life on the Mississippi: thus it may not be illegitimate to trace here precisely that inner necessity in the writing of the novel, which at this point led the writer to *realize* (and invert) in the second narrative what was metaphorical in the first, or, as Faulkner often said, to give a "counterpoint" to the story of Harry and Charlotte. In fact, the comparison occurs in the third section of the novel (the second "Wild Palms" section), that is, at a point where in the *composition* of the novel the "Old Man" section had not yet started: what is left of the typescript shows beyond doubt that the first two sections of "Wild Palms" were originally one section. So that comparison may very well have been the actual germ of the contrapuntal part of the narrative.

Later, by the lakeside, Harry soon gets into the habit of going back to bed each morning after breakfast while Charlotte goes swimming:

> Then he would sleep again (this scarcely an hour after he had waked from slumber, a habit which he formed within the first six days) to wake later and look out and see her lying on the pier on stomach or back, her arms folded across or beneath her face; sometimes he would still be there, not sleeping now and not even thinking but merely existing in a drowsy and fœtuslike state, passive and almost unsentient in the womb of solitude and peace, when she returned, moving then only enough to touch his lips to the sun-impacted flank as she stopped beside the cot, tasting the impacted sun. (p. 110)

The convergence of the nouns "womb" and "flank" and of the adjectives "drowsy," "fœtuslike," "passive," and "unsentient," and the orality of the relationship to Charlotte ("to touch his lips to the flank," "tasting") clearly evince a regressive desire, which is also a death compulsion—a desire that is expressed, too, in the description of the hospital where Charlotte is dying:

> . . . the carbolised vacuums of linoleum and rubber soles like wombs into which human beings fled before something of suffering but mostly of terror, to surrender in little monastic cells all the burden of lust and desire and pride, even that of functional independence, to become as embryos for a time. . . . (p. 299)

There is in the novel so little doubt left about the nature of Harry's desire that he himself is made to acknowledge it in his long confessional speech to McCord before leaving for Utah, where he describes his loss of virginity as a fall into a precipice:

". . . the darkness, the falling, the thunder of solitude, the shock, the death, the moment when, stopped physically by the ponderable clay, you yet feel all your life rush out of you into the pervading immemorial blind receptive matrix, the hot fluid foundation—grave-womb or womb-grave, it's all one." (p. 138)

In July 1938 Faulkner wrote to Robert Haas about the title of his novel in progress, then called _If I Forget Thee, Jerusalem:_

I think it is a good title. It invented itself as a title for the chapter in which Charlotte died and where Wilbourne said 'Between grief and nothing I will take grief' and which is the theme of the whole book, the convict story being just counterpoint to sharpen it. . . .[14]

Though apparently this title was not at hand right from the beginning of the composition, a desire to return and, more profoundly, a regressive desire certainly made up a pattern presiding over the writing of the novel and _informing_ its two narratives, which then already existed in contrapuntal relation. The discovery of the title may have been the sudden realization that the Bible was providing the adequate chart for the novel—that the intertext already at work in the text had indeed a name.

Indirectly, Faulkner's remark to Robert Haas at once confirms and specifies what has been noted at the beginning of this essay: a study of Biblical intertextuality in _The Wild Palms_ cannot be a mere search for language, images, or even patterns or charts; it provides insights into the writing of the novel, not so much its genesis as what could more exactly be called a combinative process at work in the writing. This in no way means there was a Biblical "analogy" antedating the composition: Faulkner's remark seems to testify to the emergence of a controlling principle, to his recognition of the _legality_ in his text. In other words (and the letter to Haas does support the argument), the Biblical analogy did not so much _originate_ the novel as it confirmed an organizing principle already at work, then recognized and named.

That is why Psalm 137 had, in the last analysis, to be absent from the patent, visible text of *The Wild Palms,* as though written only in invisible ink. Thus the Biblical chart loses its transitivity: it does not signify for its own sake, as its sense is disseminated into the centralizing text.

This text, that is, the contrapuntal novel, which patently maintains the "leadership" of meaning,[15] now seems to distribute the disseminated psalm back to the reader (or rather the re-reader). To take up the phrase of Borges,[16] the literary work thus comes to "influence its predecessor": Faulkner's novel now develops harmonics around the Biblical text. To a reader of *The Wild Palms,* Psalm 137 will never be the same again.

---

NOTES

1. *Lion in the Garden: Interviews with William Faulkner, 1926–1962,* James B. Meriwether and Michael Millgate, eds. (New York: Random House, 1968), p. 247.
2. The same could be said of Steinbeck, who often claimed that the operative influences upon his work were Malory and the King James version of the Bible.
3. Cf. Faulkner's well-known remark about the writing of *As I Lay Dying:* "Sometimes technique charges in and takes command of the dream before the writer himself can get his hands on it. That is *tour de force . . .*" (*Lion in the Garden,* p. 244).
4. *The Wild Palms* (New York: Random House, 1939), p. 264. Further page references will appear parenthetically in the text.
5. Roland Barthes, *Encyclopaedia Universalis* (Paris: Encyclopaedia Universalis France), vol. XV (1973), "Texte [Théorie du]": "Tout texte est un *intertexte;* d'autres textes sont présents en lui, à des niveaux variables, sous des formes plus ou moins reconnaissables . . . Epistémologiquement, le concept d'intertexte est ce qui apporte à la théorie du texte le volume de la socialité: c'est tout le langage, antérieur et contemporain, qui vient au texte, non selon la voie d'une filiation repérable, d'une imitation volontaire, mais selon celle d'une dissémination— image qui assure au texte le statut, non d'une *reproduction,* mais d'une *productivité.*"
6. In *William Faulkner: Toward Yoknapatawpha and Beyond* (New Haven and London: Yale University Press, 1978), Cleanth Brooks has an excellent study of Harry and Charlotte in the light of Rougemont's argument that romantic love (in the medieval *courtois* tradition) must needs be suffering and tragedy as the romantic lovers can only be in love with what radically transcends and finally defeats love: death, in the last analysis (pp. 214–16). Charlotte apparently acknowledges that her ideals are indeed "borrowed," when she says to Harry after the aborted hotel meeting: "'. . . the second time I ever saw you I learned what I

had read in books but I never had actually believed: that love and suffering are the same thing and that the value of love is what you have to pay for it'" (p. 48). In his musings, Harry resorts to similar (though degraded and unconsciously borrowed) clichés, such as the bohemian and "illicit" love nest, and he acknowledges that he has "*accepted completely her ideas about love*" (pp. 84–85): "*. . . the passionate idea of two damned and doomed and isolated forever against the world and God and the irrevocable*" (p. 82). This is a cross between *courtois* ideals and puritanism, which makes Harry into a hybrid of a sort between Tristan and a conscience-stricken Lothario.

7. ". . . who to say what Helen, what living Garbo, he had not dreamed of rescuing from what craggy pinnacle or dragoned keep" (p. 149).

8. According to Thomas L. McHaney, *William Faulkner's The Wild Palms: A Study* (Jackson: University Press of Mississippi, 1975), p. xiii, n. 1.

9. According to Joseph Blotner, *Faulkner: A Biography* (New York: Random House, 1974), p. 1002. Apparently, Haas made the bizarre argument that Faulkner's title would arouse anti-Semitic feelings.

10. "Les fleuves de Babylone coulent et tombent et entraînent. O sainte Sion, où tout est stable et où rien ne tombe!" (*Pensées*, p. 459)

11. In particular by Michael Millgate in *The Achievement of William Faulkner* (New York: Random House, 1966), p. 177.

12. The word "umbilical" is used for the chains pairing the convicts, at the beginning of their journey (p. 67).

13. "'I ain't coming without the boat'" (p. 238); ". . . the grapevine painter [was] wrapped several times about his wrist and clutched in his hand" (p. 239); ". . . the grapevine painter still wrapped about the convict's wrist" (p. 250).

14. *Selected Letters of William Faulkner*, ed. Joseph Blotner (New York: Random House, 1977), p. 106.

15. ". . . l'intertextualité désigne non pas une addition confuse et mystérieuse d'influences, mais le travail de transformation et d'assimilation de plusieurs textes opéré par un texte centreur qui garde le *leadership* du sens" (Laurent Jenny, "La stratégie de la forme," *Poétique*, 27 [1976], 257–81, p. 262).

16. Quoted by Laurent Jenny, art. cit., p. 260.

# Creation and Procreation: The Voice and the Name, or Biblical Intertexuality in *Absalom, Absalom!*

## Nancy Blake

What is exists at the price of an absence, a lack, a negation. Such at least is the situation as a result of our exile in a world dominated by language. Somewhere on the threshold between the realm of the *Trieb* and that of language, between what Kristeva distinguishes as the "semiotic" and the "symbolic," one might locate the experience of symbolic splitting constituted by birth. Perhaps, as some would argue, the basis of the binary opposition that characterizes our language is the radical split of sexual differentiation. Be that as it may, we are now aware of an unsatisfactory cleavage regulating our perception of reality, dividing the world into word vs. thing, name vs. body. While there is nothing new in this state of affairs, a persistent consciousness, an annoying uneasiness over it, has come to be recognized as a characteristic of modernity.

The narration of Faulkner's *Absalom, Absalom!* echoes Genesis as it recapitulates the story of creation:

1. In the beginning God created the heaven and the earth.
2. And the earth was without form, and void; and darkness was upon the face of the deep. And the Spirit of God moved upon the face of the waters.
3. And God said, Let there be light: and there was light.

Sutpen is explicitly identified with the God of Genesis: he came "out of the soundless Nothing . . . creating Sutpen's Hundred, the *Be Sutpen's Hundred* like the oldentime *Be Light*" (pp. 8–9).[1] Through the introductory pages of *Absalom, Absalom!,* Faulkner seems to propose a definition of the signifier which allows it to share in the nothingness of original chaos, the *ex nihilo* from which something was made. Like the Bible, *Absalom, Absalom!* appears to recount the stories of nothing more or less than a chain of signifiers. In Chapter 1 of Genesis and in *Absalom,* creation exists in so far, and only in so far, as it is voiced; it is as it is named.

> 5. And God called the light Day, and the darkness he called Night.

If man then is made in God's image and after His likeness, it is as namer of creation that man is creator, before becoming pro-creator.

> 2:19 And out of the ground the LORD God formed every beast of the field, and every fowl of the air; and brought *them* unto Adam to see what he would call them: and whatsoever Adam called every living creature, that *was* the name thereof.

As Sutpen stands before the "soundless Nothing," the text echoes the opening verses of Genesis. The novel underlines one aspect of emptiness however, since the origin is not so much without form as it is "soundless"; by implication then, when there will be something, that something will be a voice.

Recounting creation, Genesis enumerates a pronouncement first, and immediately following it, a division. Creation is the establishing of difference, light/dark due to the divine judgment:

> 1:4 And God saw the light, that *it* was good: and God divided the light from the darkness.

Sutpen also creates and names: Charles, Charles Bon, Charles Good. The Old Testament God is an absolute judge who proclaims the goodness of his creation. In Faulkner's text however, the biblical authority seems to be evoked as underwriter for something that amounts to a disavowal of procreation in favor of a sort of creation *ex nihilo*. As Quentin learns from his father, it was General Compson's opinion that Sutpen named Bon precisely in order to abolish any link between father and son:

> . . . [he] would not permit the child, since it was a boy, to bear
> either his name or that of its maternal grandfather, yet . . .
> would also forbid him to do the customary and provide a
> quick husband for the discarded woman and so give his son an
> authentic name. (p. 266)

Mr. Compson believes that Sutpen "named them all . . . that
entire fecundity of dragons' teeth" (p. 266; see also p. 62).

The purpose of this paper is to examine the distinction established throughout Faulkner's text between two sets of binary
oppositions: between creation and sexual reproduction on the
one hand, and between the voice that I will relate to the Lacanian signifier and the name on the other. While the first set of
terms should strike a familiar chord for the reader of Faulkner,
the second might seem to require some further definition. The
voice, in Faulkner's text, exists as an irrefutable, overwhelming
presence. There is nothing else that possesses the same force in
this fictional universe as "the voice not ceasing but vanishing into
and then out of the long intervals like a stream, a trickle running
from patch to patch of dried sand" (p. 8). This is of course the
voice of Miss Rosa Coldfield in the opening passage of the novel.
Yet while it is possible to distinguish among the book's various
speakers, the working hypothesis for the present reading is that
all these narrators are simply mouthpieces for a voice that is
unique, singular, and indivisible.

The voice is really *anonymous*. As Mr. Compson says, perhaps
"we are not supposed to know" (p. 100) who is talking. The
stories are like the trunkful of letters found in an attic, letters
without signatures revealing only initials or nicknames that have
become meaningless. When Sutpen tells the story of his own life
to General Compson, he himself becomes anonymous through
the telling: "He was telling a story. He was not bragging about
something he had done; he was just telling a story about something a man named Thomas Sutpen had experienced, which
would still have been the same story if the man had had no name
at all" (p. 247). The central figure of the novel, when he assumes
the role of narrator, becomes strangely impersonal, a simple

vehicle for the voice. Like the stream, the voice may pass under-
ground and out of sight, but it is never interrupted. Not the
voice of a character, it is that of a ghost, dead and therefore
immortal. The first pages of *Absalom, Absalom!* are presented as
Miss Rosa Coldfield's narration. They illustrate the identification
of the voice and the signifier.

"Her voice would not cease, it would just vanish" (p. 8).
Through Faulkner's rhetoric, the syntax announces an opposition that the vocabulary denies. Yet, what the text conveys is the
impression of an impersonal voice whose "effect" continues, although the individual through whom it passes has stopped
speaking. Everyone has noticed that the narration circulates in
Faulkner's text. There is however, a commitment of the subject
to the discourse. If the speaker is possessed as by a demon, or
haunted as by a ghost, comparisons that the text exploits, he or
she is also a witness to an absolute submission to the law of an
indivisible word.

While it bears witness to the subtle, yet pervasive omnipre-
sence of the voice, the text explores the meaning of the name,
which comes to represent a kind of determinism. Its power is
such that most people instinctively avoid it, using instead
metaphor and euphemism to sidetrack the danger. Sutpen, for
example, grew up among people who refused Adam's preroga-
tive, who refused to name the division between the races, "knowing that the men and the women were talking about the same
thing though it had never once been mentioned by name, as
when people talk about privation without mentioning the siege,
about sickness without ever naming the epidemic" (p. 231).

Paraphrasing Freud's quoting of Napoleon, who is supposed
to have said, "Anatomy is destiny," Faulkner's text seems to proclaim, "The name is a destiny." In doing so, the text is faithful to
the tradition which prompted the study of etymology during the
Middle Ages as a sort of equivalent to the horoscope—that is, as
a means toward understanding one's fate. Matthew of Ven-
dome, twelfth-century author of such a treatise, explained that
Caesar's crimes were somehow inscribed and foreshadowed in
his name: Caesar being derived from *caedere*—to kill, massacre.

The name is a destiny; the person is only a result, an effect, in the biblical sense, a witness to the name.

Faulkner's text proceeds to destroy any expectation of a body behind, beside, or underneath the all-powerful name. At most, the sound is accompanied by a weak, wavering, often stereotyped *image*. Of Charles we are told that "Miss Rosa . . . had got the picture from the first word, perhaps from the name, Charles Bon" (p. 75). As is often the case, the text calls upon the oxymoron to speak the disavowal of desire. Bon's name makes him *anonymous*, but first of all, he is bodiless: "*It would not even need a skull behind it; almost anonymous, it would only need vague inference of some walking flesh and blood desired by someone else even if only in some shadow-realm of make-believe*" (p. 147). The text insists constantly upon Bon's presence as that of someone born not of the body: he is "phoenix-like, fullsprung from no childhood, born of no woman" (p. 74). He is indeed Sutpen's replica in this denial of division, and he appears in the text as another demon, coming into that "isolated puritan country household almost like Sutpen himself came into Jefferson: apparently complete, without background or past or childhood" (p. 93). Bon somehow sprang forth between "two people neither of whom had taken pleasure or found passion in getting him or suffered pain and travail in borning him" (p. 339).

If the name is a destiny, it robs experience of existence. Judith, for example, as Sutpen's daughter, is reduced by Mr. Compson to the function of her name: " . . . it was not Judith who was the object of Bon's love or of Henry's solicitude. She was just the *blank shape,* the empty vessel in which each of them strove to preserve, not the illusion of himself nor his illusion of the other but what each conceived the other to believe him to be . . ." (pp. 119–20, my emphasis).

The fatal quality of the name seems to exist, as *Absalom* suggests, independently of any act of will on the part of the namer. Miss Rosa is time and again compared to Cassandra, both as prophetess of doom and as mistress to the aging enemy king. If her name, "Coldfield," is a pronouncement of sterility, "Cassandra" is not exactly a given name, but certainly a proper one to the extent that it imposes itself upon Quentin as upon his father. At the same time, if Sutpen as creator names all of his children, the text suggests that the names speak of a truth that escpaes the consciousness of the namer. He meant to name his half-Negro daughter Cassandra after the slave mistress of Agamemnon, but whether through ignorance or a slip of the tongue, he called her "Clytemnestra," thereby reversing values and giving the slave the name of the legitimate spouse. Several names in the book seem, on the other hand, to be degraded forms of originally promising destinies. Wash Jones is a degenerate Washington, a failed founding father, and Pettibone, the Tidewater planter who unwittingly fathered Sutpen's dream of an ideal identity, is in fact a diminutive and sterile Bon.

To trick fate, one may of course change names and move to Texas. This eventuality is often evoked in the novel in connection with the projected crimes of Mr. Coldfield, Bon's lawyer (another Pettibone and an unworthy foster father), as well as Sutpen and Henry. Such an attempt is desperate but doomed, for one can escape one's fate only at the price of a loss of self-hood. We will have occasion to return to this point.

If the voice is all-pervasive in Faulkner's text, the body is denied, but not ignored. Partly responsible for this contradictory state of affairs is fleshless Miss Rosa, who assures the santification of the body through her bombastic rhetoric: "*Because there is something in the touch of flesh with flesh which abrogates, cuts sharp and straight across the devious intricate channels of decorous ordering, which enemies as well as lovers know because it makes them both . . .*" (p. 139). What we have here is, however, negated by the speaker herself when she responds to Sutpen's overtures by a denial of bodily presence: "*I hold no substance that will fit your dream but I can give you airy space and scope for your delirium*" (p. 168). Such a statement as judgment upon the desire for descendants is very close indeed to the biblical message. The Old Testament is largely a treatise on genealogy. Yet, each time God or one of his messengers tells a man that he will have a son, thereby providing the proof that a child is engendered by a word, the Scriptures never fail to be very precise. The formula is: "And he knew his wife and she conceived," as if there were a danger of not understanding this link of cause and effect, as if the desire to ignore the role of sexuality could overwhelm judgment.

Deficient in symbolic presence, women in *Absalom* are either vehicles for the overpowering voice or else evanescent images; they are, at all events, bodiless. Women are always vanishing without trace. Ellen and Bon's mistress are compared to butterflies. Is there a reference here to Psyche? If so, the reference operates once more, as so often in Faulkner's text, as a contradiction in terms. These women are bodiless, but also "soulless." The Octoroon is seen as disappearing, "leaving no bones, no substance, no dust of whatever dead pristine soulless rich surrender" (p. 196). The women in the novel are not seen as anchoring man in the presence of reality. On the contrary: *"Beautiful lives women live—women do. In very breathing they draw meat and drink from some beautiful attenuation of unreality . . ."* (p. 211). Rosa and Clytie remain in the book as presences without bodies; both are compared to bundles of clothing or clean rags. Both are as "light and dry and brittle as a stick" (p. 351).

If women are essentially fleshless in *Absalom,* this state can be read as a disavowal of their overwhelming identification with matter. When the female is linked to the earth, however, the comparison is effectuated through a disavowal of any difference. Living without men during the war, Rosa, Judith, and Clytie are said to exist *"in an apathy which was almost peace, like that of the blind unsentient earth itself . . . "* (p. 155).

Symbolic existence, on the other hand, is anything but peaceful. It is always torn from nothingness through an act of violence as Sutpen's Hundred is torn from the primal Chaos. In an ironic comment on the cost of creation, Faulkner has Rosa sit in the dark in order to avoid incurring the debt for an act of violent creation. "She would have no light burning . . . the cost of electricity was not in the actual time the light burned but in the retroactive overcoming of primary inertia when the switch was snapped: . . . that was what showed on the meter" (p. 88). This is a sort of self-parody, or meta-discourse, on the fundamental theme of the debt. It shows on the meter; it is inscribed on the ledger, the account book. The inexplicable, but inexorable debt, written down, just like the genealogies recorded in family Bibles, this is the motor force driving the voice that recounts the story.

Quentin must listen to, then transmit the story because of some hereditary guilt. His grandfather had helped Sutpen, so Quentin's father tells him, "maybe she [Miss Rosa] considers you partly responsible through heredity for what happened to her and her family through him" (p. 13). Miss Rosa also postulates a sin of the father, distant and unknowable, for which she, her sister, and her sister's children are doomed to suffer: "even I used to wonder what our father or his father could have done before he married our mother that Ellen and I would have to expiate and neither of us alone be sufficient; what crime committed that would leave our family cursed to be instruments not only for that man's destruction, but for our own" (p. 21).

There are crimes committed in *Absalom;* however, they seem almost to be seen as retrospective attempts to merit or explain the hereditary guilt of the criminal. Mr. Coldfield, for example, deals with Sutpen not for money, which he refuses, but almost as though he needed the occasion to know why he was to expiate. It is of course through his descendants, his daughters, that he will pay: "It was as if he had had to pay the same note twice because of some trifling oversight of *date* or *signature*" (p. 84, my emphasis).

One must pay for the place one occupies in the world, and the problem is that one can pay only with images; money is a false substitute for the thing itself. Sutpen's mistake, his error, is his trust in the symbolic, that is to say, his ignorance of the real. General Compson understands this and attempts to explain to him the consequences of his disavowal of the rights of the body in his treatment of his first wife: "didn't the dread and fear of females which you must have drawn in with the primary mammalian milk teach you better? What kind of abysmal and purblind innocence could that have been which someone told you to call virginity? what conscience to trade with which would have warranted you in the belief that you could have bought immunity from her for no other coin but justice?" (p. 265).

Everything in this quotation deserves attention: Faulkner's emphasis on the word *virginity* as a disavowal of sexuality and procreation is, however, especially striking. By means of a certain vocabulary, Sutpen is apparently allowed to ignore the true nature of his debt. Birth is a division, violation of a primal unity and it must be atoned for in time. It is not surprising, then, that those who owe existence to this original division are held accountable, that the sins of the fathers are visited on the children. The text here makes explicit reference to a biblical authority:

> the old Abraham full of years and weak and incapable now of further harm, caught at last and the captains and the collectors saying, 'Old man, we dont want you' and Abraham would say, 'Praise the Lord, I have raised about me sons to bear the burden of mine iniquities and persecutions; yea, perhaps even to restore my flocks and herds from the hand of the ravisher: that I might rest mine eyes upon my goods and chattels, upon the generations of them and of my descendants increased an hundred fold as my soul goeth out from me.' (p. 325)

"Some things just have to be." This is what Shreve says Quentin speculates Miss Rosa said, and the chain of transmission of this truth is not indifferent to its message: "some things," Shreve continues, "just have to be whether they are or not, just to balance the books, write *Paid* on the old sheet so that whoever keeps them can take it out of the ledger and burn it, get rid of it" (p. 325). The fantasy of total destruction, the burning of the family house, is one symptom of the debt. Another response to hereditary guilt is denial. Sutpen does not acknowledge his first son; Bon does not acknowledge the fact that he had a father. Charles Bon, according to Shreve's narrative, is he "who not only had no visible father but had found himself to be, even in infancy, enclosed by an unsleeping cabal bent apparently on teaching him that he had never had a father . . ." (p. 313).

Bon's search for a father is undertaken almost unconsciously

and is seen as a search for selfhood. Charles looks at Henry to
see himself, his own image only slightly blurred by something
"alien": *"alien blood whose admixing was necessary in order that he
exist"* and from contemplation of himself, Charles passes on to
violence, "penetration," homosexual desire for the father surfaces: *". . . there—at any moment, second, I shall penetrate by something
of will and intensity and dreadful need, and strip that alien leavening
from it and look not on my brother's face whom I did not know I possessed
and hence never missed, but my father's, out of the shadow of whose
absence my spirit's posthumeity has never escaped . . ."* (p. 317). I am
not forgetting that this is Shreve speaking Charles's role as he
calls his father the "shadow of an absence." This definition of the
father is, however, very close to *As I Lay Dying*'s explanation of
the word as "just a shape to fill a lack." In the "shadow of an
absence" one may read the Lacanian definition of the phallus:
the signifier without a signified. Shreve's discourse also makes a
mysterious and somewhat contradictory reference to the "posthumeity of the spirit." The use of the present-perfect tense
maintains the curious a-temporality that is so typically Faulknerian. The real present is devoid of action since all has been acted,
spoken in the past; the text bears witness to the telescoping of
past and present. Moreover, in a supreme negation of the axiom
concerning the irreversibility of temporal sequence, the narrative present speaks the past and thus calls it into existence after
the fact.

In the above quoted phrase attributed to Bon, the spirit is
being held prisoner, denied the escape from time into immortal-
ity because of the absence of the symbolic father. Be this as it
may, however, the signifier, through its very existence, re-
pudiates eternity: it is only in the *hic* and *nunc*. What is even
more important, the signifier *is,* in, through, by, itself. As in
Genesis, creation is, exists *ex nihilo.* Thus *Absalom* creates a
genealogy of fatherless sons: Charles Bon, Charles Etienne
Saint-Valery Bon: "this child with a face not old but without age,
as if he had had no childhood . . . as if he had not been human
born but instead created without agency of man or agony of
woman . . ." (p. 196). The use of "as if" here as elsewhere in

Faulkner's text seems to have the weight of a disavowal, "as if" means "what follows is not true, yet is, that is, exists, not in life, but in language." The text presents what linguists call a "speech act."

The question of a nonfiliation comes up again in the novel when General Compson posits the separation between biological and symbolical existence. When asked about his father's identity, Charles Etienne Saint-Valery Bon affirms his ignorance, and the General replies: "What ever you are, once you are among strangers, people who dont know you, you can be whatever you will. . . ." Yet the text judges this hypothesis as "lame vain words, the specious and empty fallacies." It is not really true that one can live without one's name. As General Compson finally says of Bon's son: *"Better that he were dead, better that he had never lived"* (pp. 204–05). And once more the novel echoes the Old Testament, this time Job 3:3: "Let the day perish wherein I was born, and the night *in which* it was said, There is a man child conceived." Generation continues still as procreation, and the effort now is only to abolish, not life itself, but the name. In the fourth generation, the offspring has become a nameless "it." Judith declares: *"I will raise it, see that it . . . It does not need to have any name"* (p. 208). Yet, somehow, the child does have a name, as we learn through Luster in Shreve's narrative: ". . . *you were watching the boy, the Jim Bond* . . . you hadn't heard the name before, hadn't even thought that he must have a name that day when you saw him . . ." (pp. 214–15). No father names Jim Bond, for now the name has become an independent force. As the text puts it: ". . . the name *was* Bond now" (p. 215, my emphasis).

Such a state of affairs is, as Luster suggests, a matter of *law*, at any rate, that is his interpretation of the orphan's name: "'Dat's a lawyer word. Whut dey puts you under when de Law ketches you' . . . And that was him, the name was Bond now, and he wouldn't care about that, who had inherited what he was from his mother and only what he could never have been from his father" (p. 215). Again the reference is to Job:

14:4–5 Who can bring a clean *thing* out of an unclean? not one. Seeing his days *are* determined, the number of his months *are* with thee, thou hast appointed his *bounds* that he cannot pass. (My emphasis)

The etymology of the name follows *Bon* from "good" through *Bound* to *Bond*—fetter.

Sutpen has two sons. The first is denied the name of the father and has a descendance in opposition to the law of the symbolic. The result after four generations will be the annihilation of humanity: Jim Bond is a speechless idiot. The second son, Henry, is holder of the name, but the recognition of the body is denied him. Sutpen fathered both as if he were continuing his indivisible selfhood. He creates, does not procreate, does not accept the "agency of man or agony of woman" (p. 196).

Denying difference, Sutpen has created both his dominion and his descendants. Yet, procreation is incompatible with the integrity of his *Oneness*. To those who are marked by Sutpen's name—Judith and Henry, but Clytie as well—no offspring will be allowed. Clytie and Judith are doomed to spinsterhood. Even if Henry could be imagined as engendering children, he could do so only in the realm of the biological; symbolical fatherhood, the conferring of the name, is denied: "... *and whatever dragon's outcropping of Sutpen blood the son might sow on the body of whatever strange woman would therefore carry on the tradition ... under another name and upon and among people who will never have heard the right one*" (p. 182).

Bon's conclusion to the mystery of being is expressed as a mythological formula: "... and hence no man had a father ... all boy flesh that walked and breathed stemming from that one ambiguous eluded dark fatherhood and so brothered perennial and ubiquitous everywhere under the sun" (p. 299). Through the image of the sun the text expresses once more an identification of Sutpen to an absolute father, God: "... *if there could have been such a thing as sun to him, if anyone or anything could have competed with the white glare of his madness*" (p. 166).

Faulkner's text repeats the image of the sowing of dragon's teeth as a denial of sexual reproduction thereby illustrating Levi-Strauss's reading of the myth as an effort to narrate the unavoidable contradiction between religious belief which states that life originally sprang from the earth, and observation which teaches that life is the result of sexual union. The anthropologist suggests that all religious belief has its roots in the necessity of providing a parallel fiction to supplement the unacceptable mystery of sexual reproduction.[2]

In much the same way, while the Old Testament insists so heavily upon the absolute linearity of filial connections, the New Testament takes up this "history" only to undermine it. The beginning of the gospel according to Matthew announces "the book of the generation of Jesus Christ, the son of David, the son of Abraham." The text of chapter 1 thus enumerates relations of fathers to sons without ever mentioning the presence of the mothers. There are, however, two significant exceptions to this rule. These exceptions are situated at the two points where the enumerations are modulated by an articulation: 1:6 "And Jesse begat David the king; and David the king begat Solomon of her that had been the wife of Urias." Again 1:16 "And Jacob begat Joseph the husband of Mary of whom was born Jesus, who is called Christ." And finally the text resumes: 1:17 "So all the generations from Abraham to David are fourteen generations and from David until the carrying away into Babylon are fourteen generations and from the carrying away into Babylon unto Christ are fourteen generations." At the points of articulation, when the name of the woman is introduced, this feminine presence implies at the same time a doubt as to the absolute law of filiation. David fathers Solomon, but the woman involved belonged to another man. In the final analysis, this first ambiguity as to the identity of the father is only an introduction to the tremendous contradiction that Matthew's text must voice: an unbroken line of generation from father to son, from Abraham to Joseph, then suddenly a reversal in the discourse, for Joseph is not the father of Christ: the text states that he is the husband of a virgin with child through the agency, not of man, but of the Holy Spirit.

The biblical text can be seen to operate in favor of a return to monotheism with this denial of procreation. In much the same way, at the end of his personal story, Sutpen, denied descendance, seeks to salvage his domain. Sutpen's Hundred, the text tells us, would now be better named "Sutpen's One."

The denial of difference, of which sexual difference is only one facet, can be seen as the explanation for the analogous disavowal of time, which is so striking in Faulkner's universe. One example among many is Bon's letter referring to the war as an echo (p. 131). Another is Rosa's account of Bon's death: "*I heard an echo, but not the shot*" (p. 150).

The negation of time and of sexuality results, in a static, frozen, mesmerized world, immortal because lifeless, which is perhaps the story itself. A fitting place for its telling is the tomblike office in Jefferson or the Harvard sitting room converted into a grave. The novel is a fetish, a monument to the disavowal of procreation. Hence its title taken from II Samuel 18:18:

> Now Absalom in his lifetime had taken and reared up for himself a pillar, which *is* in the king's dale: for he said, I have no son to keep my name in remembrance: and he called the pillar after his own name: and it is called unto this day, Absalom's place.

Like the Bible, Faulkner's text bears witness to the unbearable ambivalence of desire in the death of the son preceding that of the father. Samuel 18:33 ". . . O my son Absalom, would God I had died for thee."

The abuse of the name is linked to the negation of time and to the establishing of a curious antigenealogy in which the living and the dead are confused. What is in question here is the effort to deny the difference of generations. As Quentin says, ". . . *we are both Father*" (pp. 261–62). The voice exists while its various mouthpieces lose substance. Fleshly descendance is abolished, and only the voice provides a link. But if the subject identifies himself, situates himself in connection with the narration, he remains outside of time, which has become reversible. Quentin continues: "*Or maybe Father and I are both Shreve, maybe it took Father and me both to make Shreve or Shreve and me both to make Father or maybe Thomas Sutpen to make all of us*" (p. 262). In this passage, Quentin has already succumbed to psychosis.

Bon, in remaining unaware of his need to define his origin
and to find his name, put off his search for a father, but the
repressed need erupted in the form of a mirror-double encountered in his brother Henry. Not surprisingly, then, the double
becomes murderous or, at least, presents the means toward
suicide for a self bereft of symbolic existence. The suggestions of
homosexuality in *Absalom* present in the description of Charles
and Henry on the one hand and of Shreve and Quentin on the
other, are only transformations of the repressed desire for a
symbolic father.

The conclusion to the unwilling quest for selfhood that is
Faulkner's novel is the confrontation between Henry and Quentin. Presented as dialogue, it is close to a monologue between the
subject and his alienated other:

> *And you are———?*
> *Henry Sutpen.*
> *And you have been here———?*
> *Four years.*
> *And you came home———?*
> *To die. Yes.*
> *To die?*
> *Yes. To die.*
> *And you have been here———?*
> *Four years.*
> *And you are———?*
> *Henry Sutpen.* (p. 373)

This is the encounter between a speaker and his mirror image.
The dialogue is an inverted doubling revolving around the axis
of death. "To die?" is the center of identity, the immortal phallus, Absalom's pillar. This exchange illustrates Lacan's rule of
communication: "In the unconscious the subject's message
comes back to him in inverted form."[3]

Faulkner's *Absalom, Absalom!* can be read as an examination of
the effects of the name as manifestation of the universal fear of
desire. The book presents the central figure of a primal father
outside of desire. Sutpen is eternal because he has lost everything. He has renounced, given up everything, and, at the same

time, kept a copy, a double. In all of his repeated dealings with women, he bypasses desire. Because his unions are part of a design, they are not motivated by desire, and Sutpen can ignore on each wife's face the persistent image of his own death. Avoiding the encounter with the other, denying the necessity of division, Sutpen puts off his own encounter with castration and engenders a series of doubles fixed like Henry and Quentin in a dizzying repudiation of life and light. In the final analysis then, if procreation is denied, if creation is impossible, Faulkner's text has only the power to negate, to project a series of reflections of a darkness "where light never began" (p. 300).

NOTES

1. All references to *Absalom, Absalom!* are taken from the Modern Library issue, 1951, and followed by the page number in parenthesis. References to the Bible are taken from the Authorized (King James) Version.

2. See for example *La Pensée sauvage* (Paris: Plon, 1962).

3. See especially "Le Séminaire sur 'La Lettre volée,'" in *Ecrits* (Paris: Seuil, 1966).

# Intertextuality and Originality:
## Hawthorne, Faulkner, Updike

## John T. Matthews

We have learned that the centrifugal and centripetal pressures of the intertextual project drive us first away from and then back toward Faulkner—to the Old Testament, Flaubert, Beckett, southern oratory, Horace McCoy, and some other "Faulkners" (not the first), then back to Faulkner (perhaps no longer the first). I cite this path in order to begin my own purposeful digressions: the Gospels, *The Scarlet Letter,* and John Updike's *A Month of Sundays.* My path will be circuitous in part, because in this paper I am less interested in distinguishing Faulkner from other writers than in seeing him as other writers—intent to assess the conditions for originality.

An incident in the ministry of Jesus illustrates in divine hyperbole an aspect of my topic, the speaker's position within the laws that govern what may be said. Teaching one morning, Jesus is interrupted by scribes and Pharisees who bring before him a woman taken in adultery. The Mosaic law, they remind him, requires death for such a one; let the young teacher pass his judgment. The dilemma has been neatly conceived since the Pharisees expect Jesus to choose between the harsh dictate of the religious law, which did indeed prescribe death by stoning, and the superseding authority of the Roman law, which forbade execution for offenses against Jewish law. Jesus' eloquent reversal is familiar: "He that is without sin among you, let him first cast a stone at her" (John 8:9). The woman's accusers can do no better than to leave silently and singly. But Jesus' spoken challenge is punctuated by a gesture equally eloquent and instructive; twice he stoops "and with his finger wrote on the ground, as though

Portions of this essay appeared as "The Word as Scandal: Updike's *A Month of Sundays.*" *Arizona Quarterly,* 39 (Winter 1983), 351–80.

he heard them not" (8:6). What Jesus writes we are not told. In John Updike's *A Month of Sundays,* Reverend Marshfield, adulterous and hence especially appreciative, interprets the gesture this way: "He wrote idly, irritating His vengeful questioners, and imparting to us yet another impression of our Lord's superb freedom, of the something indolent and abstracted about His earthly career."[1] Such aloofness from human interrogation and conundrum allows Jesus to point to his supernatural affiliation and authority. Jesus vaults from the status of the law's interpreters to the stature of their author; his moving finger means to imitate his father's.

The pure inscrutability of Jesus' writing makes it arresting to the Pharisees and to the readers of John's gospel. Yet, commentators have been tempted to read the writing on the ground as related to Jesus' interpretation of the Mosaic law and his refusal to condemn the adulteress. Perhaps Jesus begins to write out the law that covers adultery in the Mosaic code, or the law governing the probity of witnesses, to which he refers later when he proposes that executioners ought themselves to be sinless. In both cases Jesus' writing would be a reinscription of the law, a rewriting of the law that constitutes an interpretation or reading of it as well. (One commentator further conjectures that Jesus' writing reminds the Pharisees that the text of the law may be pronounced in varying and rival ways; writing preserves the law's ambiguity and the necessity of divine application.) Jesus' gesture emphasizes that he does not challenge the Mosaic law but actually enforces it. Once the woman's accusers have disappeared, she is exempt from the prerequisite for condemnation: two unimpeachable witnesses. By exercising the law in this manner, Jesus situates himself as its divine practitioner, not its overthrower: "Think not that I am come to destroy the law, or the prophets: I am not come to destroy, but to fulfill" (Matthew 5:17). Jesus' writing of the law assumes divine authority. St. Paul insists that though God spoke in the past through his prophets, He has "in these last days spoken unto us by His Son . . . who [is] the brightness of his glory, and the express image of his person . . . " (Hebrews 1: 1–2). Jesus construes the law through his

writing and, in doing so, constructs his divine person. The audacity of his claim is to be, at once, speaker and spoken.

The accusation of the woman taken in adultery is not an acci-
dental occasion for Jesus' only recorded act of writing. Like the
adulteress, Jesus is exposed to a potential charge of violating
civil or religious law. His insouciantly self-reflective writing resembles distantly but sharply the transgressive subversiveness of
adultery. The brillance of Jesus' gesture is to transform the appearance of shameful lawbreaking into an occasion for upholding the law, to translate apparent destruction into fulfillment. At
the same time, of course, he permits his manifest chastity to
chasten and forgive the woman's sinfulness: "Neither do I condemn thee; go, and sin no more" (John 8:11). The law's condemnation dissolves into divine forgiveness; the incident is an
emblem of Jesus' view that he lawfully supplants the Mosaic
code. I interpret Jesus' careful repetition of his enigmatic gesture as his attempt both to establish the legitimacy of repetition
(is he not a supplement to the deity that is self-sufficient?), and
to insist on the present indecipherability of his perfect reinscription of the law (his time is not yet come).

Jesus' sympathy for the adulterous woman may stem more
deeply from the paradox of his own humanity. God's incarna-
tion of himself in the person of Jesus is his sufferance of human
limitation. When He gives "an express image" to his glory, when
He speaks himself in the Word that was in the beginning, the
Word made flesh (John 1:1), God is all but adulterating himself
with human form. As we shall see, the association of adulteration and adultery is profound. For the moment I will allow Updike's Reverend Marshfield to intimate the range of its
significance. Marshfield initiates his clerical adulteries because
he hopes to rediscover the vital estrangements of illicit desire.
He and his wife, he complains, have become virtual twins after
two decades of marriage, even coming to look like each other.
Adultery becomes Marshfield's passage to the necessary other
that abrades and completes the indeterminate self. As a writer of
therapeutic reminiscences in *A Month of Sundays,* Marshfield discovers additionally that the author's world is also the other's. His

writerly ventures give him a fictional alter ego, give him the remembered alter egos of his lovers, and give him an Ideal Other, his invisible reader, whom he names Ms. Prynne. All of these others Marshfield possesses as altered, adulterous selves, constructions of a lettered self that are products of reading and writing.

The unique indifferences claimed by Jesus' writing annul all of the anxieties that other, more human forms of writing encounter. By pointing to Jesus' "superb freedom," Updike's Marshfield uses the episode to comment indirectly on the customarily compromised status of writer and written. One source of compromise for the writer arises in the intertextual situation of all subjectivity. Julia Kristeva describes the speaker's double bind: ruled by intertextuality, aspiring to originality.

> The daily attention given to the discourse of the other confirms, if need be, that the speaking being maintains himself or herself as such to the extent that he/she allows for the presence of two brinks. On the one hand, there is pain—but it also makes one secure—caused as one recognizes oneself as subject of (others') discourse, hence tributary of a universal Law. On the other, there is pleasure—but it kills—at finding oneself different, irreducible, for one is borne by a simply singular speech, not merging with the others, but then exposed to the black thrusts of a desire that borders on idiolect and aphasia. In other words, if the overly constraining and reductive meaning of a language made up of universals causes us to suffer, the call of the unnamable, on the contrary, issuing from those borders where signification vanishes, hurls us into the void of a psychosis that appears henceforth as the solidary reverse of our universe, saturated with interpretation, faith, or truth. Within that vise, our only chance to avoid being neither master nor slave of meaning lies in our ability to insure our mastery of it (through technique or knowledge) as well as our passage through it (through play or practice). In a word, jouissance.[2]

By focusing on the way *The Scarlet Letter, As I Lay Dying,* and *A Month of Sundays* present these brinks, I hope to show how the Law of others' discourse manifests itself as literary contexts for each work; and I shall argue that each novel ponders how the urge to construct an original utterance and identity is a transgression of law and convention that nevertheless depends upon it for its fulfillment. Adultery is the emblem of a flight to freedom and irreducibility that fulfills itself in the reconstitution of a contract. This emblem is also worn by writing in the three novels.

In considering the affiliations of *As I Lay Dying* and *A Month of Sundays* with *The Scarlet Letter*, I have kept in mind Jonathan Culler's recent distinction of two approaches to intertextuality:

> . . . the first is to look at the specific presuppositions of a given text, the way in which it produces a pre-text, an intertextual space whose occupants may or may not correspond to other actual texts. . . . The second enterprise . . . leads to a poetics which is less interested in the occupants of the intertextual space . . . than in the conventions which underlie that discursive activity.[3]

I suggest that the triad of works I shall discuss permits us to pursue both of these lines of inquiry simultaneously. *As I Lay Dying* presupposes *The Scarlet Letter*, as *A Month of Sundays* presupposes both; within that intertextual space, moreover, all three works confront the question of what it means simply to write. Hence these three works inquire into the conventions, the customs, of writing, and in so doing, they cast and recast the recognition that the originality of a work is constituted in the movement that displaces its origin, that textuality is always intertextuality, and that, in the master image of all three novels, adultery represents the constitution of authenticity through a proscribed act.

The law of others' discourse, which threatens to make its subject mere tributaries (as Kristeva puts it), takes several forms in *The Scarlet Letter*. As Hawthorne probes aesthetically what Kristeva has described empirically, one perilous brink emerges as familial, cultural, and literary proscription for the narrator of "The Custom-House," the autobiographical preface to *The Scarlet Letter*. The narrator recounts his indenturedness to the surveyorship of customs in Salem, an expedient made necessary by his languishing literary career, and describes the fortuitous discovery of a predecessor's papers in the custom house, papers that deliver to him the scarlet letter and an accompanying narrative. Newly possessed of so promising a literary property, Hawthorne's narrator welcomes the change in federal administrations that deprives him of its patronage and returns him to the life of letters. Though there has been a peacefulness in his retirement from the toils of publishing, the narrator looks upon his surveyorship as having been a painful curative for literary ambition:

> It is a good lesson—though it may often be a hard one—for a man who has dreamed of literary fame, and of making for himself a rank among the world's dignitaries by such means, to step aside out of the narrow circle in which his claims are recognized, and to find how utterly devoid of significance, beyond that circle, is all that he achieves, and all that he aims at.[4]

Rather than seeing his name "blazoned abroad on titlepages," the narrator sees it stamped on the merchandise he processes. Such a life threatens him with an absolute absorption by the conventions of usage; one veteran compatriot in his office strikes him as having become a "nonentity" (p. 18). The narrator is endangered by the prospect of becoming nothing other than a surveyor of customs.

The narrator discovers his salvation in the private papers of a predecessor, Mr. Surveyor Pue, whose private researches into local history have produced a written corpus that preserves "the traces of Mr. Pue's mental part, and the internal operations of his head" (p. 30). Pue's papers body forth the renewed enticements of the literary career, especially when the narrator re-members that a Mr. Pue's literal remains had been dug up during an excavation and that nothing but fragments survive of the corporal Pue. Moreover, Hawthorne's predecessor had conducted his private writing during public hours (Hester's story is discovered among cast off, unofficial documents). Pue's salutary career, then, emerges in his transgression of the proscriptions

against a private self in a public occupation. The narrator redis-
covers writing as a fugitive routing back to another self that is his
authentic self. His surveyorship having threatened to become a
permanent disaffection, the narrator's mind is "recalled . . . in
some degree, to its old track" (p. 33). When the narrator begins
to exercise his fancy on the scarlet letter and its history, however,
he discovers that his "imagination was a tarnished mirror"
(p. 34). Disuse has imperiled his ability to see himself as a con-
struction of the literary imagination.

Despite its rewards, the recalling of the narrator to his proper
life makes him suffer. Before he reads Pue's accompanying account of Hester Prynne's disgrace, the narrator notices the rem-
nant of the scarlet letter and instinctively places it on his own
breast. A painful thrill "as of burning heat" (p. 32) causes him to
shudder and involuntarily let the letter drop to the floor. The
narrator identifies himself with the sign of Hester's shame, then,
before he even knows its significance. I shall argue that, although the shamefulness of writing has circumstantial links to
Hester's career for Hawthorne, the central relation of the two
wearers of the letter is that they are authors of themselves. The
exercise of fancy produces shame.

For the narrator to write about Hester's adultery is for him to
incur shame in several ways. His evident sympathy for Hester's
plight in the romance censures his own ancestors, the notorious
judges Hathorne of Salem: "I, the present writer, as their representative, hereby take shame upon myself for their sakes, and
pray that any curse incurred by them . . . may be now and
henceforth removed" (p. 10). Inversely, Hawthorne's writing
also makes him the object of reproof. Those very ancestors
would "scorn" his "degenerate" occupation as a "writer of story-
books" (p. 10). In doing so, they might find reinforcement in the
opinions of Hawthorne's townsmen, who find his description of
official life in Salem shameful. The writer defends himself from
the shamefulness of his circumstances, but a more treacherous
brink opens within the general conditions of writing.

Pointing to patronage's practice of "beheading" its official re-
tainers as a consequence of political disfavor, the narrator is only

a little surprised to be sent to his writing desk in a "decapitated state" (p. 43). The narrator elaborates on his figure of speech when he describes his renewed literary life: he is now a "gentle-man who writes from beyond the grave. Peace be with all the world! My blessing on my friends! My forgiveness to my enemies! For I am in the realm of the quiet! . . . I am a citizen of somewhere else!" (p. 44). The narrator describes his recovery of his "old track" in imagery violent and strained. His resurrection is a kind of death, his new self a no self, his recovered place a displacement. The atopic writer, moreover, may only be fathomed by an anonymous reader, and then only in part. Haw-thorne rejects the indulgence of revealing "confidential depths" in his text: "It is scarcely decorous, however, to speak all, even where we speak impersonally" (p. 4). He addresses an ideal reader who is a friend, "though not the closest friend," and who will listen to his talk while respecting the author's "inmost Me behind its veil." The narrator betrays a latent shame over the writer's need to publish abroad the embodiments of his most private fancies.

The narrator likewise deliberates the compromises of literary proprietorship. Surveyor Pue has not only preserved the scrap of Hester's badge, he has written a "reasonably complete expla-nation of the whole affair" (p. 32). The narrator assumes the right of "dressing up" the affair, to ascribe motivation and "modes of passion" (p. 33), but he insists that the "main facts of that story are authorized and authenticated by the document of Mr. Surveyor Pue" (p. 32). Hawthorne will create within an "out-line," with "nearly or altogether as much license as if the facts had been entirely of my own invention" (p. 33). Since Haw-thorne's account of Pue's manuscript is perfectly fictional, I sug-gest that the narrator is describing the condition of all literary invention. The law of letters—both the language in which it is written and the body of its literary tradition—has already "au-thorized and authenticated" what may only be invented "as if" it were original. We may appreciate Hawthorne's anticipation of Kristeva's "vise"; the narrator approaches his task with the sting-ing glee of one who must maintain the shame of being a tributary to the laws of composition and also the urgency to create the "irreducible" difference of his own speaking self. To write his story the narrator must read Pue's; it is no wonder that he lingers over the "traces" of Hester's scarlet letter. Only his predisposed and active fancy leads him to study the scrap in such a way that it "assumed the shape of a letter." And his reading of the letter's art suggests that not even its unraveling can reconstruct it completely: "the stitch . . . gives evidence of a now forgotten art, not to be recovered even by the process of picking out the threads" (p. 31).

Having confronted the writer's self-adulteration, Hawthorne pursues his affiliation with the adulterous heroine in the story proper. There are two synonymous signs of Hester's adultery: her child Pearl and the scarlet letter. The narrator equates them, allowing Hester to point out that her offspring "is the scarlet letter" (p. 113). Hester goes so far as to attire Pearl's "rich and luxuriant beauty" in a garb that "allowed the gorgeous tendencies of [Hester's] imagination their full play" (p. 102). Like the luxuriously and ornately embroiderd scarlet "A," Pearl is curiously both the product of Hester's rich imagination and the emblem of her shame. Dimmesdale observes that Hester's artistry (as it is embodied by Pearl and the letter) is both an "ever-recurring agony" and a "troubled joy" (p. 114). Her badge strikes the gray Puritans as "artistically done, . . . with so much fertility and gorgeous luxuriance of fancy" (p. 53). The narrator's appreciation of Hester's art recalls his own "striving to picture forth imaginary scenes . . . on the brightening page in many-hued description" (p. 35). Indeed, the narrator implicates himself repeatedly in Hester's crime, suggesting that she too senses the "red-hot brand" of the letter (p. 163), and that Hester's more dangerous sins are intellectual, not carnal. We may notice that Hawthorne's own authorial dilemma is pointed out by his description of Hester's: "The world's law was no law for her mind. . . . She assumed a freedom of speculation . . . which our forefathers, had they known of it, would have held to be a deadlier crime than that stigmatized by the scarlet letter" (p. 164). Like her author, Hester strives to transgress the very

Law that gives her her richest self. Pearl is the embodiment of the impulse toward freedom, private irreducibility: "There is no law, nor reverence for authority . . . mixed up with that child's composition" (p. 134). Hester and Dimmesdale's adulterous passion embodies their "black thrust" toward a world that is the "solidary reverse of our universe." The two yield themselves to the dark desires of the forest in the adultery that has, as Hester says, "a consecration of its own" (p. 195).

Faulkner and Updike each originates his novel in part as a rewriting of *The Scarlet Letter*. *As I Lay Dying* centers on Addie Bundren's perverse request to be buried far from home in her town of origin and on her mysterious speech from afterlife in which she explains her mistrust of language and convention and her yearning for something more authentic. How closely Addie's situation resembles the narrator's in *The Scarlet Letter:* like him, she speaks from the other side of life, as a "citizen of somewhere else." Her complaints about marriage echo Hester's dissatisfaction with the cold monasticism of Chillingworth's scholastic devotions, but Faulkner allows Addie to make the connection between the laws of marriage and language more explicit. Addie insists that any word is "just a shape to fill a lack," that words are no good, that "words dont ever fit even what they are trying to say at."[5] Words, according to Addie, are just the dead containers of actual experience, and she associates her platitudinous husband, Anse, with the betrayal of life by language: "It was as though he had tricked me," she says about her first pregnancy, "hidden within a word like within a paper screen and struck me in the back through it" (p. 164). Addie's despair that she will be able to find nothing that is not already deadened by the laws of usage and convention brings her to contemplate the ecstatic brink of authentic difference that Kristeva describes. Addie tries to recall the time before she has been lost to the customs of marriage and talk: "The shape of my body where I used to be a virgin is in the shape of a        and I couldn't think *Anse*, couldn't remember *Anse*" (p. 165). The blank space in Addie's speech demarcates the "black thrust" toward the authenticity of the "unnamable" that threatens aphasia. Addie reaches for an au-

thentic knowledge before and outside of language, for an immanent word that is not *déja lu,* for an original, virginal intactness
before loss. Yet the blank space in Addie's section inescapably
functions as an inscription, a citation of lost virginity and innocence. Remembering that *Anse* is the word for the shape of her
body where it used to be a virgin, Addie demonstrates how the
instrument (language) that names innocence names its loss in
the same motion—just as Anse is the male member whose shape
describes, as it despoiled, Addie's virginity.

Addie's name predicts her dream of adulterous self-recovery.
Perhaps the name "Addie" derives from "AD," the initials that
were a much more common badge for adultery among the Puritans than the "A" that Hawthorne has Hester wear.[6] The missing
"D" on Hester's breast suggests the anonymous paternity of her
child since "AD" would publish abroad Arthur Dimmesdale's
initials. Like Hester, Addie refuses to divulge the author of her
secret sin, the Reverend Whitfield, who is the father of Addie's
Jewel (a name that incidentally points to Hester's Pearl). Addie
recalls her adultery with Whitfield as a way of stripping off "the
clothes we both wore in the world's face" (p. 166), and she wants
her adultery to cure a problem that is as much verbal as domestic: "I would think of the sin as garments which we would re-
move in order to shape and coerce the terrible blood to the
forlorn echo of the dead word high in the air" (p. 167). Addie's
spectacular sin requires the complicity of the one figure, the
preacher, who is an emblem of the only possible marriage of self
and speech—through the emptying of the individual and the
filling of the Word. But Whitfield and Dimmesdale parody their
divine precursor; their grotesquely hypocritical words magnify
the estrangements of self suffered by all but miraculous speakers. Tull notices that Whitfield's "voice is bigger than him. It's
like they are not the same. It's like he is one, and his voice is one,
swimming on two horses side by side across the ford and coming
into the house, the mud-splashed one and the one that never
even got wet, triumphant and sad" (p. 86). Jewel embodies what
Addie has made of her adultery; he is a "living lie," as Whitfield
says, a representation of Addie's fugitive jouissance that, on the

one hand, powers her to the brink of the unnamable and, on the other, returns her to the security of other's discourse, Anse's domain of usage, fidelity, and death. Addie summarizes, "I could just remember how my father used to say that the reason for living was to get ready to stay dead a long time" (p. 161).

*A Month of Sundays* completes a triangular meditation on the scarlet letter by recurring to its instigators. Although Updike once decried "the carnival of French Existentialists and Mississippi stream-of-consciousness purveyors who have recently degraded" the Nobel Prize in literature,[7] he nevertheless depends on one of them to differentiate one of his contributions to the novel of adultery. Marshfield, who is sent to a spiritual sanitorium for clergymen in the southwest to recover from his assorted theological and carnal infidelities, may strike us as extending Addie Bundren's metaphysics of adultery and as bearing touches of Whitfield in his name and his rationalized hypocrisy. But his predicament also prompts Marshfield to recollect *The Scarlet Letter,* and soon we notice that his past intimates bear names like Chillingworth, Prynne, and A for Adulterous Alicia. Updike amplifies the writer's implication in adultery in ways that Hawthorne only begins to grasp. Updike's Marshfield is both a writer and an adulterous preacher. The sanitorium's regimen requires that every morning be spent writing although there is no prescribed subject. Marshfield's winging his way into his book introduces him to the conditions of writing. Like Hawthorne's narrator, he approaches it with anticipated shame: "I write these pages at some point in the time of Richard Nixon's unravelling. Though the yielding is mine, the temptation belongs to others: my keepers have set before me a sheaf of blank sheets—a month's worth, in their estimation. Sullying them is to be my sole therapy" (p. 3). Particularly at the outset Marshfield depreciates writing, thinking it onanistic and solipsistic. The prevailing imagery for writing depicts it as pollution since Marshfield senses that his written confession is a kind of self-encoding, a transmutation of his familiar self and loves into the unworldly and unfamiliar regions of the page.

Precisely this strangeness for the writer, the equivalent to

Hawthorne's decapitation or Addie's aphasia, comes to consti-
tute Marshfield's recuperation. His manuscript teaches him that
he cherishes the adulteration of self in adultery; Marshfield's
apologetic argues that adultery is a flight from the coincidence
of self in married partners who have become identical to joyful
self discovery in self-abandonment. Alicia, Marshfield's first
lover, is "the body . . . of my soul" (pp. 85–86), and he sees her as
occupying "the otherworld in which my supine otherform lay
transfigured" (p. 97). Having lost this familiar world of
otherness, however, the writer Marshfield only slowly understands that writing repeats a kind of adultery at the same time it
is to cure it: a recuperation in two senses. His text, indeed,
reconstitutes his adulterous partners (even restoring momentarily his happy unfamiliarity with his wife during their courtship),
but it also constructs people made of words, a different but
corresponding order of alterity. Marshfield notices that he has
taken on a second "I" as he becomes character and narrator and
that his cohorts threaten to become literary properties (he knows
that their names are lifted from Hawthorne and Richardson, for
example). Marshfield's writing allows him another form for his
adultery; it justifies the sacrament of marriage as a condition for
the sacrament of adultery; and it deepens and complicates the
affiliation of adultery and writing suggested by *The Scarlet Letter*
and *As I Lay Dying*.

Naturally, Marshfield also rebels against the uxorious duties
to his typewriter; he worries that "now the danger is it [the
sanitorium] has become the only place. And this accounting the
only accounting, and you my reader my only love" (p. 181). To
cure himself he fancies seducing the mistress of the place, who
has also been his imagined ideal reader; their climactic lovemak-
ing not only conflates the acts of writing and adultery but also
prepares Marshfield for his return to a familiar world now made
strange by its having been written. The novel suggests that human writing, unlike Jesus's divinely intended writing, always in-
curs shame, adulteration, lawbreaking, and the flight toward
black, unnamable, lawless idiolect. As Marshfield has it, "The
Word is ever a scandal" (p. 46).

NOTES

1. John Updike, *A Month of Sundays* (New York, 1975), p. 42. I shall quote from this edition throughout.

2. Julia Kristeva, *Desire in Language: A Semiotic Approach to Literature and Art,* ed. Leon S. Roudiez, trans. Thomas Gora, Alice Jardine, and Leon S. Roudiez (New York: Columbia University Press, 1980), pp. ix–x.

3. Jonathan Culler, *The Pursuit of Signs: Semiotics, Literature, Deconstruction* (Ithaca: Cornell University Press, 1981), p. 118.

4. Nathaniel Hawthorne, *The Scarlet Letter,* vol. 1, *The Centenary Edition of the Works of Nathaniel Hawthorne* (Columbus, Ohio: Ohio State University Press, 1962), pp. 26–27. I shall quote from this edition throughout.

5. William Faulkner, *As I Lay Dying* (New York, 1930; Modern Library edition, 1967, photostatically reproduced from the text published by Random House, Inc., 1964, edited and corrected by James B. Meriwether), pp. 162–63. I shall quote from this edition throughout.

6. See, for example, Nina Baym, "The Romantic *Malgré Lui:* Hawthorne in 'The Custom-House,'" *ESQ: A Journal of the American Renaissance,* 19 (1973), pp. 14–25; as reprinted in *The Scarlet Letter* (New York, 1976; Norton Critical Edition, eds. Sculley Bradley, Richmond Croom Beatty, E. Hudson Long, and Seymour Gross), p. 24.

7. John Updike, *Assorted Prose* (New York: Knopf, 1965), p. 30.

# "Motion" and the Intertextuality
in Faulkner's Fiction

## Kenzaburo Ohashi

In an article of mine, entitled "Creation Through Repetition or
Self-Parody: Some Notes on Faulkner's Imaginative Process,"
which I wrote in 1980,[1] I pointed out some interrelations of
certain scenes, characters, and images that appear in various of
William Faulkner's works. For example, I found the comical
triangular relationship of Eula Varner, Jody Varner, and Hoake
McCarron in *The Hamlet* to be a kind of repetition as well as a
self-parody of that romantic and tragic relationship of Caddy
Compson, Quentin Compson, and Dalton Ames in *The Sound
and the Fury*. Quentin runs after Dalton Ames in order to accuse
him of corrupting his sister, but he, who is a local intellectual of
the town of Jefferson, Yoknapatawpha County, is quite meek
and impotent and faints in the end without even hitting Ames. It
is farcical, indeed, but the situation is tragic in its essence, as we
know from the text of the Quentin section. On the other hand,
Jody in *The Hamlet* cannot even run after Hoake McCarron with
the ancient pistol in his hand, because his father, Will Varner,
who, unlike Mr. Compson, is robust enough to be "engaged at
present in a liaison with the middle-fortyish wife of one of his
own tenants," treats him like a child, preventing him from pursuing Eula's lover.[2] This is essentially a comic presentation of a
situation similar to that of *The Sound and Fury*, his earlier work
published eleven years before.

The above is only one example of many in which Faulkner
creates a new scene with new significance by repeating a scene or
situation he has used in an earlier novel. But though I do not
enter into a full discussion of the matter at present, more details,
which I pointed out in my article beyond the example cited
above, can, I believe, prove that there can be found out an

intertextual network of scenes, characters, or images inherent in the working of Faulkner's imagination.

The repetition might have been either conscious or unconscious—it is very difficult to judge that, but there certainly *is* repetition, which is in some cases a kind of self-parody. I cannot help thinking that Faulkner *was* often conscious of reusing his own material in a new work of fiction—for example, when he wrote that scene in which Jody was prevented by his father from pursuing Hoake McCarron—especially because he seems to have been always conscious or aware of the whole world he had already created. I do not know if I can properly call that self-parody or not, but at any rate there is, or must be, indeed, a close intertextual relationship in the whole world of Faulkner's novels—if not literally *whole,* yet whole in the sense that he continuously summed up what had been already created.

I will not enter into a discussion of the details of the relationship now, because I have another problem in my mind, which is as important to me, and which I want to discuss here above all other things. Moreover, it is, I believe, closely related to the problem of the details of the intertextual network. The question is: if we can trace the intertextual relationship or network in Faulkner's fiction, how can we treat the dynamics of the relationship? I mean that powerful creative energy of Faulkner's which would not stand still, but would be always on the move. Faulkner himself declared that "life is motion"; " 'motion' is change and alteration and therefore the only alternative to motion is unmotion, stasis, death. . . ."[3] The intertextual relation or network, then, cannot be static, especially in Faulkner's case, but must be kinetic or dynamic. This, of course, is quite different from that idea of "development" or "growth," which had been quite familiar until not so long ago—a kind of diachronic concept—but the fact does not exclude, we must admit, the element of "time" or change or transformation, or what we may call a "temporal intertextual relationship."

Faulkner himself never completely abandoned a *chronological* coherence in his works, although he destroyed and disorganized the chronology itself uncompromisingly. It is significant, as well as curious, that the more he tried to destroy the chronological order in his novel, the more obsessed he seemed to be with it. In *The Sound and the Fury,* for example, the chronology is foreshortened, as it were, in a reverse order, as can be seen from the fact that we can reconstruct the story chronologically, coherently enough, even from Quentin's deranged *monologue intérieur.* This was, in a sense, a kind of time obsession on the part of the writer himself, just like that of Quentin Compson. But Faulkner tried gradually to conquer the obsession, or what Jean-Paul Sartre called his "métaphysique du temps,"[4] in writing his novels one after another. The following may sound like a rough description, but it is certain that Faulkner succeeded in conquering or transcending the time obsession after writing *Absalom, Absalom!* (1936). Here, he confronted the extremity of his time obsession with the whole historical context of the American south and the world since the Civil War as its actual burden. Perhaps the same occurred in *The Wild Palms* (1939), in which Harry Wilbourne finally chose some final positive value, though paradoxically enough, as he declared in the end, "*Yes, between grief and nothing I will take grief.*"[5] Faulkner could make him choose it by reversing his concept of value or his concept of time—from the negative toward the positive, from the past toward the future, though, of course, after that, he had to confront many strong counter-forces.

The following facts may serve as further evidence of the reversal of concepts of "value" and "time" in Faulkner's imaginative world: in "Lion,"[6] which was probably written in the early part of 1935, and which was incorporated into "The Bear" of *Go Down, Moses* (1942), Quentin Compson narrates his experience of the deep mysterious life in the wilderness just like Isaac McCaslin's in "The Bear," but he is not himself a mystic like Isaac. He is rather a rationalistic person and, in that sense, an intellectual not unlike the Quentin who appears in *The Sound and the Fury* and *Absalom, Absalom!* He does not, as Isaac later does, cast away his compass and watch, to say nothing of his gun, when he goes into the heart of the wilderness. Far from that. He actually reassures himself of his wise rationalism in depending on his gun so that he can conquer the irrational fear of the bear. This Quentin of the wilderness was *not* incorporated into *Absalom, Absalom!*, however, which was being written in the same period, but later into *Go Down, Moses,* where the character is transformed into Isaac, a kind of mystic who has some sense of a positive value and of future time. And the role of the intellectual Quentin seems to have been consumed completely in *Absalom, Absalom!* He disappears from Faulkner's works after that novel, together with other Quentins or his variants. Consider, for example, his variants in the original versions of "Fool about a Horse," written about the same time and later incorporated into *The Hamlet,* or "The Old People," written later, probably in June 1939, and then incorporated into *Go Down, Moses.* What are left are Quentin's doubles or *alter egos,* such as Harry Wilbourne, or Isaac McCaslin, a transformed figure of Quentin in "Lion," or Gavin Stevens, and a few others.[7] These new characters are all eager to find new values and future time, even if their trials finally end in errors or failures.

There are a few more little facts, which are quite significant, that reinforce the evidences of Faulkner's new positive attitude. "Was," the first story of *Go Down, Moses,* was originally titled "Almost" and narrated by Bayard Sartoris of *The Unvanquished.* When it was incorporated into *Go Down, Moses,* the narration was changed to that of an omniscient author, who told the story to Isaac and the reader as that of an experience of Carothers Edmonds, Isaac's cousin, when he was a boy. Moreover, the rascal hero of the title story of *Go Down, Moses* was originally a descendant of the Negro genealogy of Thomas Sutpen. Thus, *Go Down, Moses* is actually a collage, not just of different stories, but of different stories belonging to different genealogies in Faulkner's fiction.[8] This shows how dynamic the working of Faulkner's imagination was in creating the world of a new novel out of different elements covering many important phases of the world already created, and how significant all those transformations are that absorb all the different elements. In these transformations also are contained germs of the reversal of the author's concepts of "time" and "value."

And the "time" element which, as can be seen from the facts given above, was working dynamically in Faulkner's imagination, must have had an especially close relationship with that whole intertextual network inherent in Faulkner's works. How can we explain these relationships and grasp their collective significance as one of the most important characteristics of Faulkner's works and also as one of the inescapable literary problems of today?

Faulkner, while collaborating with Malcolm Cowley in editing *The Portable Faulkner* in the 1940's, perplexed the critic by insisting on changing some details written in his previous works. For example, in the "Appendix" to *The Sound and the Fury*, he changed the pear tree by which Jason's niece Quentin escaped from her uncle's room to a rainspout and changed the amount of the money stolen by her from $3,000 to $2,840.50. Not only did he change them, but he explained the reason for the changes in his peculiar and unique way. He compared himself to the "Garter King-at-Arms, heatless, not very moved, cleaning up 'Compson' before going to the next 'Co-o' or 'C-r.' "[9] As Cowley interprets this comparison, his new role as the "Garter King-at-Arms," besides providing him with a fresh approach to the Compson story, had another great advantage. "This Garter K/A didn't know about the monument and the slipper," Faulkner said. "He knew only what the town could have told him: a) Benjy was an idiot. b) spent most of his time with a negro nurse in the pasture. . . ."[10] That is, he knew things only according to what the town told him afresh from day to day.

Although Cowley interprets this episode, which is important as well as interesting, as a kind of excuse on Faulkner's part for changing freely what he had written before, I believe that this is inseparably connected with his time concept, especially as represented in his later works. He was always trying to stand in time present, which he characteristically called "*is*" or "*now.*" During the period when he was trying to complete his *magnum opus, A Fable,* he was always trying also to sum up his image of the world, his vision of the whole world, which he had studied, analyzed, and reconstructed in his imaginative works, as is typically and definitively shown by the novel, published in 1954. He tried to sum up not only his image of the world-at-large, but also the image of the particular Yoknapatawpha world that is closely related to that of the whole universal world created in his imagi- nation. It is significant that his efforts to create the world of *A Fable* went side by side with his efforts to write the "Golden Book" or the "Domesday Book" of Yoknapatawpha County, some early realizations of which were, indeed, the "Appendix" to *The Sound and the Fury,* which appeared in 1946, and those prologues located at the beginning of each act of *Requiem for a Nun.*

Faulkner's efforts to sum up had been continuous since the establishment of his County, but his attitude of summing up what he had written of Yoknapatawpha County before, coinci- dent with his summing-up of the conception of the world at large, definitely began to assume a more explicit and fuller form after *A Fable*—that is, in *The Town* and *The Mansion,* the last two novels of the Snopes trilogy. The following may be just a minor evidence, but it is quite significant that the number of the characters that appear in *The Town* is the largest among the novels of Faulkner—131 altogether, according to Robert W. Kirk's *Faulkner's People.*[11] Next to *The Town* stands *The Mansion,* whose dramatis personae number 125. Compare these figures with 31 in *Absalom, Absalom!,* 76 in *Go Down, Moses,* and 63 in *A Fable.* The fact helps to show that Faulkner in these two Snopes novels was trying to build up *anew* the whole world of Yok- napatawpha as an actual local image of the universal world he had tried to grasp in *A Fable.* Moreover, even if there is a con- tinuation of story from *The Town* to *The Mansion,* the latter still seems to be yet another summing-up of the world of the County on a different level from that of the former; there are, indeed, continuity and discontinuity between the two novels. That is, in his later works Faulkner tried to, and did, stand always in time *present,* recreating each time the image of the whole world, either abstractly as in *A Fable* or concretely as the world of Yok- napatawpha in *The Town* and *The Mansion.*

And his method, his way of doing so, was repetition or self-parody, as in those cases I referred to in the beginning of this paper concerning the relationship between the Caddy-Quentin-Ames triangle in *The Sound and the Fury* and that of Eula-Jody-McCarron in *The Hamlet*. The repetition had been continuing steadily, changing now and then the names of the characters and their backgrounds. The repetition was inevitable and necessary for Faulkner because he not only stood always in the present time, but also wanted to reconstruct again and again the whole world that he had created before in order to ceaselessly search for new possibilities of art and life. In the sense that he stood in present time each time, the repetition implied a *dynamic* reconception of the world, the implication corresponding to Faulkner's belief that "life" must be "motion," and that the work of art should contain the motion like the figures on a Grecian urn. The movement in the repetition can be linear and forward, trying to reach some point in the future. But in the sense that he wanted to *reconstruct* the whole world of his imagination, he inevitably had always to return to the world that he had already created and to return to the themes of eternity. The motion, which is still there, is, we must admit, in this sense circular or cyclical, like that procession of figures on the Grecian urn as John Keats sang in one of those odes Faulker liked so much, and the presentation might become repetitive and even occasionally parodic.

To conclude my paper, I will give here one example of such repetition or self-parody, which is very important as well as quite remarkable. In *The Mansion* Gavin Stevens visits Linda Kohl at Pascagoula, where she has been working as a riveter. On the beach Linda gives Stevens a beautiful shell, and the two are on the brink of becoming true lovers, spiritually as well as physically. Remember that this Pascagoula is the place Harry and Charlotte of *The Wild Palms* repaired to after the unsuccessful abortion. And here in *The Mansion* also are "the tall and ragged palms and pines fixed by that already fading explosion until the night breeze would toss and thresh them."[12] And although they know that their marriage is prohibited and that their love should be purely platonic, Stevens knows and understands that Linda wants to "marry" him. This is quite paradoxical, but the two proceed to realize the "marriage": at a hotel Linda arranges things so that

> Our rooms are next door with just the wall between and I had both beds moved against it so after we talk and are in bed any time during the night I can knock on the wall and you can hear it and if I hold my hand against the wall I can feel you answer.—I know, I wont knock loud enough to disturb anybody, for anybody to hear it except you.[13]

And they do exactly as Linda has prepared for the occasion.

This certainly is a parody of Tristan and Iseult, Pyramus and Thisbe, or Romeo and Juliet. It even possesses a little of the burlesque and the grotesque. But is that all? Paradoxically enough, that "courtly love" to which Cleanth Brooks refers in his chapter on *The Town* in *William Faulkner: The Yoknapatawpha Country*," introducing Denis de Rougemont's *Love in the Western World*,[14] seems here to be rather purified somehow or other through this very burlesque and grotesquerie and appeals to the reader unexpectedly from behind him, so to speak, or from the bottom of the grotesqueness itself. The pseudo-marriage that they celebrate seems to be a kind of incantatory ritual by which to evoke afresh the image of "pure love" in this mechanical, artificial, and impersonal world of modern civilization and of Snopesism.

And we should remember that this love between Linda and Gavin Stevens is itself a parodic repetition of the love between Eula and Gavin in *The Town*. So, inevitably, the later love affair has to become in its appearance more vulgar, or even more obscene than the earlier one, probably because the world in which Linda is left alone by the suicide of Eula, who was a kind of goddess of nature, is actually more vulgar and obscene than the world where Eula had a brief love affair with Hoake McCarron. Linda, who is deaf and has great difficulty in *human communication,* uses "four-letter words" in her "duck voice"[15] while courting Gavin Stevens. This is, indeed, the opposite of the old "courtly love," but by these very vulgar repetitions or self-parodies, Faulkner returns to that theme of eternity, "love," in this sordid world of the latter half of the twentieth century.

Not only that. Through such repetitions, as well as self-parodies, he seems to have returned at the same time to his earlier conception of human relationship, especially of "love," in this last period of his literary career. In their last rendezvous (this is after Stevens has actually married Melisandre Backus), Linda and Stevens once more repeat their gesture of love, and this time also they are on the brink of a physical intercourse. But of course they must inevitably refrain from it. Linda sympathizes with Stevens because he hasn't "had anything," because he has "had nothing"; that is, he has gotten physical satisfaction neither from Eula nor from Linda.

> He knew exactly what she meant: her mother first, then her; that he had offered the devotion twice and got back for it nothing but the privilege of being obsessed, bewitched, besotted if you like; Ratliff certainly would have said besotted. And she knew he knew it; that was (perhaps) their curse: they both knew any and every mutual thing immediately. . . .[16]

And Stevens, admitting that he has "just finished being accessory before a murder" (he is referring to the fact that he connived at Linda's helping Mink to shoot Flem to death through realizing a petition), insists that he has "everything" and they have had "everything."[17] This affirmation of love through the awareness of "curse" and "sin": is it not certainly a return, say, to the love of Quentin and Caddy in *The Sound and the Fury*? Not a simple return, to be sure, but a return after the novelist's career of life and writing since his early period. What the return draws upon flows from a broad and deep reservoir of the memory of "life in motion," from which may pour new and positive values and a reversal from the time past to the time present and future.

I am not speaking only of those novels I referred to so far but of the probable whole network of intertextual relationships in Faulkner's fiction. At its core, somewhere within its static structure, lies the motion of life. Thus with its circular or cyclical movement, the world of William Faulkner emerges as profound and dynamic, both temporally and spatially.

---

NOTES

1. *William Faulkner: Materials, Studies, and Criticism*, vol. 2, no. 1 (Tokyo: Nan'undo, December 1979), pp. 34–47.

2. William Faulkner, *The Hamlet* (New York: Random House, 1964), p. 140.

3. From the "Preface" to *The Mansion* (New York: Random House, 1959).

4. Jean-Paul Sartre, "A propos de *Le bruit et la fureur*. La temporalité chez Faulkner," *Situations* I (Paris: Gallimard, 1947), p. 71.

5. *The Wild Palms* (New York: Random House, 1939), p. 324.

6. Published first in *Harper's*, December 1935.

7. The short story, entitled "Snow," which was sent to Harold Ober, Faulkner's agent in 1942, had a variant of Quentin as narrator character, but the story may have been written quite early (in 1926) when Faulkner wrote "Mistral" (cf. "Notes" in Joseph Blotner, ed., *Uncollected Stories of William Faulkner* [New York: Random House, 1979], pp. 711–12).

8. Cf. Joanne V. Creighton, *William Faulkner's Craft of Revision: The Snopes Trilogy, "The Unvanquished" and "Go Down, Moses"* (Detroit, Michigan: Wayne State University Press, 1977), p. 146.

9. Malcolm Cowley, *The Faulkner-Cowley File: Letters and Memories, 1944–1962* (New York: The Viking Press, 1966), p. 44.

10. *Ibid.*, p. 44.

11. Robert W. Kirk, *Faulkner's People: A Complete Guide and Index to Characters in the Fiction of William Faulkner* (Berkeley & Los Angeles: University of California Press, 1963), pp. 157–77.

12. *The Mansion*, p. 248.

13. *Ibid.*, pp. 249–50.

14. Cleanth Brooks, *William Faulkner: The Yoknapatawpha Country* (New Haven & London: Yale University Press, 1963), pp. 196–201.

15. *The Mansion*, p. 238.

16. Pp. 424–25.

17. Pp. 425.

# A Polyphonic Insert:
## Charles's Letter to Judith[1]

## Olga Scherer

In an earlier Bakhtin-inspired study of Faulkner and Dostoyevsky, I tried to show that the apparent stability and immediate
intelligibility of information claimed by pieces of written evidence—such as newspaper articles, diaries, printed announce-
ments, engraved inscriptions, and, above all, personal letters—
deliberately signified as *put down on paper,* and so suggesting
immovable and lasting semantic values, necessarily lose their
"reliable" character in polyphonic fiction, where they invariably
slip into ambiguity as they undergo various processes of *reseman-
tization.* By focusing on Mr. Compson's letter, which informs
Quentin of Miss Coldfield's death—a document that I called the
*syntagmatic frame* of *Absalom, Absalom!*—I attempted to demonstrate how the destabilizing power of external interferences
made its message ambiguous. The single message of this would-
be document, refracted (partly contested, in fact) by the fully
competent voices of various protagonists, becomes as mobile and
unfinished as the relationship among all the connoted utterings
it absorbs.[2]

The doubt, eventually elaborated in *Absalom, Absalom!,* about a
document's reliability, which the first reading of the novel would
misleadingly make us accept, is perhaps even more clearly illustrated by Charles Bon's letter to Judith Sutpen.[3] The ensuing
dialogue between Charles and Judith, which actually never takes
place, brings out the complexity of the polylogue—i.e., of the
numerous, mutually overlapping messages that contest and miti-
gate each other—which the letter conveys. In other words,
Charles is not its only author, just as Mr. Compson is not the
only author of the letter to his son. Both letters are polylogical,
even though unlike Mr. Compson's written document, which

virtually *frames* the body of the novel, as its two parts are separated by over two hundred pages, Bon's letter *is framed* by the
body of the novel.

Using two different methods, the author thus achieves a similar effect: he upsets the semantic stability of a seemingly rigid
documentary truth. In both cases an apparently firm or valid
judgment turns out to be both inconclusive and not entirely
reliable. The only material vestige of the young hero's existence,
which, as such, carries a great deal of signified narrative weight,
is made entirely relative by a dense network of interferences its
body reveals and which emanate from other speakers, such as
Mr. Compson, his son, and even Miss Coldfield, but especially
from the addressee of the letter, Judith herself.

I shall not at present go into the intricate dialogical relationship established between Miss Rosa and Charles Bon, two
characters who, like Judith and Bon, have never met. Let me just
state that this relationship conclusively shows that what counts
for the meaning of a polyphonic text is not a series of relationships elaborated and *signified* on the basis of a plausible set of
realities, but on the contrary, that it is the plausibility of an
artistic vision which sets up these relationships as *signifiers* of the
realities. I shall concentrate on the coauthorship that Judith's
response posthumously supplies to Bon's statement and, second-
arily, on Mr Compson's contribution to the mysterious young
man's dialogical challenge; in the order of presentation, both
precede the challenge itself.

In his lengthy introductory comment about Bon's written leg-
acy, Mr. Compson insists on the utmost importance of its epic
and classically tragic aspects; its protagonists are deliberately
presented as giants, "larger, more heroic, not dwarfed and involved but distinct, uncomplex": they are for him dehumanized,
hyperbolized creatures, subject to elevation through myth. What
emerges in the end contradicts this epic dimension specifically,
though to be sure, this reservation is already present in Mr.
Compson's statement, since he also emphasizes, in his dialogically sensitive, hesitating way, the utterly fortuitous, if not altogether arbitrary, character of the only remaining letter among

what he suggests were many others written by Charles to Judith, most of them intercepted, read, and torn up by Henry. The letter's value as a trustworthy document is thus contested before we (and Quentin) ever learn its content. Torn out of a possibly larger epistolary context, it bears the mark not so much of either chance or tragic necessity, but rather that of ambiguity and incompleteness, which its graphic form itself will only confirm. The letter is neither dated nor signed, and it includes no salutations. Mr Compson's introduction, and in particular his comments on certain fragments of the letter, which he tears out of their context, makes of the document a meeting place of the heroic-epic, which belongs to the utopian character of the letter's ideological historical dimension, with the factual-psychological, which is justified by Charles's indirect acquaintance with Judith as with a representative of a social type: a young girl of a good family, possibly in love in a romantic way, but chiefly anxious to get married. And so, even before we know the content of the letter, we can distinctly recognize in it the simultaneous presence of two criss-crossing voices belonging to Charles, and a third, Mr. Compson's, which helps to bring them out.

The attempt to bestow prestige on the would-be heroic aspect of the event clashes with a counterattempt within the same text. Judith's subsequent tirade, as it emphasizes the part played by each of the voices it contains, sets the relatively small importance of the meanings fixed in written form against the colossal significance generated at the points of their intersection with her own words. By reversing the chronological order of the presentation of the two statements and so bringing Judith's reaction to the reader's knowledge first, the author enables us to notice that much of the girl's interpretation is already contained, by anticipation of its eventual formulation, in Bon's own document. In order to study the various stages of this operation, I have italicized them in Judith's statement. Her reply to Grandmother Compson is actually addressed to her dead fiancé, that silent listener, that invisible interlocutor—that other self perhaps—

whom Dostoyevsky has taught us to appreciate as one possessing the greatest contaminating *and* contesting capacity.[5]

Grandmother Compson, surprised by Judith's intention to entrust her with Charles's letter, asks the girl whether she expects her to keep it. As we read this passage, easily absorbing its immediate meanings (left-hand column), let us try to listen to the multiple connotations conveyed by the fragments that I am italicizing. Let us now give these connotations a reading (one of several possible ones) which would yield Faulkner's idea about his own polyphonic poetics (right-hand column):

" 'Yes,' Judith said. *'Or destroy it. As you like. Read it if you like or dont read it if you like.* Because you make so little impression, you see. You get born and you try this and you dont know why only you keep on trying it and *you are born at the same time with a lot of other people, all mixed up with them,* like trying to, having to, move your arms and legs with strings only the same strings are hitched to all the other arms and legs and the others all trying and they dont know why either except that *the strings are all in one another's way like five or six people all trying to make a rug on the same loom only each one wants to weave his own pattern into the rug; and it cant matter,* you know that, or the Ones that set up the loom would have arranged things a little better, and *yet it must matter* because you keep on trying or having to keep on trying *and then all of a sudden it's all over* and all you have left is a block of stone with scratches on it *provided there was someone to remember to have the mar-*

A word by itself is of no importance. Learning its content in this form would be a slim contribution to knowledge.

A character's voice is necessarily accompanied by other voices.

A text is fed by various discourses, which are neither complementary nor fused together, but most often in conflict.

Far from satisfying the characters committed to such a relationship, this contradictory state of affairs is nevertheless indispensable if we are to avoid undesirable finality and completeness.

Finality in the form of death is naturally inevitable, but in the realm of meaning it is only an illusion.

Someone somewhere will always remember a meaning provided the dead man's word is preserved.

*ble scratched* and set up or had time to, *and it rains on it and the sun*

*shines on it* and after a while *they dont even remember the name and what the scratches were trying to tell,*

*and it doesn't matter.* And so maybe

*if you could go to someone,* the stranger the better, *and give them some-*

*thing—a scrap of paper—something,*

*anything, it not to mean anything in itself and them not even to read it or keep it,* not even bother to throw it away or destroy it, at least it would be something just because it

would have happened, *be remembered even if only from passing from one hand to another, one mind to another,* and it would be at least a scratch, something, *something that might make a mark on something* that

*was* once for the reason that it can die someday, while the block of stone cant be *is* because it never

can become *was because it cant ever die or perish . . .'"*
(pp. 127–28)

Many situational contexts then introduce new codes, which will be used to graft new messages onto the original one.

The polylogue that follows may appear poorly fitted to a given set of realities, chiefly because of the temporal dispersion of its original participants.

But nothing is lost since reality cannot be defined by a single discourse produced by a single voice. The verbal heritage that is suggested here has a better chance of reproducing faithfully the ambiguity of the truth.

It is therefore necessary to engage someone else in a dialogue.

The text as such, a text free from interferences, is just a deaf and dumb thing and consequently remains insignificant. If such a text never came into existence, it would not make any difference.

It acquires significance only in contact with other people's replies.

By grafting itself on the denoted text, the connoted text engenders meaning.

Underlined by the author, the words *was, is, was,* show that Judith has learned Bon's dialogical lesson.

The deep nature of things always remains unfinished, incomplete.

It is in the light of this poetics that Bon's letter, which follows at last, will solicit our attention, making us at once distinguish a great number of overlapping voices, each fully endowed with authority, each questioning and at the same time contaminating the others, all simultaneously active and equally valid. Let us now examine at least a few instances of the letter's ceaseless shifts in the questioning and contaminating process.

The admittedly conventional opening of the letter sets an object of high quality against an object of low quality, an old one against a recently manufactured one, a ruined southern manorhouse against a northern factory:

| | | |
|---|---|---|
| *a sheet of notepaper with, as you can see, the best of French watermarks dated seventy years ago, salvaged (stolen if you will) from the gutted mansion of a ruined aristocrat;* | as opposed to | *and written upon in the best of stove polish manufactured not twelve months ago in a New England factory. Yes. Stove polish. We captured it: a story in itself.* (p. 129) |

The letter, to be sure, starts out as an avowedly dramatic dialogue. As such, it is by definition free from ambiguity and necessarily monological.

Yet, it promptly sets up an opposition between a salvaging or stealing action carried out by the old—an effect of actualized irony—and a capturing action of the new by the old. Since this pathetic capture will obviously not prevent the ultimate defeat, and Bon knows it, the effect of irony (a virtual one) releases, next to Bon's two already existing aspects (namely that of a character belonging to the southern world and that of a character who is able to regard that world with a sense of distance), still another position, that which expresses a man on his way to liberate himself of existing cultural constraints, just as the three-word cluster, "*a woman, lady or female,*" by ringing a familiar bell, brings back Mr. Compson's authority in its full, already dialogically tested form. We now discover that this all-encompassing definition of the Old South's feminine world—which Mr. Compson had several pages above somewhat sarcastically attributed not only to Henry, but to the whole society of southern gentlemen, whose ideology Mr. Compson partly shares and which includes at least one of Charles Bon's facets—had obviously been borrowed from Bon's letter.

At the same time we notice that Mr. Compson had introduced a significant modification in the consecutive order of the three components of the loan-phrase, which in his mouth had read: *ladies, women, females.* What we now take to be Mr. Compson's partly inaccurate quotation follows its original logic, the logic of Bon striving towards a world of social freedom. By setting *lady* discreetly in the middle, Bon deprives that category of the possible prestige implied by the priority Mr. Compson had given it in his modified version. One of the ideological positions voiced by Charles thus expresses disagreement with Mr. Compson's position, which, however, is at the same time contaminated by another of Bon's facets, that of the critical observer. In a polyphonic novel indeed, as Bakhtin points out, man never coincides with himself.

Furthermore, the two distinguishable sets of realities in crisis, one material and denoted, the other ideological and connoted, possess, by the time the first paragraph of the letter ends, enough referential stability for Charles to make the purely factual meaning, involving the preparation for the wedding, converge with the deeper, ideological meaning; he begins the second paragraph with the words: "We have waited long enough" (p. 131). And just because Judith's comments had by anticipation depolarized the would-be antithesis *past/present,* Charles, on the verge of submitting its terms to a contrasting analysis, will prefer to leave it open-ended by means of a characteristically Faulknerian parenthesis, which goes on for nearly a whole page. One of the functions of the parenthesis is to take us back to Bon's wartime context in which he actually wrote the letter; it begins with the words: "There. They have started firing again. . . ."

It is precisely in the subsequent part of the parenthesis that Bon's utopian challenge is born or at least comes to a verbal surface. For if his return is uncertain (the first sentence following the parenthesis reads: "I cannot say when to expect me"), it is not so because the past is dead: Charles knew before opening the parenthesis that the past had been dead ever since the beginning of the hostilities. Nor is it so for practical reasons, such as being wounded on the battlefield. The parenthesis will have served as a tool to reshuffle the relationship between WAS and IS, which ultimately becomes a curiously inconclusive one. The pseudo-causal series of clauses beginning with the word *because* within Judith's statement is now taken up following her own syntactic pattern (*because . . . because . . .* in one sentence) and breaks away from its original direction, i.e., the one it had taken prior to the opening of the parenthesis:

> *Because I cannot say when to expect me. Because what* WAS *is one thing, and now it is not because it is dead, it died in 1861, and therefore what* IS——(*There. They have started firing again. . . .) I cannot say when to expect me. Because what* IS *is something else again because it was not even alive then. And since because within this sheet of paper you now hold the best of the old South which is dead, and the words you read were written upon it with the best (each box said, the very best) of the new North which has conquered and which therefore, whether it likes it or not, will have to survive, I now believe that you and I are, strangely enough, included among those who are doomed to live. (pp. 131–32, emphasis mine).*

With *therefore what* IS becoming *because what* IS, cause and effect are inverted, and Bon's last sentence acquires a vestige of Judith's general idea of survival.

In a monological novel we might have expected victory in defeat—for instance, the victory of Bon's utopian idea in the defeat of the values set down by a community or even in his own material defeat. If Faulkner's dialogical hero falls short of any triumph, it is so on the surface chiefly because he remains, as he says within the parenthesis, "still immersed and obviously bemused in recollections of old peace and contentment the very names of whose accents and sounds I do not know that I remember" (p. 131). Bon, the cool observer, comes close to Bon, the southern gentleman, but being exhausted by the war and (at least according to Mr. Compson) lazy by nature, he attempts to push away the new idea of social freedom, which the apocalyptic reality releases in this philosophically-minded fatalist. Hope becomes even more vague, as a possible "fourth" voice of Bon is heard at the intersections of the other three—a voice rejecting all social classification, transcending all the historically determined notions of freedom. Could it be the author's voice, telling us that nobody knows, unless it is the dialogical hero himself, whether his unacceptability stems from bigamy alone, from bigamy and incest, or from racial impurity to which bigamy and incest have merely been added? If the hero knows the answer, he will keep the secret from all, even from the author.

All we know after having read his letter is that, on the one hand, he admits the active presence of the past in the present and that, on the other hand, he is reluctant to negate, or to confirm, the contrary (i.e., the presence of the present in the past) for fear of resolving the WAS in his consciousness. If this kind of negation or confirmation on his part had not already been contested by Judith—who, so to speak, corrects the possible error he might commit by yielding to such a temptation, as she states that only a future fed by the past can revive a dead meaning—the novel would have verged on the monophonic genre, with Bon's last word about himself acquiring the value of the author's word. Such a composition would necessarily have re-created a finished hero, a hero closed in by a finished idea. Taking up his word, Judith salvages the hero's hesitation, possibly his secret knowledge. It is in fact she who, by recuperating the overlapping zones of her fiancé's different facets, makes it possible for him to speak chiefly through those zones.

As for Faulkner, he achieves this feat without having recourse to denotation. The ambiguous idea is conveyed almost entirely through a signifier, which is probably the noblest principle active in the dialogical way of narrative life.

---

NOTES

1. This study was prompted by Mikhail Bakhtin's dialogue theory as applied to narrative fiction and developed in his work *Problems of Dostoyevsky's Poetics* (1929/1962, translated by R. W. Rotsel, Ann Arbor: Ardis, 1973). I borrow such notions as *polyphony, dialogism, unfinished character, refracted discourse, overlapping utterances*, directly from Bakhtin. As for the word *polylogue*, it was coined by analogy with *dialogue* in Bakhtinian usage, by Iuri Lotman ("Znakovyi mekhanizm kul'tury" in *Semeyotikhe. Sbornik statei po vtorichnym modeliruyushchim sistemam*, Tartu, 1973, p. 198).

2. "La contestation du jugement sur pièces chez Dostoïevski et Faulkner", *Delta*, 3 (1976), pp. 47–62.

3. This apparently stable and trustworthy second piece of written evidence in Faulkner's novel is reminiscent of Mrs. Raskolnikov's letter informing her son of his sister's "scandalous" engagement project in that it similarly challenges the addressee by soliciting her response to her correspondent's potentially existing doubts about his own statements.

4. William Faulkner, *Absalom, Absalom!* (New York: Random House, 1936), p. 89.

5. Let us, for instance, consider, in Ivan Karamazov's story of the Grand Inquisitor, the powerful verbal presence that emanates from the perfectly silent Christ whose words—those actually recorded in the Gospels, as well as other possible ones—His interlocutor Torquemada integrates, as independent and fully authoritative utterings, into his own discourse. Something similar, and even more polyphonic, happens to Tikhon's ideas in the text of Stavrogin's written confession, as the old clergyman reads it and comments upon it while facing its author's silent presence in the controversial chapter "At Tikhon's" *(The Possessed)*. The famous missing page is not—as might be surmised—alone responsible for the plurality of overlapping meanings present in the confession, although it certainly has a share in their operations.

# Searching for Jason Richmond Compson: a Question of Echolalia and a Problem of Palimpsest

## Patrick Samway, S.J.

"ergo age, care pater, cervici imponere nostrae; ipse subibo umeris nec me labor iste gravabit; quo res cumque cadent, unum et commune periculum, una salus ambobus erit."

*(Aeneid,* 11, 707–10)

"TO A FATHER BY A SON"
(Inscription on the Anderson Bridge, Cambridge, Mass.)

For centuries, scripture scholars and dogmatic theologians have had to cope with the problems created by the large-scale diversity of letters, gospels, and narrative accounts that proclaim the "good news" of Jesus of Nazareth. Because of the fragmentary nature of many early papyrus manuscripts, scholars have created vast genealogical trees whose spreading branches testify to an overwhelming desire: to understand Jesus, the culture of his day, and the message(s) he preached.[1] Certain segments of these scriptural texts, or pericopes, show that the oral narrations upon which they were based were widely shared, while others were circulated only within limited groups. Of the total number of verses in the synoptic gospels (Matthew 1070, Mark 677, Luke 1150), approximately one third of Matthew's gospel, one tenth of Mark's and one half of Luke's contain material unique to these three redactors; the rest consists of shared material. Were one to consider the possible variants (the narrative material that Matthew and Mark or Matthew and Luke have in common, for example), then the solution becomes more complicated; explanations and descriptions of the life and times of Jesus depend to a great extent upon the number of manuscripts and texts studied, keeping in mind that each presents a congeries of semantic, historical, theological, structural, and thematic problems. Athanasius and Augustine, Bultmann and Bornkamm,

178

Cullmann and Conselmann, and countless others, have developed methodologies which, through an intricate, though unprogrammed, series of checks and balances, allow the cumulative wisdom of archaeology, history, linguistics, literature, and theology to have full play in the exegetical process; above all, these scholars attempt to understand the formation of these theological texts so that the stories and sayings of Jesus, and the narrative accounts and letters about him, can be interpreted in ways that respect both the faithful experience of the early followers and the developing experience of believing Christians today.

With the exception of Chaucer, Shakespeare, Milton, Joyce, and perhaps Faulkner, no writer in the English literary tradition, it seems to me, offers the critic the multiplicity of problems faced by scripture scholars. From one perspective, scripture scholars are literary critics as they account for the dramatic tension, understatement, structure, and calculated ambiguity that are part of the very fabric of the parables and sayings of Jesus. They must avoid the tendency to turn a story into a religious maxim; rather, their task is to assist the reader in appreciating the fullness of the story, relating it both to imagery and stories in the Old Testament and to Near Eastern mythology whenever necessary. Likewise, these scholars must refrain, contrary to the wishes of many pious churchgoers, from harmonizing in a too-facile manner the four gospels and twenty-one letters of the New Testament, thereby presenting a Jesus whose biography, like his robe, lacks unsightly seams and whose theological views show logical and systematized development, even when the texts might indicate otherwise.[2] Heretical as it may seem, there is no one way, the same for all, of looking at Jesus of Nazareth: we peer alternately through both ends of the binoculars, locating the configurations on the horizon, pausing here and there to observe specific scenes, which undergo subtle changes as we move from text to text. Or fixed on certain passages, which we sometimes consider proof-texts to pinpoint what is essential to Christianity, we forget the sweep and flow of the Old and New Testaments, the confluence of many rabbinical and literary currents, as we try to articulate something whose meaning is inferential and related to many divergent sources.

It could readily be argued that searching for Jason Richmond Compson, like searching for Jesus of Nazareth, need not be undertaken; Mr. Compson is definitely present in "That Evening Sun," *The Sound and the Fury*, and *Absalom, Absalom!*, and only the obtuse reader would not feel his palpable, overwhelming presence in these three texts. The Compson Appendix, for example, graphically portrays him sitting all day under the portico of the Compson house drinking his whiskey from a decanter and composing, perhaps in the manner of Horace, Livy, or Catullus, caustic and satiric eulogies about Jefferson's living and dead. Yet, this portrait, one among many in a gallery of Compson failures, is impressionistic and sketchy and not completely consistent with other views we have of him, though admittedly it does not contradict these other views. The first three sections of *The Sound and the Fury* dramatically portray the last surviving males in the Compson family who deal, one way or another, with Caddy, whose portrait, like Picasso's attempts at three-dimensional painting, is created by the various features each of the brothers gives her. More central to our understanding of Mr. Compson, however, is to realize that wherever Quentin is, his father is close by; only through Quentin's eyes and ears do we perceive Mr. Compson with any degree of clarity. As father, Mr. Compson is the natural one Quentin turns to for advice and for an understanding of the history of Jefferson and Yoknapatawpha. Yet, as André Bleikasten and others who have studied *The Sound and the Fury* point out, Quentin hears his father offering a wisdom rooted in death, cynicism, and nihilism concerning degrading relationships between women and sex.[3] The question inevitably arises, since so much of our understanding of Mr. Compson comes through Quentin: did Quentin fabricate his father's views, did he create a personal cacodemon, a ghostly dybbuk, or are we warranted in believing that we can depict, discern, and describe a figure from whom these words emerge?

During his peripatetic wanderings on June 2, 1910, Quentin

encounters three boys enjoying an edenic pastime of trying to catch a large trout that has been avoiding capture for a quarter of a century. While the boys talk about the reward for capturing this illusive treasure, Quentin characteristically withdraws into the inner reaches of his mind and ponders the discussion he overhears: "They all talked at once, their voices insistent and contradictory and impatient, making of unreality a possibility, then a probability, then an incontrovertible fact, as people will when their desires become words."[4] This reflection paradigmatically embodies Quentin's confused state in *The Sound and the Fury:* the chorus of voices, past and present, as exemplified particularly in the sequence of interior and exterior events that occur during the car ride with Gerald, Mrs. Bland, Spoade, and the Misses Daingerfield and Holmes, create repetitious analogues, which ultimately trap Quentin to such an extent that he can only extricate himself—and stop these voices—by committing suicide. He seems incapable of halting his progress from unreality (Caddy not pregnant) to fact (Caddy pregnant), from reliving past events and conversations which lead to the decision to take his own life.

Yet Faulkner, at least in one other story, saw Quentin in quite a different light. Though Quentin narrates "Lion" and "A Justice," as well as "A Bear Hunt," "The Old People," and "Fool About a Horse," his narration of "That Evening Sun" is the first time he incorporates his father into one of his narrations.[5] This story exhibits almost perfect recall of the conversations Quentin heard or took part in; though twenty-four at the time when he narrates the story, Quentin assumes the posture of a nine-year-old and keeps the perspective from that point of view. Since Quentin was either nineteen or twenty when he committed suicide in *The Sound and the Fury,* it could be argued that Faulkner, at this point in his writing career, had no intention of developing Quentin as the type of young man we find in the two later novels.[6] Neither Caddy's virginity, nor incessant thoughts of suicide, nor the confusion caused by obsessive inner voices, are alluded to; rather Quentin artistically creates an atmosphere of fear and terror as he relates matter-of-factly the story of

Nancy dreading the return of Jesus, her common-law husband.[7]
During the course of this story, Mr. Compson tells his sickly wife
with a tinge of premeditated sarcasm that he will accompany
Nancy and the Compson children to Nancy's cabin; his walk to
the cabin symbolically represents the journey of a man who
brings his children to the threshold of a potentially evil world,
one they could not at this point understand. Though he does not
abandon his three children (Benjy is not mentioned), Mr. Compson
son does not give them the necessary attitudes and information
to cope adequately with this particular situation. Quentin believes
lieves that his mother thought "all day father had been trying to
think of doing the thing she [Mrs. Compson] wouldn't like the
most, and that she knew all the time that after a while he would
think of it."[8] Yet when questioned by his wife why he would leave
the children unprotected with her in the house, he replies:
"What would he [Jesus] do with them, if he were unfortunate
enough to have them?" (p. 294). Caddy, however, perceives the
real danger and perspicaciously asks two parallel questions,
neither of which is answered: "Why is Nancy afraid of Jesus?"
and "Are you afraid of father, mother?" (p. 299). During one of
their trips to Nancy's cabin, Caddy remarks that Nancy compensates
sates for the anxiety she experiences and defends herself by
constantly speaking with the children and attempting to engage
them in play. Though Caddy penetrates Nancy's ruse, she can
offer no more real comfort than her father can when he says
that Nancy's fears are unfounded—a comment that shows his
utter lack of sympathy for her plight. Mr. Compson's final words
to Nancy are that she lock the door, put out the lamp, and go to
bed; in a more confused way, Benjy and Quentin hear the same
words at the end of their respective sections in *The Sound and the
Fury*. As narrator, Quentin observes his father carefully, and
though he does not single him out for special consideration, he
does remark that as they walked back to the main house that
against the sky it "looked like father had two heads, a little one
and a big one" (p. 309), an undeveloped image foreshadowing a
dichotomy found later in *Absalom, Absalom!:* "Then hearing
would reconcile and he [Shreve?] would seem to listen to two

separate Quentins now—the Quentin Compson preparing for Harvard in the South . . . and the Quentin Compson who was still too young to deserve yet to be a ghost. . . ."[9] Perhaps this double-headed image enigmatically reveals the relationship Faulkner thought Quentin might have with his father, who, in *Absalom, Absalom!,* is later identified with Shreve. Does Mr. Compson become in some way for Quentin a two-headed monster without any discernible body, a Hydra who, when one of its heads is cut off, finds it replaced by two others?

In all, Mr. Compson in "That Evening Sun" helps no one—neither Nancy, nor his wife, nor the three children. The key questions concerning infidelity and revenge are posed by Caddy, and because of Mr. Compson's abdication of his parental obligations, Caddy does not profit from the guidance her father could have given her. We cannot even say that the words written in the story and attributed to Mr. Compson are actually, to use scriptural methodology and terminology, his *ipsissima verba;* the evidence is just the opposite since the story is told fifteen years after the events took place. What is achieved in this story, to shift the problematic from the "real" to the realm of the "possible," is the illusion that Mr. Compson has a type of existence we can assent to, based not on the verifiable data (the writings of Josephus give a type of extra-biblical evidence helpful to biblical scholars), but upon the power of the human imagination to create characters who act and speak like people we know in everyday situations. Quentin, as narrator, speaks words that Faulkner, as author, "ad-scribes" to Mr. Compson, words that seem to be the ones he might have spoken, ones appropriate to the character Quentin dramatically is trying to present. Ironically, the more faithful Quentin is to the mimetic voice he employs, the less we plumb the inner depths and motivations of the characters involved. Mimesis accentuates the external, the observable, the sequential nature of a story, whereas that other voice, which does not appear to simulate normal speech, but searches out the cerebral core of thought and speech, the constitutive voice, if you will, focuses on ideas and language before they have been organized into logical and rational patterns.

As we move from the mimetic voice in "That Evening Sun" to the constitutive voice of Quentin in *The Sound and the Fury,* we find ourselves in a linguistic environment akin to poetry, where, through distortion, dislocation, hyperbole, suffused images, and metaphors, we push the nature of language and the ability to communicate and understand to undelineated boundaries where words take on new vitality, weight, and shape precisely because they could disappear and fail to communicate should they fall off the brink and disappear into the void. Unlike "That Evening Sun," the more we search for Mr. Compson in *The Sound and the Fury,* the more difficult it is to locate him with any precision. Are the words Quentin employs in recounting the words his father speaks in this novel to be attributed fully to Mr. Compson or only partially? To what degree can we make any sort of evaluation like this since father and son are inextricably linked? How do we deal with the problem of echolalia in this novel? Quentin's voice in this novel, André Bleikasten asserts, comes out of nowhere; it is nobody's voice: "Deciphering it is no easy matter, yet, reading and rereading it, we eventually make out the pattern of a trajectory, tortuous, shadowy, paradoxical, headed for death, and we also come to see where and when this lethal course begins."[10] Surprisingly, if there is any initial point of contact between "That Evening Sun" and *The Sound and the Fury* in searching for a discernible Mr. Compson, it occurs not in the Quentin section but in the Benjy section. Among other events and situations important to him, Benjy remembers the time when Caddy, Jason, Quentin, and Versh were down at the branch and then were summoned back to the main house where Damuddy's wake was in progress, a definite reversal of the Nancy episode in "That Evening Sun." In the branch scene and others, Benjy is not unaware of his father and occasionally gives us glimpses of him. Once, after Benjy's name change, when Mrs. Compson insists that her side of the family was as good as the Compson side, and that Uncle Maury suffers from bad health, Mr. Compson replies: "Bad health is the primary reason for all life. Created by disease, within putrefaction, into decay."[11] These words recorded by Benjy, the idiot, provide initially the key for analyzing Mr. Compson in the Quentin section. As an idiot, the ideal who absorbs his surroundings into himself directly and with no conscious effort, Benjy could not have either initiated this type of thinking nor chosen and structured this type of vocabulary. Though there is a likelihood that Benjy might have overheard Mr. Compson speak these words to Quentin when Quentin returned home for Christmas in 1909 from Harvard (and subsequently associated them with Uncle Maury's sickness), it is more likely, I believe, that he recalls them and places them in their original context since they fit this context.

These sixteen words (all *ipsissima verba,* since Benjy repeats them exactly as he heard them) give the first indication that the ideas and language purported to be Mr. Compson's do originate with him, though not necessarily, I would claim, in the exact linguistic and semantic patterns Quentin employs. In a revery in which Quentin quotes and refers to his father, he too uses the word "putrefaction" (thus this word is used only twice in the entire novel, both times in a context of death):

> Because women so delicate so mysterious Father said. Delicate equilibrium* of periodical* filth* between two moons balanced. Moons he said full and yellow as harvest moons her hips thighs. Outside outside of them always but. Yellow. Feet soles with walking like. Then know that some man that all those mysterious and imperious concealed. With all that inside of them shapes an outward suavity waiting for a touch to. Liquid *putrefaction* like drowned things floating like pale rubber flabbily filled getting the odour of honeysuckle all mixed up. (p. 159, emphasis mine)[12]

In general, Quentin's rendition of his father's views, while not in conflict with those of Mr. Compson as recorded by Benjy, blend together many more factors, suggesting that these words/ideas were not spoken at a specific time, but were selectively fused by Quentin after any number of conversations with his father. Irena Kaluza, in her fine study of the sentence structure in the stream-of-consciousness techniques in *The Sound and the Fury* notes that the memory and reflection idiom, and she uses the

Mr. Compson-Quentin relationship, is characterized by unorthodox and inconsistent punctuation and printing devices, which cannot be used as formal criteria in grammatical classification. Likewise, the change in typeface is of little help because it marks only a shift in the time of the experience in question. Using unequal syntactic, lexical, morphological, and phonemic devices, Faulkner spins out interlocking repetitious patterns that have a tendency to create new structures of the same nature, which ultimately produce a mental process that is continuous, unceasing, persistent, associative, and sometimes downright circular. Form and content so blend in the Mr. Compson-Quentin dialogues as to make these distinctions relatively minor; the syntactic units are vague and ambiguous, though Quentin is careful to use pronouns throughout which demarcate the dialogue and set up signals for the internal dialogue.[13] Thus, by analyzing Mr. Compson's vocabulary (and not the sentence structure), it is possible to determine the words that only he uses which occur as hapax legomena in this novel. And precisely because of the distinctive nature of this vocabulary used only by Mr. Compson, Quentin, in *The Sound and the Fury,* with the recall he displayed in "That Evening Sun," shares directly with the reader his father's words, thus showing that Mr. Compson's voice is ultimately different from Quentin's and has its own originating source. As in *Hamlet,* we are dealing with a father's voice from the past, which now commands the death of the usurper, in this case Quentin himself. Tragically, the father's voice cannot respond to new questions, and so the conversation, like a scratched and warped record, repeats itself.

Fatherhood can be considered not only a physical act that generates, nourishes, and supports, but a voice that summons, instructs, and counsels, until it drifts off asymptotically to become a memory once the child has found his own words and mode of existence, commensurate with the past and suitable to react to the vagaries of the future. The second section of *The Sound and the Fury* begins and ends in a cyclical fashion with a conversation between Quentin and his father. In a surrealistic

mode, the watch Quentin receives from his father is transformed into a mausoleum, a final resting place for the dead
members of the Compson family; this watch is meant to reduce
human experience to its most absurd dimensions: the void, the
lack of significance in life, death. With such morbid defeatism,
Mr. Compson hopes that Quentin might forget the minute progression of time and thus not try to conquer that which is beyond conquering. Relying on military imagery, Mr. Compson
marshals forth empty words and images dreamt up by the master controllers of language, those philosophers and fools who, in
his opinion, are one and the same: "conquer," "battle," "won,"
"fought," "[battle]field," "victory." The pervasive notion of
"death" is not mentioned; it is the absent word, the unspeakable
void, the ineffable vortex which beckons and which must inhabit
the mausoleum and give it its purpose and meaning. Quentin
must supply this word, and then experience its meaning; in
doing so, he will rest with his ancestors who have profited no
more from life's experiences than he will have.

Quentin identifies his anxiety with the sense of loss Jesus must
have felt; such an identification is made by the shifting of tiny
gears whose synchronizing motion transposes him from one
realm of experience to another. On the other hand, according to
Mr. Compson, Jesus' passion and crucifixion had little or nothing to do with redeeming sinners from their wretched condition,
something that might have been a source of hope for Quentin
had it been otherwise. Rather, Jesus, like Quentin, was exhausted by the passing of time as signified in the "clicking of
little wheels" (p. 94). The watch, a real and symbolic talisman,
becomes the object associated with Mr. Compson as the instrument of the death he wishes for his son. Quentin, unlike the
Corporal in *A Fable,* is not given a choice by his father; rather,
his father becomes a type of executioner unparalleled in the
history of American literature. The "arbitrary dial" (p. 94) of the
watch (Quentin is exhorted not to speculate about the position
of the hands on the dial) links the beginning and end of Quentin's last conversation with his father: "every man is the arbiter

of his own virtues" (p. 219), and "every man is the arbiter of his own virtues" (p. 221). Time is not fair and will take one when one least expects it.[14]

With the same intense emotion that the Tall Convict felt at the end of "Old Man" when he exclaimed "Women—!", Quentin, upgrading his father's language, utters in disgust "Excrement" (p. 94), thus providing a *sforzando* to the transition from time to sordidness to women. When Quentin finally summons up the nerve to play his last card and to confess to incest, Mr. Compson trumps him: ". . . men invented virginity not women" (p. 96). Virginity, the pure, undefiled, uncompromising condition, is like death. The trajectory of Mr. Compson's psyche becomes clear: time, defeat, women, sordidness, virginity, death. What is so sad is that "nothing is even worth the changing of it" (p. 96); the only possible pattern for life is to backloop, the unceasing repetition of what has already been spoken. Lending credence to the verisimilar quality of this conversation is the manner in which Mr. Compson repeats three times the word "dreadful" (p. 98), a word he first hears from Quentin; this indicates that at this point in the conversation there is a certain amount of give-and-play. Mr. Compson believes that yesterday passes into today and prefigures tomorrow, yet human beings cannot remember tomorrow what they considered dreadful today. Unlike men, women in Mr. Compson's estimation are attracted to evil, and where it is lacking, they supply it: they surround themselves with it and even absorb it into themselves, like sleep, the quintessential image of death. Against this denigrating view of womanhood, there is no defense because men and women exist in separate realms. Even when considered a composite, they are the sum of their misfortunes: "Man the sum of what have you. A problem in impure* properties carried tediously* to an unvarying* nil*: stalemate* of dust and desire" (p. 153). Through linguistic sorcery Mr. Compson keeps Quentin suspended in a cynical state of mind in which nature and virginity are not seen as being natural to the human condition. Mr. Compson creates a mental prostitute, where the mysterious delicacy of the sexual organs achieve a monthly equilibrium which Quentin cannot

emotionally cope with, even through language. He remains passive before this type of feminity which, having no face or
warmth, becomes the antithesis to the Caddy he so fantasizes
about. His father's concoction of a woman as a toxic mixture of
bodily fluids which animals find attractive supplants finally
Quentin's image of Caddy, one that loses human definition and
unfortunately becomes a mere pronoun which father and son
bandy about.

In his final revery, Quentin goes limp before the onslaught of
Mr. Compson's driving barrage of words, which when added up,
are a clarion call for suicide. Supposedly as a college student
Quentin is responsible for his actions, but given his mental condition—suicidal people do not act normally—it could be said
that his father's views created an environment whereby the only
genuine response would be self-imposed death. Mr. Compson
insists that each person creates his own virtues—and courage is
what you make of it; death in Quentin's case is not a disvalue or a
passing from one state to another, but a "virtue" and the coura-
geous man is not afraid of it. Quentin's father takes his son very
seriously because he knows Quentin has the inner courage of
confessing that he committed incest; he perceives Quentin's tormented logic and knows too how his mind can make the
transpositions from folly to horror to truth. Mr. Compson tells
Quentin that he is blind to the nature of his condition: "you are
contemplating an apotheosis in which a temporary state of mind
will become symmetrical above the flesh . . ." (p. 220). Repeating
the word "temporary" four times, as a head-bobbing refrain
which through the power of association transports us back to the
images of the watch and mausoleum in the first conversation
Quentin had with his father, Quentin realizes that his limited,
finite condition can only be halted by going out of his body in an
ecstatic, exalted state, where he would be himself and not himself, and thus beyond his present predicament. With wily, in-
sinuating language Mr. Compson circles around "it," thus re-
moving the sting from this word and giving Quentin the ghastly
freedom of naming "death" for himself. Death has nothing to do
with growing old, in Mr. Compson's mind, or being changed

into a white-haired, elderly gentleman; instead, death involves risk and decisive action. One does not commit suicide at the first experience of disgust or disappointment even when one senses that the Other, the diceman, is indifferent to how one feels. Life's experiences, including love and sorrow, have a finality built into them which must be respected and accepted. The golden clasp to Mr. Compson's nihilistic string of comments is to suggest that even Caddy was not worth the anguish and despair Quentin suffers. What more need be said? Not only does Mr. Compson refer to "floating" (p. 221) (image associated with death), but he instructs Quentin to go to Cambridge (the place of his death), and not disappoint a lady, obviously his mother, but by extension his sister (motive for death). Words have rendered the death-experience acceptable; the father has led the son to the brink of death and prepared a mausoleum for him to rest in with his ancestors, spectres who lingered in Faulkner's mind until they were finally included in the Compson Appendix. Death has been talked about, analyzed, probed, and rendered harmless; Quentin's suicide is not an irrational act because he understood and followed the suggestions of the authoritative voice of his father. Though Quentin might be considered Hamlet purging Denmark of its rottenness, he is actually Ophelia drowning out the inner, constitutive voices of the romantic past which prevent any future growth in love.

Like the father of Captain Paul Morache in the screenplay, *Road to Glory*, which Faulkner worked on with Joel Sayre in late 1935 or early 1936, Mr. Compson leads his son off camera.[15] In the final shots of the screenplay, we see two men at the head of the fifth company: an old man leading his blind son. Replacements march forward to continue the war with the Germans. One of the other characters, Lieutenant Delaage, had previously said that this company would receive a decoration at the death of the father and son, thus inferring, as in a Greek tragedy, that their deaths will take place off stage as, in fact, they do in *The Sound and the Fury*. Quentin reminds us of the type of person Harold Bloom is thinking about when he says that a poet (even *un poète manqué?*) is not speaking to others so much as he is rebelling against being spoken to by a dead man, the precursor who is outrageously more alive than he is. "A poet dare not regard himself as being *late,* yet cannot accept a substitute for the first vision he reflectively judges to have been his precursor's also. Perhaps this is why the poet-in-a-poet *cannot marry,* whatever the person-in-poet chooses to have done."[16] Though the last scene of *The Sound and the Fury* portrays Benjy and Luster on their way to the cemetery to visit Quentin's and Mr. Compson's graves, Faulkner did not let either the unmarried Quentin or his father rest in peace.

Unlike the Snopes clan in the Snopes trilogy which took over twenty years to write and see through the press, and which *as a trilogy* has a certain linear, expected, chronological progression, Mr. Compson and Quentin in *Absalom, Absalom!* are presented to us as a second moment of reflection on *The Sound and the Fury* (or third if one counts "That Evening Sun"). Albert Guerard insists that we are dealing with two different Quentins in these two novels:

> The actual connections [between the two novels] come down, very nearly, to a home town, a father, a freshman year at Harvard; and, briefly, Luster. *The Sound and the Fury* and *Absalom, Absaslom!* are (like *Heart of Darkness* and *Lord Jim*) great autonomous novels, not two fragments of a *roman-fleuve* or a Balzacian series, and our feelings for one Quentin should not control our feelings for the other."[17]

Estella Schoenberg, on the other hand, is quite willing to connect the two novels: "Neither Quentin's sister nor his suicide is mentioned in *Absalom, Absalom!* but they are both so important to the novel . . . Faulkner must have assumed that his readers would know the earlier novel and that the images would be as evocative for them as for Quentin."[18] Faulkner himself talked about Quentin as a consistent character: "To me he's consistent. . . . Quentin was still trying to get God to tell him why, in *Absalom, Absalom!* as he was in *The Sound and the Fury*."[19] A third critic, John T. Irwin, who has written an intriguing book relating *The Sound and the Fury* and *Absalom, Absalom!,* assumes that we are dealing with the same Quentin in both instances. As a consequence of such a view, each novel can be read as a chapter in a psychological textbook (mostly Freudian); and when both novels are analyzed together, we have a total picture of the case studies under observation.[20] Granted that Faulkner understood his characters better as he thought and wrote about them, we create, in my opinion, two imaginary, pseudo-intertexts by assuming that a true and undifferentiated harmony exists between these two novels:

*The Sound and the Fury*—(Intertext 1)—*Absalom, Absalom!*
*Absalom, Absalom!*—(Intertext 2)—*The Sound and the Fury*

The supposition of the first intertext argues that Faulkner went back and, relying on the storytelling techniques of the "Don and I" stories, created the multiple narrators in *Absalom, Absalom!*, especially Shreve and Quentin, not only to portray the history of the South in larger terms than those provided by the Compsons in *The Sound and the Fury*, but to explore and extend narrative techniques. Quentin listens to his father and Miss Rosa as they tell what they know and think about Thomas Sutpen and his family, and then Shreve continues on his own, with occasional comments by Quentin to probe a central issue in the novel: why Henry shot Charles Bon. What Quentin hears and discusses, particularly in terms of the discussion of incest and imagination, is responded to by Shreve, who has no immediate ties with the South and who, through leaps of logic and fancy, fabricates a lawyer in New Orleans to provide a causal link between Bon and Henry. The supposition of the first intertext sees the Henry-Charles-Judith love relationship as a modification of the Quentin-Dalton Ames-Caddy relationship, even though neither Ames nor Caddy is mentioned in *Absalom, Absalom!* By abandoning the structure of both novels and creating an oscillating third text, which is conceived of as a composite of the two novels Faulkner did write, Irwin has created a curious, but dubious methodology:

To speak to the *elements* of the structure is simply to speak of various limited perspectives of the whole, and to say that this structure in Faulkner's works is intertextual and its meaning interstitial is simply to evoke the effort to see the structure from all of its various perspectives at once, to see the structure as epistemologically created by the simultaneous interaction of all its individual limited perspectives, its *elements*. And it is precisely the impossibility of seeing the structure from all sides at once that allows us to take a further step, allows us to see why structures are always virtual, always *to-be-known*, or more exactly, always *to-be-inferred*. (p. 6)

To put it another way, Irwin maintains that the structure of the text(s) was deferred to some never-to-exist future "as if the structure is both before and after without ever having been here and now" (p. 9). Irwin opts for an unidentified intertext that is the fusion of both novels since the structure he discusses resides neither in one nor the other, nor even in the cumulative effect of both: it exists, rather, in the imaginative space that the novel creates *in between* themselves by their interaction. And the only way to assess critically his intertext is to solve the simultaneous equation that unites these two texts. What Irwin forgets is that there are real intertexts between these two novels: *As I Lay Dying, Sanctuary, Light in August, Pylon,* plus more than fifty short stories published between 1929 and 1936.

To omit these tangible intertexts from a discussion of the relationship between *The Sound and the Fury* and *Absalom, Absalom!* is to deny effectively the growth that Faulkner experienced during this time period in which he prepared himself to write *Absalom, Absalom!* Yet, common sense would tell us that a study of both novels demands multiple readings of both texts; this does not necessarily mean, *eo ipso*, our critical analysis should follow the sequence which we pick up and read these two novels. Michael Millgate has made the following helpful observation:

Whether it is useful, or critically permissible, to work backwards in Faulkner's career is another question. I have never, for example, found it very illuminating to think of *Absalom* as fitted into the temporal framework of *The Sound and the Fury,* to try to feed into Quentin's act of suicide the supplemental motivation that might be reckoned to flow from his recent exposure to the final stages of the Sutpen tragedy. Given that he wanted to use Quentin in *Absalom,* Faulkner in order to avoid absurdity had to place the Harvard portions within Quentin's lifetime as already established by *The Sound and the Fury,* but the ghost of *Absalom* seems simply not to be there in *The Sound and the Fury,* even if the earlier novel cannot help but be a shadowy presence on the sidelines of the later. . . . It seems to me, then, that each Faulkner text must be considered a unique, independent, and self-sufficient work of art, not only capable of being read and contemplated in isolation but actually demanding such treatment.[21]

Would that the opposing views of Irwin and Millgate—the first seeks a radical fusion of the two novels while the second opts for a deliberate separation—could be harmonized. The human imagination cannot deny what it has read and absorbed, and thus, Millgate's views, while ideally desirable, are almost impossible to maintain in terms of a practical, comprehensive approach to Faulkner's works. The second intertext proposed above allows our knowledge of Quentin, acquired from initial readings of the *The Sound and the Fury* and *Absalom, Absalom!,* to be used for a third (or fourth?) moment of reflection on *The Sound and the Fury* where the Caddy-Quentin relationship changes considerably in light of the discussions of incest/miscegenation in *Absalom, Absalom!* For Irwin, these two intertexts are really one, since they can be read backwards or forwards to support the type of clinical analysis he wants undertaken. What is lacking in Irwin's methodology is a normal reckoning of the distinctions that should be made if these two novels, as Millgate infers, are to have any structural integrity at all. As in scriptural studies, the critical methodology one employs will be directly related to the real and implied questions one asks about the text involved. In my opinion, it is quite legitimate to move along a critical continuum to allow the imagination to experience and probe the depths of the fictive text, provided that the text is rich enough that it can be approached, as Faulkner hinted at in his mention of Wallace Stevens in connection with *Absalom, Absalom!,* from thirteen *or more ways.*[22] Ultimately what is at stake in all of this is the ideology (singular/plural) about the world we live in and fiction's place in this world.

Like names and dates etched on tombstones, emblems of a person's life which Mr. Compson keeps track of, the most specific and authentic voice we have of Mr. Compson in *Absalom, Absalom!* is provided in the letter in Chapter VI he wrote to Quentin, postmarked January 10, 1910: these words addressed to Quentin, unlike the fragment purportedly written by Charles to Judith and entrusted to General Compson's wife, are indeed the genuine *ipsissima verba* of Mr. Compson. They will not change nor are they subject to modification by Quentin's whirling imagination. Unfortunately, the letter trails off into a spoken version of it, which emerges with the discussion Quentin had with his father before he went to Sutpen's Hundred and perhaps after he returned. Not a philosophical treatise on life, which would provide a framework to work from, but a timely report on Miss Rosa's death and burial, the letter fragment focuses neither on the reaction of the community nor the specifics of the funeral, but with the act of death itself: painless death takes *"the intelligence"* by surprise and, at most, can be said to be a *"brief and peculiar emotional state . . ."* (p. 173). For someone like Miss Rosa, forty-three years of suffering and distress militate against a peaceful death. A swift death in such a case seems preferable; this *"irrevocable and unplumbable finality"* (p. 173) is not the type of experience that warrants a long period of bewilderment and reflection. Without losing the authorial voice, that of the father instructing the son, the predominant voice in *Absalom, Absalom!* is the mimetic, narrative voice, quite unlike Miss Rosa's tormented and highly interior narrative voice. Spoken from the third-person point of view, "Mr Compson told Quentin" (43), it is clear that we can take Mr. Compson's narration as fairly normal conversation as he burdens Quentin with Miss Rosa's demise: "So maybe she considers you partly responsible through heredity for what happened to her and her family through him [Sutpen]" (13). Focusing on Sutpen, a man he admires because of the gigantic, almost impossible task he had undertaken, Mr. Compson is curious about the Coldfield-

Sutpen relationship. Though never fully explained, the town sent a "vigilance committee" (45) to force the zealous newcomer to modify his behavior; yet Sutpen merely stares down the committee and dances to his own tune: "He was like John L. Sullivan having taught himself painfully and tediously to do the schottische, having drilled himself and drilled himself in secret until he now believed it no longer necessary to count the music's beat, say" (46). Mr. Compson's frequent refrain of "doubtless" reveals the inquiring, speculative dimension of his imagination as he seeks to recreate a story from a psychological viewpoint, making commentaries as Shreve does but without Shreve's flippancy.

Above all, he probes the inner heart of Sutpen in order to make sense of his external actions; he refrains from being apodictic or philosophical, contrary to the view we have of him in the letter fragment. Sutpen's entrance into Jefferson has the drama of a Western film as he walks "erect" with his "new hat cocked" (47) and has a show-down with the local townsfolk who oppose him more out of fear of the unknown than anything else. Sutpen enters the Coldfield house with flowers, makes a deal, and exits from the house engaged to Ellen. Mr. Compson has a sense for detail not seen in *The Sound and the Fury;* he mentions, for example, people involved in this drama who were to become sources who had information: Old Ikkemotubbe, Mr. Coldfield, Akers, Judge Benbow, Quentin's grandmother and grandfather. In addition, he has an extraordinary sense of sequential time: "good while," "when he reached the courthouse," "but by that time," "five years ago," "after the three years," "late that afternoon," "Two months later" (pp. 47–48). His fixation on Sutpen becomes sharper as he narrates the wedding ceremony, not from the viewpoint of a spectator inside the church, but from without, noting particularly its Gothic elements: the ghoulish torches held by the blacks, the garbage thrown at the couple, and the tearful eyes of Ellen, which are reflected in the dismal, rainy atmosphere. In an almost chatty manner, he compares church weddings with those presided over by a justice of the peace: "So is it too much to believe that these women come to long for divorce from a sense not of incompleteness but of actual

frustration and betrayal?" (p. 49). Coldfield's "tedious and unre-
mitting husbandry" or "some innate sense of delicacy and
fitness" (p. 50) prompted him to want the wedding, even though
Sutpen, recently released from jail, would probably not have
pushed for such a ceremony. Sutpen is exonerated from any
blame since Coldfield is an honorable man; yet, his honor has
been besmirched by his relationship with Sutpen. Investigating
the female mind, he speculates about how women think: "Or
maybe women are even less complex than that and to them any
wedding is better than no wedding and a big wedding with a
villain preferable to a small one with a saint" (p. 52). Working
from various accounts, some of them told by eye witnesses, Mr.
Compson circles around the scene he believes he is reconstructing to probe reasons that validate and give coherency to the
scene before his eyes. His mind restlessly searches out the psychological "truths"; they are not the starting point of his imaginative investigation, but the final result.

In an image reminiscent of Jewel on his horse, Mr. Compson
struggles with a multitude of demons and shows none of the
terrible defeatism that he has been accused of:

> —that unsleeping care which must have known that it could
> permit itself but one mistake; that alertness for measuring and
> weighing event against eventuality, circumstance against hu-
> man nature, his own fallible judgment and mortal clay against
> not only human but natural forces, choosing and discarding,
> compromising with his dream and his ambition like you must
> with the horse which you take across country, over timber,
> which you control only through your ability to keep the
> animal from realizing that actually you cannot, that actually it
> is the stronger. (53)

There is no clear victor in this confrontation of two opposing
forces; rather there is a type of respectful reconciliation whereby
man, through his own interior power, keeps the brute force of
the horse from overpowering him. It is not a question either of
mind over matter, nor one of division within man that is suggested; what we see is Sutpen as a congeries of conflicting ten-

dencies, each of which seeks dominion, but none actually achieve it. Though Mr. Compson's account of the wedding is detailed, brooding, prolonged, personal (curiously, without any use of "I"), he sees the bridal couple involved in life's cosmic battle. In fact he raises the participants to new abstract, benevolent heights, and thus creates a chasm between what they are and what they could have been:

> '. . . people too as we are, and victims too as we are, but victims of a different circumstance, simpler and therefore, integer for integer, larger, more heroic and the figures therefore more heroic too, not dwarfed and involved but distinct, uncomplex who had the gift of loving once or dying once instead of being diffused and scattered creatures drawn blindly limb from limb from a grab bag and assembled, author and victim too of a thousand homicides and a thousand copulations and divorcements.' (89)

In line with this type of categorizing, Mr. Compson imagines Bon the "intending bigamist" (p. 90) while Henry is the dutiful son "doomed and destined to kill" (p. 91). Ironically they form a single personality who, through letter writing, seduces Judith, though Judith does not really know Bon. Henry would never have told Bon anything since the code of the southern gentleman would have prevented that; yet, Bon guessed that Sutpen knew about his mistress and child in New Orleans. Though Mr. Compson never considered Charles as having black blood (his son has sixteenth-part black blood [p. 194]), he does state, perhaps relying on Quentin's knowledge, that Bon was Sutpen's son:

> "Yes," Quentin said. "Father said he probably named him himself. Charles Bon. Charles Good. He didn't tell Grandfather that he did, but Grandfather believed he did, would have." (p. 265)

Mr. Compson never doubts that Bon loved Judith, and thus Bon becomes Henry's source of despair; yet Bon remains a fascinating character, a "hero out of some adolescent Arabian Nights who had stumbled upon a talisman or touchstone . . ." (p. 96). The attracting and repelling human forces, for Mr. Compson and, as Shreve later says, for Quentin too, interpenetrate one another in an incestuous manner: "In fact, perhaps this is the pure and perfect incest: the brother realizing that the sister's virginity must be destroyed in order to have existed at all, taking that virginity in the person of the brother-in-law, the man whom he would be if he could become, metamorphose into, the lover, the husband; by whom he would be despoiled, choose for despoiler, if he could become, metamorphose into the sister, the mistress, the bride" (p. 96). Here, Mr. Compson explicitly points to the seemingly homofilial love of Charles and Henry, and ultimately he proposes that it is Henry who seduces Judith. The key to the imagination here is deductive logic which is fascinated by a triangular love relationship; unlike Dalton Ames or Herbert Head, however, Charles is very much part of the relationship and is not forgotten. Judith and Charles saw each other three times in two years for a total of seventeen days and thus can only be pictured in the most ethereal of terms: ". . . the same two serene phantoms who seem to watch, hover, impartial attentive and quiet, above and behind the inexplicable thunderhead of interdictions and defiances and repudiations out of which the rocklike Sutpen and the volatile and violent Henry flashed and glared and ceased . . ." (p. 97). Unlike the situation in *The Sound and the Fury* when Quentin wants to confess an actual incestuous relationship he had with Caddy, Mr. Compson in *Absalom, Absalom!*, rhapsodizes about a theoretical, spiritual incestuous relationship, and as he has done previously in this novel, he only concerns himself with an abstract solution by which opposing forces can be reconciled. As Joseph Reed observes, "Mr. Compson's peculiar fixations distances his information even more than his remote sources will account for. His heavy emphasis on realization, his concentration on his own powers of ironic observation, his affected moralization lead to overcomplexity and oversubtlety, and ultimately to cold remoteness."[23] What Quentin understands and interiorizes at this point goes beyond the evidence of the text. What Mr. Compson says, however, is clear: the image of incest does not provide a solution to the love triangle that he has been describing all along. It is but one of several hypotheses that might make sense in this case.

Trying to penetrate the concept of pure incest, Mr. Compson deals with the mentality of the individuals involved: "this girl," "this father," "this brother," "this lover" (pp. 99-100). He accounts for the possible variables and assumes the points of view that would be helpful in explaining the actions that resulted in the shooting of Bon by Henry. With all his highly developed, skillful, imaginative ratiocination, he arrives at a sound conclusion, one difficult to accept, but one that is honest and truthful:

> It's just incredible. It just does not explain. Or perhaps that's it: they dont explain and we are not supposed to know. We have a few old mouth-to-mouth tales; we exhume from old trunks and boxes and drawers letters without salutation or signature, in which men and women who once lived and breathed are now merely initials or nicknames out of some now incomprehensible affection which sound to us like Sanskrit or Chocktaw; we see dimly people, the people in whose living blood and seed we ourselves lay dormant and waiting, in this shadowy attenuation of time possessing now heroic proportions, performing their acts of simple passion and simple violence, impervious to time and inexplicable— Yes, Judith, Bon, Henry, Sutpen: all of them. They are there, yet something is missing; they are like a chemical formula exhumed along with the letters from that forgotten chest, carefully, the paper old and faded and falling to pieces, the writing faded, almost indecipherable, yet meaningful, familiar in shape and sense, the name and presence of volatile and sentient forces; you bring them together in the proportions called for, but nothing happens; you re-read, tedious and intent, poring, making sure that you have forgotten nothing, made no miscalculation; you bring them together again and again nothing happens; just the words, the symbols, the shapes themselves, shadowy inscrutable and serene, against the turgid background of a horrible and bloody mischancing of human affairs. (pp. 100-01)

Mr. Compson has thought of love in its various modalities, he has considered the proper porportions of human motivations without going beyond the evidence, and he has raised the issues to abstract levels when appropriate. He has come to the end of his logical probing; he cannot go beyond Quentin's statement that no one ever did know whether or not Bon knew that Sutpen was his father. He is willing to admit that he is stymied, that implicitly his theory of spiritual incest might not provide the answer he is looking for. Rather, he returns to the flimsy evidence ("mouth-to-mouth tales," "letters without salutation or signature," "dimly [seen] people"). The chemical formulas which normally give certitude fail here since parts of the equation are unobserved or omitted. No amount of recalculation can help: we have all the evidence—interpreted as symbols and shapes—set against the background known to the narrators. Thoughts of incest cede to considerations of chemistry and mathematics. The answer apparently lies beyond Mr. Compson's grasp, though he has given the reader in the above paragraph a marvelous theory of writing, an *ars poetica*, which might well be the central focus of the novel.

In reviewing this narrative tale a second time, Mr. Compson focuses on three aspects of the story he is reconstructing (two new ones and one already considered): Judith buying a trousseau, Sutpen's trip to New Orleans, and the marriage ceremony. In this version, he sees Ellen, not Henry, as the matchmaker. However, Bon's dead body lies at the center of his musings, and whatever he dreams up must account for this reality. The anticipated marriage cannot be separated from Bon's death. Yet, what if Henry himself had gone to New Orleans and discovered the mistress and child? For Mr. Compson, Henry would not be upset by the possible bigamy, but by the fact that it was his father, Sutpen, who told him: ". . . the father who is the natural enemy of any son and son-in-law of whom the mother is the ally, just as after the wedding the father will be ally of the actual son-in-law who has for mortal foe the mother of his wife" (p. 104). The culmination of this type of speculation is the Christmas eve scene of 1860, the results of which are known but not what transpired.[24] At most, we have a stand-off: Bon does not know how much Henry knows, yet Henry will not question Bon. On the

other hand, Charles learns from Henry because Henry would
have to have told him, and "in his fatalism he loved Henry the
better of the two" (p. 108)—thus leaving out the sister. Once Bon
has told Henry, in Mr. Compson's mind, it is the "puritan heritage" (p. 108), "the puritan mind" (p. 109), and "puritan's
humility" (p. 111) that cause Henry to react so violently. Not the
miscegenation, nor the incest, but the ceremony itself is again
seen as the stumbling block, this time, as is Mr. Compson's wont,
transformed into a surrealistic abstraction:

> A formula, a shibboleth meaningless as a child's game, per-
> formed by someone created by the situation whose need it
> answered: a crone mumbling in a dungeon lighted by a hand-
> ful of burning hair, something in a tongue which not even the
> girls themselves understood anymore. . . . (p. 117)

Mr. Compson's visual imagination creates complicated
scenarios, which help him to understand the situations he is
probing, culminating in this case in the picture of "a corridor of
doomed and tragic flower faces walled between the grim duenna
row of old women and the elegant shapes of young men trim
predatory and (at that moment) goatlike" (p. 112). Like Sutpen,
turned away from the mansion door, Mr. Compson cannot get
beyond "a wall, unscalable, a gate ponderously locked" (p. 112).
His imagination sees finally, but I don't think really accepts, an
action that is more compromise than a solution: two men opposing one another in a casual, romantic duel.

Ironically, the more Henry followed Charles about and saw
him in his local habitat, the less he knew about him. What he
ultimately sees is

> . . . a place created for and by voluptuousness, the abashless
> and unabashed senses, and the country boy with his simple
> and erstwhile untroubled code in which females were ladies or
> whores or slaves looked at the apotheosis of two doomed races
> presided over by its own victim—a woman with a face like a
> tragic magnolia, the eternal female, the eternal Who-
> suffers. . . . (p. 114)

Yet, Bon protests vehemently against this puritanical view of octoroons, since their condition was created by white men. Even with this, Mr. Compson fitfully proclaims there is something more: the four years, the time of testing and waiting for the dissolution of the relationship with the octoroon woman. Like this woman, Judith has been patient and has had no real notion of what transpired between her father and Charles. Love, as Addie Bundren knows, demands a correlation between the word and the experience, with the word emerging from the experience itself. Ironically, Judith is described in a way that parallels Addie's description of Anse:

> She was just the blank shape, the empty vessel in which each of them strove to preserve, not the illusion of himself nor his illusion of the other but what each conceived the other to believe him to be. . . . (pp. 119–20)

Throughout, Judith remains steadfast: "*I love, I will accept no substitute . . .*" (p. 121). The Civil War takes on the atmosphere of a dance in which Mr. Compson watches the partners on the floor, and those such as Ellen, Clytie, Wash Jones, his daughter, and his granddaughter, who stand at the edge. Or switching metaphors, the participants are like puppets, and then suddenly the show is over; all that is left from this is a stone with scratches on it: ". . . something that might make a mark on something that *was* once for the reason that it can die someday, while the block of stone cant be *is* because it never can become *was* because it cant ever die or perish" (pp. 127–28), words which reflect some of Charles's sentiments to Judith, or Darl's thoughts as he listens to the rain outside his bedroom, or even Mr. Compson's own fascination with tombstones.

In trying to determine the nature of the Henry-Bon-Judith relationship, Mr. Compson freely determines what he wishes to discuss, and thus we have a greater, more controlled sense of his personality that we do in *The Sound and the Fury*. Not only does he fail to solve the problem of why Henry murdered Bon or why Sutpen refused to allow the marriage of Bon and Judith, but he fails to see the subtlety of the moral and racial issues involved, and so reveals that he is surprisingly closer to the Mr. Compson in "That Evening Sun" than to the Mr. Compson in *The Sound and the Fury*. Try as he may, he cannot enter Sutpen's mind fully. Though Mr. Compson creates an agile *bon vivant* in the person of Charles, whose sensuous passivity he finds attractive, he cannot understand why it was carried to such an extreme, why Bon allowed himself to be murdered. Thus, he is a far richer character in his novel than Joseph Reed admits because he enjoys the narrative powers of a quick imagination, which step-by-step looks at the characters in the Sutpen story and invents *personae* for them that are worthy of the best storytellers:

> Mr. Compson is trying to sell his brand of resigned, ironic morality more than he is attempting to grasp the shape of the Sutpen story. His narrative is undertaken for the wrong reason: he wants the fiction to fit his rather tired philosophical bromides so that he can feel superior not only to the story but to the men and women who originally enacted the events which form it." (p. 163)

Even when he cannot make all the pieces fit in the characters he establishes, he circles around again to try a different approach, never forgetting the final, unrelenting, undeniable fact: Bon's death. He becomes one of several co-creators of the Sutpen story, and his final role is to be identified with Shreve and then with Shreve and Quentin together, emphasizing that his role is one primarily of storyteller: "*Or maybe Father and I are both Shreve, maybe it took Father and me both to make Shreve or Shreve and me both to make Father or maybe Thomas Sutpen to make all of us*" (p. 262). The paternal voice that Quentin hears in *The Sound and the Fury* is filled with both sound and fury; not so in *Absalom, Absalom!*, where the voice selects, discerns, interprets, but never demands or commands anything that resembles death.

Establishing intertexts, which lack structural definition, focuses not on the art of storytelling, but on characters who are treated as if they were real—a point that Faulkner seems to strain against precisely because they are not created uniquely

through dramatic action but through voices, moments of speculation, narratives of brilliant creativity. A search for Jesus of
Nazareth is normally undertaken because his friends and their
disciples, and the communities he came to know, have be-
queathed to us written documents that proclaim that he actually
lived, died, and rose from the dead. Modern hermeneutical
studies attempt to give the *Sitz im Leben* of Jesus' sayings, and the
cultural and theological climate of his day, in ways that can be
understood today. The venture is assumed with utmost
seriousness because of the profound metaphysical and theological implications of who Jesus was/is and what he preached/
preaches. Above all, there is a reverence for the written text, for
each word, that is not normally found in other disciplines. As
Paul Ricoeur reminds us, "Writing creates a new kind of being, a
being which originated in an event, the act of composition, but
perdures as ideal meaning, that is, as meaning liberated from its
originating event and capable of being reactualized in new ways
in subsequent events of understanding."[25] The Jesus "event" differs significantly from the Mr. Compson "event" in that the latter consists solely of the act of the creative imagination in the act
of writing; we cannot look through the various layers of Faulkner's works and discover a person who once had an ontological
existence. Nor can we locate Mr. Compson as he existed in
Faulkner's mind and imagination. His only "reality" can be dis-
cerned in the possible situations in the three texts in which he
appears. Since he lacks a verifiable, historical existence, we look
on him, not with the same sense of eschatological dulia with
which biblical scholars look at their subjects, but with a type of
respect that questions whether or not he is consistent as a possible human being. By looking closely at his vocabulary and behavior, we see that Mr. Compson differs considerably in *The
Sound and the Fury* and *Absalom, Absalom!,* and any attempt to
reconcile these differences does harm to that which makes each
text so distinctive and rich, especially as Mr. Compson emerges
from the disturbed shadows of Quentin's mind in *The Sound and
the Fury* and takes on more recognizable human attributes in
*Absalom, Absalom!* Yet, Mr. Compson never ceases to be Quen-

## 206   Patrick Samway, S.J.

tin's father, sharing his views on life, death, history, women, problem-solving, and philosophy. As we go from a general view of him to a specific, more focused view, we must be more conscious of both the exact nature of the text and context we find him in. When zeroing in on a specific issue that Mr. Compson discusses, whether it be incest, virginity, or marriage, one should avoid using a string of quotes, as if they were proof-texts which have the same weight, since the surrounding events and structure of the overall passage will provide clues and questions for ways to interpret these views. As in all literary masterpieces, we will never locate a real person in a fictive text; what we will discover is a character who leads us into realms of further discovery as we follow closely in his footsteps.

---

NOTES

1. For a further explanation with a supplementary bibliography, I suggest consulting the excellent essays in *The Jerome Biblical Commentary*, ed. Raymond E. Brown, S. S.; Joseph A. Fitzmyer, S. J.; Roland E. Murphy, O. Carm. (Prentice-Hall: Englewood Cliffs, New Jersey, 1968). The Rylands Papyrus 457, the earliest of any fragment of the New Testament, is among the more than seventy-five manuscripts of the New Testament that have been discovered in the last one hundred years. With this manuscript, and others found at Qumran, our knowledge of the formation of the gospel texts is contantly being expanded and revised.

2. The New Testament abounds with sayings that show divergent theological views. Notice, for example, the saying in Matthew (5:17–20) that Jesus came to fulfill the Mosaic law of the Old Testament, whereas St. Paul in his letter to the Galatians (3:7–22) says that Jesus came to do away with the Mosaic law and replace it with the law based on love.

3. See particularly the remarks in Bleikasten's book about Quentin's suicide as a predictable end of his long journey. André Bleikasten, *The Most Splendid Failure: Faulkner's "The Sound and the Fury"* (Bloomington: Indiana University Press, 1976), p. 137. For three fine discussions of Quentin, see Warwick Wadlington, "*The Sound and the Fury:* A Logic of Tragedy," *American Literature,* 53 (November 1981), pp. 409–23; Jane Millgate, "Quentin Compson as Poor Player: Verbal and Social Clichés in *The Sound and the Fury,*" *Revue des langues vivantes,* 34 (1968), pp. 40–49; Judith Slater, "Quentin's Tunnel Vision: Modes of Perception and Their Stylistic Realization in *The Sound and the Fury,*" *Literature and Psychology,* 27, No. 1 (1977), pp. 4–15.

4. William Faulkner, *The Sound and the Fury* (New York: Modern Library, 1954, p. 145. This edition is reproduced photographically from a copy of the first edition. All future references will be to this issue.

5. For various discussions about Quentin's role as narrator in "That Evening Sun" and elsewhere, see Estella Schoenberg, *Old Tales and Talking: Quentin Compson in William Faulkner's "Absalom, Absalom!" and Related Works* (Jackson: University Press of Mississippi, 1977), pp. 16–20; James B. Meriwether, *The*

*Literary Career of William Faulkner: A Bibliographical Study* (Princeton: Princeton University Press, 1961), p. 175; Leo J. M. Manglaviti, "Faulkner's 'That Evening Sun' and Mencken's 'Best Literary Judgment,' " *American Literature*, 43 (January 1972), pp. 649–54; Norman Holmes Pearson, "Faulkner's Three 'Evening Suns'," *Yale University Gazette*, 19 (October 1954), pp. 61–70; May Cameron Brown, *Quentin Compson as Narrative Voice in the Works of William Faulkner* (Diss: Georgia State University, 1975); Michael Millgate, "William Faulkner's Point of View," *Patterns of Commitment in American Literature*, ed. Marston La France (Toronto: University of Toronto Press, 1967), pp. 181–92; Thomas D. Young, "Narration as Creative Art: The Role of Quentin Compson in *Absalom, Absalom!*," *Faulkner, Modernism, and Film*, ed. Evans Harrington and Ann J. Abadie (Jackson: University Press of Mississippi, 1979), pp. 82–102. See also the biographical details discussed by Joseph Blotner, *Faulkner: A Biography*, I (New York: Random House, 1974), pp. 565–67. May Cameron Brown believes Ike McCaslin narrates the original version of "The Old People" (*Quentin Compson as Narrative Voice*, pp. 86–87); see Estella Schoenberg's *Old Tales and Talking*, p. 19, for her interpretation of this point. Two German studies are worth noting: Dieter Meindl, *Bewusstein als Schicksal: Zu Struktur und Entwicklung von William Faulkners Generationenromanen* (Stuttgart: J. B. Metzlersche, 1974), especially Chapter Two, "*Absalom, Absalom!: Genese eines Kunstwerks*," pp. 31–62; also, Jürgen Peper, *Bewussteinslagen des Erzählens und erzählte Wirklichkeiten—Dargestellt an amerikanischen Romanen des 19. und 20. Jahrhunderts. Insbesondere am Werk William Faulkners* (Leiden: E. J. Brill, 1966), especially Chapter Seventeen, "Der Aufbau eines Romanes: *Absalom, Absalom!*," pp. 238–67. Also two unpublished essays by a Japanese scholar, Professor Ikuko Fujihira ("From Voice to Silence: Writing in *Absalom, Absalom!*" and "Truth in Uttering: The Speaking Voice in *The Sound and the Fury*"). I am grateful to Mrs. Fujihira for sharing her insights with me. See also the views of James Watson in "Faulkner's Short Stories and the Making of Yoknapatawpha County," in *Fifty Years of Yoknapatawpha: Faulkner and Yoknapatawpha, 1978*, ed. Doreen Fowler and Ann J. Abadie (Jackson: University Press of Mississippi, 1980), pp. 202–25, especially p. 218.

6. I would hold a view slightly different from May Cameron Brown's: "A study of Faulkner's careful technique and revisions in relation to Quentin's role in the story and to the voice in which he tells it supports the view that Quentin, whatever his age, is the same as the sensitive character who narrates section II of *The Sound and the Fury*." (*Quentin Compson as Narrative Voice*, p. 63.)

7. Joseph Blotner, *Faulkner: A Biography*, II, p. 1309, comments on the relationship of Nancy in "That Evening Sun" and Nancy Mannigoe in *Requiem for a Nun*.

8. William Faulkner, "That Evening Sun," *Collected Stories of William Faulkner* (New York: Random House, 1950), p. 294. All future references will be to this edition.

9. William Faulkner, *Absalom, Absalom!* (New York: Random House, 1936), p. 9. All future reference will be to this edition.

10. *The Most Splendid Failure*, p. 96.

11. *The Sound and the Fury*, p. 53.

12. The words followed by an asterisk here and in the rest of the text and ones listed in the columns below, attributed to Mr. Compson by Quentin, occur only once in *The Sound and the Fury* and thus indicate that Mr. Compson has a distinctive vocabulary in this novel. For further information concerning the vocabulary in *The Sound and the Fury*, see "*The Sound and the Fury*": *A Concordance to the Novel*, ed. Noel Polk and Kenneth L. Privratsky (Ann Arbor, Michigan: University Microfilms, 1980).

| | | |
|---|---|---|
| mausoleum | harp | symmetrical |
| excrutiating-ly | purity | discard |
| apt | climatic | overnight |
| fitted | impure | whiten |
| conquer | properties | conditions |
| victory | tediously | gamble |
| philosophers(a) | unvaringly | dice |
| crucified | nil | diceman |
| speculation | stalemate | assuredly |
| symptom | equilibrium | essaying |
| Excrement | periodical | ranging |
| sweating | filth | violence |
| refund | fishbone | disgust |
| nowadays | alarm | bond |
| fertility | expedient | design |
| suspicion | expedients | matures |
| affinity | sublimate | willynilly |
| bed-clothing | exorcise | maine(b) |
| slumber | sequence | pennies(a) |
| fertilizing | finitude | disappointed |
| shortcomings | | prescribe |
| misfortunes | | wellbeing |

(a) singular not used in the novel
(b) the state of Maine

The following words are used twice in the novel, and both times they are attributed to Mr. Compson:

| | | |
|---|---|---|
| idle | misfortune | folly |
| acquire | arbiter | virtues |
| affinity | | |

Also, it should be noted that the word "despair" is used five times in the novel, and in each case it is attributed to Mr. Compson.

13. Irena Kaluza, *The Functioning of Sentence Structure in the Stream-of-Consciousness Technique of William Faulkner's "The Sound and the Fury"* ([n. p.] Norwood Editions, 1969), pp. 71, 87ff.

14. This point is made by Mark Spilka, "Quentin Compson's Universal Grief," *Contemporary Literature*, 11 (Autumn 1970), pp. 451–69. Five other essays that deal with Quentin and the problems of structure and interpretation are worth noting: (1) Stephen M. Ross, "The 'Loud World' of Quentin Compson," *Studies in the Novel*, 7 (Summer 1975), pp. 245–57; (2) John A. Hodgson, "'Logical Sequence and Continuity': Some Observations on the Typographical and Structural Consistency of *Absalom, Absalom!*," *American Literature*, 43 (March 1971), pp. 97–107. I find intriguing his notion that Chapter 3 of *Absalom, Absalom!* "is not continuous and contemporaneous with Chapters 2 and 4 but represents a conversation taking place at a later date, after Quentin has returned from Sutpen's Hundred" (p. 104); (3) François Pitavy, "Quentin Compson, ou le regard du poète," *Sud* 14/15 (Marseille, France [n.d.]), believes that "*Certains moments de l'ultime conversation avec le père, en particulier lorsque Quentin 'avoue' une dernière fois l'inceste avec Caddy, font bien voir que les remarques ou objections de Mr.*

*Compson sont finalement celles du fils à lui-même, que son dialogue est dès lors dialogue avec sa conscience . . ."* (p. 78); (4) Arthur Kinney, *Faulkner's Narrative Poetics: Style as Vision* (Amherst: University of Massachusetts Press, 1978), especially p. 39; (5) Donald M. Kartiganer, "The Sound and the Fury and Faulkner's Quest for Form," *ELH*, 37 (December 1970), pp. 613–39. I particularly appreciate his view that a "fluid, durational reality, in other words, could be suggested in an act centering on the very process of the work's emergence into being, its confrontation with the difficulties of its own achievement of form. In this sense process and stream of consciousness have identical aims: a literature which suggested mind in the act of knowing and the poet in the making of order" (p. 616).

15. See Joel Sayre and William Faulkner, *The Road to Glory: A Screenplay*, afterword by George Garrett (Carbondale: Southern Illinois University Press, 1981), p. 158. Along these lines, Bruce Kawin's observation is worth noting: "*Today We live* and *The Road to Glory* are more a diptych than a double feature, very much like *The Sound and the Fury* and *Absalom, Absalom!*, both intra- and infra-structurally." ("Faulkner's Film Career: The Years with Hawks" in *Faulkner, Modernism, and Film*, ed. Evans Harrington and Ann J. Abadie (Jackson: University Press of Mississippi, 1979), p. 178.

16. Harold Bloom, *A Map of Misreading* (New York: Oxford University Press, 1975), p. 19.

17. Albert Guerard, *The Triumph of the Novel: Dickens, Dostoevsky, Faulkner* (New York: Oxford University Press, 1976), p. 311.

18. Schoenberg, *Old Tales and Talking*, p. 95.

19. Gwynn, Frederick L. and Joseph Blotner, eds., *Faulkner in the University* (Charlottesville: University Press of Virginia, 1959), pp. 274–75.

20. John T. Irwin, *Doubling and Incest/Repetition and Revenge: A Speculative Reading of Faulkner* (Baltimore: Johns Hopkins University Press, 1975). All future references to Irwin's book will be to this edition.

21. Michael Millgate, "Faulkner's First Trilogy: *Sartoris, Sanctuary,* and *Requiem for a Nun*," *Fifty Years of Yoknapatawpha: Faulkner and Yoknapatawpha* (Jackson: University Press of Mississippi, 1980), p. 105.

22. See *Faulkner in the University*, pp. 273–74.

23. Joseph Reed, *Faulkner's Narrative* (New Haven: Yale University Press, 1973), p. 163.

24. See my article, "Storytelling and the Library Scene in Faulkner's *Absalom, Absalom!*," *William Faulkner: Materials, Studies, and Criticism* (Tokyo, Japan), 2 (December 1979), pp. 1–20.

25. See the excellent essay by Sandra M. Schneiders, I. H. M., "The Pascal Imagination: Objectivity and Subjectivity in New Testament Interpretation," *Theological Studies*, 43 (March 1982), pp. 52–68, especially her reference to Ricoeur, p. 59. See also Professor Schneiders' essay, "From Exegesis to Hermeneutics: The Problem of the Contemporary Meaning of Scripture," *Horizons*, 8, No. 1 (1981), pp. 23–39.

# Contributors

**Nancy Blake** teaches at Paul Valery University in Montpellier, France.

**André Bleikasten** is the author of *Parcours de Faulkner* (Paris: Ophrys, 1982), *Faulkner's "As I Lay Dying"*, and of *The Most Splendid Failure: Faulkner's "The Sound and the Fury"* (Indiana, 1973 and 1976). He has also written many articles and essays on Faulkner and other southern writers, which have been published in French, American, and German periodicals. He is Professor of American literature at the University of Strasbourg, and is working on the second volume of Faulkner's works to be published in the Pléiade edition.

**Richard Godden** is Lecturer in the Department of American Studies at the University of Keele, England. He has published numerous essays on Faulkner.

**John T. Matthews,** Associate Professor of English at Boston University, is the author of *The Play of Faulkner's Language* (Cornell, 1982).

**Michel Gresset,** Professor of American literature at the University of Paris VII, is editor of the first volume of the Pléiade edition of Faulkner's works (Paris: Gallimard, 1977) and has published *Faulkner ou la Fascination* (Paris: Klincksieck, 1982), which will be published in translation by Duke University Press. He has also translated *Selected Letters* (Paris: Gallimard, 1981) and *Unpublished Stories* (1985), as well as novels and stories by younger southern writers, from Flannery O'Connor to Heather Ross Miller and Fred Chappell. Coeditor of *Delta,* he has established the Maurice Edgar Coindreau Prize for the best translation of an American book into French.

**Kenzaburo Ohashi,** Professor of English at Tsurumi University, is one of Japan's leading scholars in American Literature. He has translated Faulkner into Japanese, and has written a massive three-volume study. He is coeditor of the journal *William Faulkner: Materials, Studies, and Criticism.*

**François Pitavy** is the author of *Faulkner's "Light in August"* (Indiana, 1973) and many articles on Faulkner in French and American periodicals. He has also translated some of Faulkner's unpublished stories. He teaches American literature at the University of Dijon and is working on the second volume of Faulkner's works to be published in the Pléiade edition.

**Noel Polk** is Professor of English at the University of Southern Mississippi. He has published numerous articles and books on Faulkner, including *Faulkner's "Requiem for a Nun": A Critical Study* (Indiana, 1981). He has edited *Faulkner's Marionettes* (Virginia, 1977) and *Sanctuary: The Original Text* (Random House, 1981).

**Pamela Rhodes** is a postgraduate student in the Department of American Studies at the University of Keele, England.

**Stephen M. Ross** is Associate Professor of English at the United States Naval Academy. He is the author of several essays on Faulkner.

**Patrick Samway,** S.J., is literary editor of *America.* He is author of *Faulkner's "Intruder in the Dust": A Critical Study of the Typescripts* (Whitston, 1980) and is coeditor of *Stories of the Modern South* (Bantam, 1977).

**Olga Scherer,** through her publications in French periodicals, is working out an application of Mikhail Bakhtin's methodological concepts to a comparative study of Dostoevski and Faulkner. She teaches American literature at the University of Paris VIII.

# Index

This is a highly selective index, designed to give access to significant discussions of major issues involving intertextuality in Faulkner's works.

## II.  Index to names